The Literary History of Alberta

Volume One:
From Writing-on-Stone
to World War Two

The Literary History of Alberta

George Melnyk

Volume One
From Writing-on-Stone
to World War Two

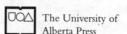 The University of
Alberta Press

First published by
   The University of Alberta Press
   141 Athabasca Hall
   Edmonton, Alberta, Canada T6G 2E8

Copyright © George Melnyk 1998
A volume in (cuRRents), an interdisciplinary series. Johnathan Hart, series editor.
Softcover/ISBN 0–88864–296–2
Hardcover/ISBN 0–88864–316–0

Canadian Cataloguing in Publication Data

Melnyk, George.
   The literary history of Alberta

   Contents: v. 1, From Writing-on-Stone to World War Two.
   Includes bibliographical references and index.
   ISBN 0–88864–296–2

   1. Canadian literature—Alberta—History and criticism. I. Title.
PS8131.A43M44 1998   C810.9'97123   C97–910821–7
PR9198.2.A4M44 1998

∞ Printed on acid-free paper.
Printed and bound in Canada by Friesens, Altona, Manitoba.

The University of Alberta Press acknowledges the financial support of the Government of Canada through the Book Publishing Industry Development Program for its publishing activities. The Press also gratefully acknowledges the support received for its program from the Canada Council for the Arts and the Alberta Foundation for the Arts. This volume was published with financial support from the Alberta Historical Resources Foundation.

COMMITTED TO THE DEVELOPMENT OF CULTURE AND THE ARTS

To Alberta Writers Past, Present, Future

Contents

Alberta 2005

Alberta Reflections

THE YEAR 2005 will mark the centennial of the Province of Alberta. In 1988, a group of Albertans from various backgrounds met in Red Deer to discuss the possibility of producing a multi-volume history of the province in time for its hundredth anniversary. The result was the creation of the Alberta 2005 Centennial History Society, a nonprofit association devoted to producing a history that is both accurate and accessible. The principal work of the Society since 1991, apart from fund-raising, has been to identify the areas of Alberta's past most in need of further research and to sponsor a series of studies aimed at filling in the blanks.

Our intention has been to commission specialized studies for publication in the series that we call Alberta Reflections. We are pleased to add George Melnyk's *The Literary History of Alberta, Volume One* to the series. Melnyk is a well-known Alberta writer and has been instrumental in the development of Alberta's recent literary culture.

A large portion of the funding for the Alberta 2005 project has come from the Alberta Historical Resources Foundation, and we gratefully acknowledge this support.

CARL BETKE
President, Alberta 2005
Centennial History Society

Acknowledgements

A BOOK SUCH AS THIS could not have been written without the support of many people and institutions. Those who read individual chapters of the book in draft form and who assisted in clarifying my thoughts were in the front lines of making the manuscript publishable.

Dr. Olive Dickason, Professor Emeritus of History, University of Alberta, read chapter one. Dr. I.S. MacLaren, Canadian Studies, University of Alberta, and Dr. Barbara Belyea, Department of English, University of Calgary, commented on chapter two. Dr. Susan Jackel, Canadian Studies, University of Alberta, read chapter three. Dr. Richard Harrison, Professor Emeritus of English, University of Alberta, reviewed chapter four. He also kindly allowed me to review the original research notes for his seminal work, *Unnamed Country: The Struggle for a Canadian Prairie Fiction* (1977). Dr. Donald Smith, Department of History, University of Calgary, brought his scholarly expertise to bear on chapter five. Professor Tamara Seiler, Faculty of General Studies, University of Calgary, read chapter six; Mr. Jars Balan was of particular assistance for the Ukrainian section of that chapter. Dr. Francis Kaye, Centre for Great Plains Studies, University of Nebraska, commented on chapter seven, and Dr. Sarah Carter, Department of History, University of Calgary, provided valuable reflections on the conclusion. Also of great value were the comments of the anonymous readers for the University of Alberta Press, who reviewed the first draft of the manuscript. Their critical eyes assisted me in making significant editorial improvements. Fellow historian and writer Walter

Hildebrandt of Calgary was the first to read the draft manuscript in its entirety. I thank them all for their kind assistance and accept full responsibility for the text as it now stands.

Throughout the process of researching and writing this volume, there were those who offered special assistance. Donald Smith was particularly enthusiastic in offering useful bits of information on individual authors. His generous support for the project and his desire to ensure it was as comprehensive as possible were exemplary. Without his involvement, this volume would have been less than it is now. My wife, Julia, read various chapters as they came off the printer and offered insights and editorial observations that proved most valuable.

I also received institutional support. The Faculty of Humanities at the University of Calgary appointed me a Research Associate for two years while I researched and wrote this book. The appointment came with an office, library privileges, and support services. I am most grateful to Dr. Ronald Bond, Dean of Humanities, Dr. Hermina Joldersma, Acting Dean, and Dr. Adrienne Kertzer, Chair of the Department of English, for their kindness and patience. Special Collections at the University of Calgary Library became my home away from home. Here I had an opportunity to leaf through many original volumes. Special thanks are owed to Ms Apollonia Steele of the University of Calgary Archives and Special Collections.

The Local History Room at the Calgary Public Library was also a useful source of early volumes that supplemented microfiche records at the University of Calgary and its Margaret P. Hess Collection. The University of Manitoba Archives assisted me with a grant to research the papers of Ralph Connor and other Alberta writers in their possession. In their archives I also read Gordon Duncan McLeod's dissertation, "A Descriptive Bibliography of the Canadian Prairie Novel 1871-1970," which served as a valuable introduction. Ms Anne Morton of the Manitoba Provincial Archives assisted my research of exploration literature. The Archive has a large number of early volumes, including the Hudson's Bay Company collection.

Of course, this literary history would not have been written without substantial financial support, which allowed me to work on the project more or less full-time and so complete it speedily. Initial and ongoing funding was provided by a generous, multi-year grant from the Alberta 2005 Centennial History Society. The goal of the Society is to fund books on Alberta's history in honour of the province's centennial in 2005, and its committee of Alberta scholars, formerly chaired by Dr. Rod MacLeod, Department of History, University of Alberta, made this volume possible. Further funding was provided by a senior writing grant from the Alberta Foundation for the Arts.

All the above assistance has made the research and writing of this volume a positive experience. After the writing was completed and the scholarly commentaries, recommendations, and advice were duly incorporated into the text, Ms Leslie Vermeer, projects editor at the University of Alberta Press, took over in a spirit of diligence and commitment to the text, guiding the author through the vicissitudes and rewards of an intense editorial process. Her manner would please any writer. Finally, I would like to thank Mr. Glenn Rollans, Director of the University of Alberta Press, for his belief in the importance of this project to Alberta letters.

Introduction

IN HIS AFTERWORD to the 1993 edition of Robert Kroetsch's 1967 book *Alberta*, novelist Rudy Wiebe describes the province as that "land on the mountain backbone of the continent sloping both north and east and south towards three very distant oceans."[1] What he describes in geophysical terms is the way the province's landmass clings like flesh to the skeletal spine of the continental body, and is, in turn, surrounded by salt water as the human body is surrounded by air. To think of oceans when thinking of landlocked Alberta may seem peculiar, but oceans define the context of landlocked areas. Their absence makes them a determining presence in the province's identity. When we think back to those who came here in ships a few hundred years ago or across the Bering Strait thousands of years ago, we acknowledge the role of oceans in forming Alberta's history.

The role of writers in our history may be even less obvious than the distant oceans, because writers form the forgotten underpinning of our cultural consciousness. As a determining factor in Alberta's identity, they too are acknowledged more by their absence than by their presence. Writers and their books were an integral part of defining the geophysical and social space that is now Alberta, but many of them have since been relegated to obscure and specialized interests. It is the purpose of this book to make these writers and their literary achievements more widely known and to acknowledge their roles in creating images of Alberta that continue to influence us.

What has come to be "written," primarily in books, in or about Alberta by those who lived here either permanently or temporarily, and by those who were born and raised here but went elsewhere, constitutes the basic limits of this text. The key element linking these writers is their contact with the physical and social landscape that is known to us today as Alberta. Kroetsch suggests that Alberta's identity is that of a place of meeting, of colliding contrasts, of differences articulated.[2] To his mind, it is a place where opposites meet, where migration determines reality. The literary history of Alberta is full of intermingling, identities formed through differences and the clash of cultures.

History is about change, both evolutionary and cataclysmic. Historical writing seeks to articulate social memory; literary history documents and analyzes the historical changes in one particular aspect of a culture. History, through those who write it, not only names things, people, and times, but unnames them by destroying old names and once-dominant languages and by introducing new concepts and different ways of grasping the past. The literary historian, in arranging his story, rearranges other people's stories, defining and selecting what he thinks is important for the reader to know or remember. The literary historian unites disparate fragments to create a social memory by asking what is worth remembering.[3] Memory creates a self, and the memory of Alberta writing formed in this text moulds a sense of what it means to be an Albertan.

The attention paid to each writer in this history depends on the historian's subjective view of the "value" of the writer's work. That valuing comes from the opinions of previous critics who have evaluated the writer, the historian's personal assessment of the original texts, contemporary cultural values, and the goals of the text itself. In the end, more may be put aside than is presented. The search for what is hidden in narrative is an important theme of postmodern writing. This seeking to reveal basic assumptions in previous narratives, to expose the values and biases of past generations, also serves to deflect attention from our own biases. Surely, we are equally unaware of our own hidden agendas. The challenge to the reader is to take up the search begun by the historian, then to begin to question the historian's text, and finally to enter into dialogue with these multiple, created histories.

The Literary History of Alberta comprises two volumes, this volume ending with World War Two and the second beginning in 1946 and coming up to the present. The history itself begins, however, before the formal concept of history existed in Alberta. It begins in what may be termed "mythopoetic time," expressed in the paintings and carvings of Writing-on-Stone in southern Alberta. It ends in the postmodern present, when the dominant, Eurocentric worldview that displaced the mythopoetic is being questioned with critical self-consciousness.

The consciousness that informs this text is that of the postmodern present, with its sense of multiple and contradictory narratives. Beginning this text at the time when oral transmission was the prime expression of "literature" means going beyond the common view of literature as language inscribed on paper. This history must deal with that oral tradition, because it expands our understanding of the human response to the Alberta landscape and offers the possibility of multiple origins for Alberta writing. Oral storytelling and the printed word are thus thrown together, with print clearly privileged because the ancient oral narratives are accessible to us only through published translations or syllabic renderings. The result is a transposition of meanings from different cultures and different historical sensibilities into a contemporary historical narrative which transforms those narratives into something literate culture comprehends as familiar—a written text.

This is but one example of the contradictions the postmodern historian creates. Another is chronology. The linear chain of causation, in which one or another event seems to affect later events, can no longer hold. In this text, Alberta's literary history does not follow one step after another, but, rather, moves all over the temporal map, even as it presents itself as chronological. For example, some exploration literature that describes events in Alberta was published in its own day and so formed part of the literary canon of the explorer's home culture in Europe. Other exploration literature remained hidden from public view until the twentieth century, when it was finally published. Yet, organizationally, both are assigned in this narrative to the time in which they were written.[4] The issue gets even more complicated when we discuss aboriginal oral tradition, some of which texts were not published until the late twentieth century and yet originate in pre-contact times. Works first published in the twentieth century end up being discussed in this history at the very beginning of volume one, when the printed word did not yet exist in Alberta. Through such shuffling, chronology becomes artificially neat and tidy.

The postmodern challenge to the modernist sense of historical narrative problematizes the very project of a literary history of Alberta. Since no literary history of Alberta has been written before, this text sets out to define what has previously been undefined. In a sense, this text creates the very idea of an Alberta literary history, an idea which did not exist previously. What did exist, prior to this literary history, were scattered observations on individual writers or anthologies that included Albertans under such rubrics as "prairie writing" or "Canadian literary history."[5] *The Literary History of Alberta* thus turns out to be an exploration, a naming, a creation of history that had not previously been named *a history*. Philosopher Jacques Derrida wrote that when a name comes, "...it still remains alien to the person, only naming immanence...."[6] There is a tentativeness in any new naming, including this one. But Derrida continues, "A name should only be given to what deserves it and calls for it."[7] This narrative is motivated by the belief that Alberta writing deserves a sense of history.

The postmodern historian is aware of contradictions, slippages, limitations, and interpretative methodologies as he creates his narrative. What holds literary phenomena together as a historical whole is the existence of the field itself. Literary history as a discipline takes the dynamic flow of literary phenomena and turns them into something stable and graspable as a single entity, while at the same time revealing the irregularities and contradictions of that entity.

We know from a single beginning filled with presumed certainty come multiple reinterpretations. Robert Kroetsch says, "I don't trust the narrative of history because it begins from meaning instead of discovering meanings along the way."[8] For Kroetsch, the historical task seeks *a priori* to order the universe with a predetermined plot. He believes the honest approach is to let chaos unfold in myriad ways. Of course, this approach challenges the literary historian, who seeks to impose order upon chaos, to mould a vessel in which the phenomenon of literature may be safely contained and understood.

A literary history that brings selected information to the foreground also slips other information into the background. All telling, according to philosopher Martin Heidegger, is a gathering up, a putting together of what was apart; but in the act of putting together, we simply create another piece, another part and not the whole we think we have.[9] Thus, closure is elusive, probably even impossible, and so this text attempts to be comprehensive but not definitive.

Representation (in a postmodern sense) is an issue for Alberta literature because Alberta as a milieu is difficult to define. What constitutes Alberta writing? Other concepts have been applied to Alberta writing, such as "English," "prairie," and "Canadian," which are valid in their ways. They draw their defining power from areas much broader than the political boundaries associated with the word *Alberta*. Alberta's contributions to Canada's national literature and to the cultural tradition of the English language are an integral part of this literary history, but they are not its main focus. Perhaps a more pressing questions is, why do we need to distinguish some writings as Albertan? Those writers who live and work in Alberta see themselves as Albertans and would appreciate a deeper sense of their literary heritage.

Alberta is a province of Canada. This text explores the provincial identity, something distinct from region, nation, empire, or world. This book claims there is such an entity as "Alberta literature" that can be discussed in a coherent manner, but who or what is entitled to be called Albertan is approached in a preliminary way. In this volume of literary history, an example of Alberta writing may be work done by someone born and raised here but living elsewhere, who does not even write about Alberta. It may include someone not born here but educated in Alberta. It may also include someone who travelled through the area now called Alberta and then wrote about it for a non-Alberta audience. It could be a book or a long unpublished manuscript recently come to light. It could be something in a language other than English that is unknown to the dominant culture. All these are possible elements when discussing Alberta literature.

Because of the uncertainty, cultural bias, and relativity inherent in all historical claims, this volume uses an elastic definition of Alberta that includes what happened here before Alberta was "Alberta"; that includes an aboriginal oral tradition in translation; that includes non-English literatures; that includes literary outsiders as well as canonical figures, myths as well as facts.

As the first literary history of Alberta, this book is a pioneer effort, with all the exhilaration and limitation that image suggests. For too long, Albertans have thought more of other places, other people, other literatures; have been enthralled by narratives produced by others; have felt that indigenous writing is little more than rough-hewn literary pioneering; have believed that greatness lies elsewhere. The purpose of this book is to give depth and history to our literary identity and thereby challenge some of these assumptions and prejudices.

By defining the basic canon of Alberta writing, *The Literary History of Alberta* intends to establish the value of this literary tradition in both a national and international context and to encourage current and future generations of writers to view their work as Albertan. As the founding literary history, this text is both exploratory and originating. It is exploratory in the sense that it is aware of its limitations and knows there is more to be revealed about Alberta writing than is contained here. It is originating in the sense of naming the origins of Alberta writing and claiming that this place has an identifiable literary *originality*, distinct from other places and cultures. This text makes three fundamental claims: that Alberta has a literary history that is definable and worth knowing; that Alberta's literary identity is multicultural and polyphonic; and that Alberta's literary history is now moving toward a global synthesis.

In articulating a tradition, this history becomes a text about texts, a narrative about narratives, a discourse about discourses. Its discourse constitutes a path that leads us through historical time. To gather up individual names of writers, place them and their books within historical epochs, identify them with one another, and claim they may be called "Albertan," is to acknowledge a certain unity and value in that identity. By drawing each writer's fragmentary understanding of Alberta, as they experienced then wrote about it, into a unified whole, the historian creates his own narrative about what those before him have created. From their individual voices arises a collective spirit of a place.

What the reader will find reading this text is a compression of authors' lives and their texts into a paragraph or a page. The narrative whole the historian is obliged to create from many random pieces sometimes reduces the subjects of his writing to abbreviated elements. This severe reduction is regrettable but necessary to achieve a coherent narrative. It must be recognized, however, that for those truly interested in the literary history of Alberta, this text is merely a map to greater discoveries and revelations. With it, they can begin their own journeys into Alberta's immensely rich and varied literary terrain.

1
Writing-
on-Stone

WRITING-ON-STONE is a small provincial park along the Milk River in southern Alberta that contains a site sacred to aboriginal peoples.[1] The site contains a large number of images, some dating from the pre-European contact period, either carved (petroglyphs) or painted with ochre (pictographs). Some images seem to represent human figures, animals, and birds, while later images also depict horses and guns. Current estimates date the oldest images to about 400 A.D., although specific dating is problematic, except for post-European contact images of horses and guns.[2]

The Blackfoot name for the place is *aysin'eep,* which one writer translates as "is being written."[3] Another translates the name as "it has been written," with an emphasis on the past.[4] This divergence in translation indicates the problem of rendering concepts from the oral to the literate tradition, from one culture to another. The western literary tradition has developed from a linear understanding of both reading and writing. The written line in English suggests both a beginning and an end, with a straight-forward logic between them. Pictographs may not express this thought pattern.

Literate cultures make a strict distinction between writing and art, but in oral cultures this distinction may not be present. Can we call the images at Writing-on-Stone writing? Are they literature or are they art? Are they both? Or neither? Is it possible to "translate" what the images represented to their creators into literary concepts, designations, and meanings? If we take Writing-

1

on-Stone as the beginning of the literary history of Alberta, these are questions we must examine.

A series of seemingly simple images at Writing-on-Stone may represent the equivalent of a poem, a prayer, a song, a story, or, more likely, something quite unlike what these words suggest in the English language. Anthropologists call oral culture "high context" culture, because a complex of meanings and associations is transmitted and understood in each word. Alphabet-based, literate culture is "low context," because it depends more on the intricacies of linguistic divisions and categories than on social context. Meaning is more closely linked to the language itself than to its use. Derrick de Kerchove, a scholar of culture and technology, emphasizes the difference when he writes, "oral listening tends to be global and comprehensive, while literate listening is specialized and selective."[5] He goes on to say that in an oral culture, "the presence, the energy and the reputation of the speaker" are paramount, but in literate culture, the spoken word has less value than the written word.[6]

In the 1980s, journalist Mark Abley described the Writing-on-Stone images as "foreign stories," while his guide noted that deciphering them is "like learning a foreign language."[7] Abley uses terms like "visual grammar" and "graphic vocabulary" as he struggles to describe the images using western literary norms.[8] Archaeologist Grace Rajnovich, who has studied similar images in the Canadian Shield from Quebec to Saskatchewan, believes "Indian rock painting is picture writing, not art...."[9] "To begin to comprehend the concepts of Indian picture writing...is to understand the character of the languages spoken by the painters," she says.[10] Rajnovich supports her interpretation by quoting from George Copway's book *The Traditional History and Characteristic Sketches of the Ojibway Nations* (1850):

> There are many Indian words which when translated into English lose their force and do not convey so much meaning in one sentence as the original does in one word.[11]

Aboriginal scholar Leroy Little Bear of the University of Lethbridge makes a similar observation:

> We can find in the English way of thinking a very linear way of thinking...but a line lends itself to polarized thinking.... But for aboriginal

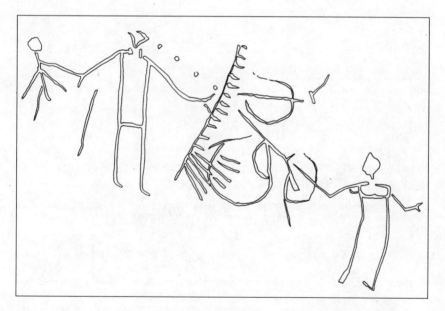

A sampling of pictographs from Writing-on-Stone, from Mystical Themes in Milk River Rock Art *(Edmonton: University of Alberta Press, 1991). Reproduced by permission.*

A sampling of pictographs from Writing-on-Stone, from Mystical Themes in Milk River Rock Art *(Edmonton: University of Alberta Press, 1991). Reproduced by permission.*

people that's not the thinking process....The other aspect of the English way of thinking is that English is largely noun or object-oriented. In Blackfoot, most of the words are action-oriented words....[12]

Copway tried to show the linguistic elements in pictographs by creating a dictionary equating English words with single pictographs. But much of the nuanced meaning and symbolic significance of the pictographs were lost in creating this one-to-one correspondence.

Pat Barry writes extensively about Writing-on-Stone in *Mystical Themes in Milk River Rock Art* (1991), calling the images "precious documents...cloaked in a language of symbols."[13] She considers them more a form of religious art than literature, although the post-contact images may have had a storytelling element. Barry associates the glyphs with a shamanistic tradition going back to the beginnings of human religion, and says their purpose was to depict a supernatural reality experienced in the shaman's vision.

Grace Rajnovich considers pictographs "sacred signs" and characterizes aboriginal thought as "poetic and complex."[14] Gerald Conaty, of Calgary's Glenbow Museum, considers the images both religious symbolism and story-telling. "Thousands of years ago," he writes, "people recorded their history and beliefs on stone outcrops which dot the Canadian plains."[15] The pictographs of Alberta may not be as extensive as those of Ontario (there are seventy-two confirmed sites in Alberta, of which fifty-nine are on the cliffs of the Milk River), but their quality is high.[16] Although representative of Plains cultures, Writing-on-Stone is related to a wider tradition of aboriginal expression in North America.

The Blackfoot Confederacy was well known for storytelling on buffalo robes and tipis. Conaty writes that "Siksika, Blood and Piegan...painted their stories on tipi covers and liners, bison robes, and even the pages of ledger books...."[17] Ledger drawings are coloured sketches of buffalo hunts and battles, created in ledger books in the 1880s. The ledger drawings of Assiniboine artist Hongeeyeesa are called *woknagabi okmabi* in Assiniboine, which has been translated as "stories that have been drawn."[18]

At the turn of the twentieth century, artist Edmund Morris asked several southern Alberta chiefs to tell their stories on buffalo robes. One of the chiefs, Bull Plume, responded that he would rather "paint on a story paper in book form."[19] Morris, however, preferred robes and commissioned five of them.[20]

▤ *Running Rabbit (right) at work on a buffalo robe. His son is taking notes of the explanation.*
Photograph by Edmund Morris, 1909. Provincial Archives of Manitoba, N 16344.

While the robes were being prepared in 1909, translators recorded the artists'
explanations of their creations. For example, Running Rabbit's words and
pictures were translated from Blackfoot into English by his son, Houghton,
while Running Rabbit created the images and explained their meaning.[21]
Should we think of this complex interaction between storytelling, oral
culture, and alphabet-based, literate culture as the "writing" of the buffalo
robes? Arni Brownstone, author of a book on the buffalo pictographs, argues
they are more art than writing, because of their pictorial quality, use of colour,
and lack of alphabetic words.

An important use of pictographs is the winter count, "a record of tribal
history maintained over a period of perhaps 150 years, each year marked by a
pictograph representing an outstanding event."[22] Bull Plume (Stumikisisapo),
who told his story on a buffalo robe for Edmund Morris, "was the last Piegan
to keep up the tribal Winter Count."[23] Hugh Dempsey, an authority on the
nations of the Blackfoot Confederacy, described a winter count by the
Blackfoot Bad Head (Pakap-otokam) that covered the period 1810 to 1883.

Although Bad Head died in 1884, his relatives maintained the winter count until 1906, by which time it was kept in a school scribbler.[24]

Ted Yellow-Fly, a Blackfoot, wrote about pictographs in a 1929 article on tipi designs.[25] Yellow-Fly divided the designs into a series of symbols, then explained how they came into being, either through tradition or visions, and how they were passed down from generation to generation. War exploits were the "most prominent subject of Blackfoot pictographic art," writes Arni Brownstone, who claims the Blackfoot "read" pictographs the way we view maps or shorthand.[26] War histories were usually autobiographical accounts, signed by name glyphs.[27] Yellow-Fly notes that a number of people collaborated on a "war deed" design, each contributing his part of the story. These early chronicles represent the first national and military histories produced in Alberta.

To treat aboriginal pictographs and petroglyphs as part of Alberta's literary heritage requires that we view them in their own cultural context and consider how their role in that context approximates the role of written language in literary culture. Derrick de Kerchove goes back to the beginning of writing in distinguishing between literal representations and stylized ones in the development of Sumerian pictograms, based on the work of Denise Schmandt-Besserat.[28] Both literal and stylized elements could have existed at Writing-on-Stone. De Kerchove recognizes that the "ideographic representations of languages" created a different mindset from alphabet-driven languages.[29]

The concept of hieroglyphics may help us understand pictographs, whether done on stone, buffalo skins, or ledger pages, more as a form of writing than of art. The word *hieroglyphics* combines the Greek words *hiero* (sacred) and *glyphe* (carving). Archaeologists use the term to describe the symbol-based pictorial language of the Egyptians or Mayans. If the images at Writing-on-Stone could be "read" by others in the culture that created them, they can be said to function the way a written language does. Thus, the pictographs and petroglyphs of Writing-on-Stone and other sites in Alberta may constitute our earliest literary heritage.

It may be as problematic to call the images of Writing-on-Stone "rock art" as it is to call them "picture writing," because neither concept existed in the languages of those who created the images. The literate tradition defines pictographs as art because it tends to privilege writing over image. But

Methodist missionary John Maclean, who was stationed at Fort Macleod from 1880 to 1889, suggests multiple uses of these images in oral culture. In his book *Canadian Savage Folk: The Native Tribes of Canada* (1896), Maclean notes that "when the South Piegan visited these rocks...they used them as models when they returned home, drawing figures on robes similar to those they had seen."[30] Such usage suggests a more complicated form of textual transmission at work than either the categories of "art" or "writing" can convey.

To claim the images of Writing-on-Stone as Alberta's earliest writing is an appreciative gesture toward a consciousness rooted in this place, ultimately beyond the grasp of western literary tradition. It recognizes that there are knowledges and practices we may not understand and cannot easily categorize, yet they shape us just the same, because we share the same landscapes. The images of Writing-on-Stone may have functioned in oral culture the way sacred scriptures have in literate cultures. Placing Alberta's literary origins outside the history and traditions of English language and literature is not an act of cultural appropriation but a recognition of the cultural diversity this land has spawned.

The Alphabet

As many as five hundred languages may have existed in North America when the Europeans first arrived; of those, some two hundred remain.[31] Prior to the arrival of the Europeans, these languages had no written alphabets. Pictorial representations, such as those found at Writing-on-Stone, are the closest we have to a written literature of these pre-contact cultures. While pictographs are limited in number in Alberta and difficult to date, orally transmitted aboriginal stories are becoming increasingly abundant. Indeed, the dominant society is just beginning to acknowledge their cultural value and difference.

North American culture has long privileged writing over oral telling. Thus, the circulation of native stories, songs, and prayers outside of aboriginal cultures has been restricted, either ignored by the general literary community or kept the preserve of ethnographic and archaeological experts. Aboriginal literature reached the dominant culture primarily through transcriptions and translations into English or French. In her contemporary study of European consciousness in the exploration period, feminist literary critic Mary Louise Pratt discusses "the perils of writing in what I like to call 'contact zones,' social spaces where disparate cultures meet, clash, and grapple with each other, often in highly asymmetrical relations of domination and subordination."[32] The act of translation from aboriginal oral cultures into European languages participates in the power relationship of dominance and subordination.

In *The Voice in the Margin: Native American Literature and the Canon*, his analysis of aboriginal literatures, cultural historian Arnold Krupat sets out the parameters of oral and written cultures. "For oral societies without alphabetic 'letters' literature is whatever language is deemed worthy of sufficient repetition to assure that it will be remembered and passed along. From a quantitative point of view, oral cultures will inevitably have less literature than chirographic and print cultures."[33] In the twentieth century, the transmission of native culture has followed two paths: Westernized forms or a newly invigorated oral tradition.[34]

Jacques Cartier, the French explorer of the St. Lawrence, was the first to create a Northern Iroquoian word list in the mid-sixteenth century. A half-century later, Marc Lescarbot collected some Micmac songs in Acadia. Both men were French speakers. In the nineteenth century, various aboriginal languages were recreated in Westernized form through syllabic alphabets, created by missionaries, and through phonetic transliteration. This imperial process of acculturation was meant to force oral cultures to conform to both Western written culture and its education system.[35] When we discuss the Westernized forms of native culture, we must be aware of both their ancient oral roots and their historic transformations.

The issue of translation is central to a discussion of aboriginal oral and written literature from Writing-on-Stone to contemporary Cree stories printed in the syllabic alphabet. Critic Eric Cheyfitz calls translation "the central act of European colonialization and imperialism in America," while Tejaswini Niranjana says it raises profound questions about "representation, power, and historicity."[36] Brian Swann, the editor of an anthology of native literatures of North America, considers the results of translation to be "fictions of the Euro-American consciousness"[37] that simply reinforce an already existing dominant view of native culture.

Krupat observes that translation creates a *bicultural* reality, especially when stories are presented as personal histories or autobiographies.[38] In the bicultural reality, the dominant culture subordinates the other. An example of this process is Father Albert Lacombe's *Dictionnaire de la langue crise* (Dictionary of

Father Lacombe, c. 1860.
Courtesy of the City of
Edmonton Archives,
EA 43-87.

the Cree Language), published in Montreal in 1874. The purpose of the dictionary was not to further Cree culture but to advance Catholic missionary work. Its intended reader was the Quebec seminarian coming west to prosely-tize. In the *Dictionnaire*, Lacombe translates the Cree word *Okitchiokimaw* as "le grand chef" and "le roi."[39] The French concept of monarchy, with all its regal and medieval connotations, is far from the aboriginal concept of *Okitchiokimaw*, but the translation provides a sort of cultural shorthand that conforms to the expectations and uses of its intended reader.

In discussing the Cree story "Mistacayawasis" (Big Belly Child), anthropol-ogist Robert Brightman explains the difficulty of grasping another consciousness through the reductive act of translation. "In oral performance of myths and folktales," he writes, "the narrator's choices from among 'different ways of saying the same thing' directly influence how the audience interprets and appreciates the story."[40] A written text cannot convey either the variable grammatical structures or audience interpretation of an oral performance. The following excerpt from a Woodland Cree story in contemporary translation attempts to be both literal and literate:

Ikwani,
those people there in that camp feared Mistahooowatimwa,
'Great Howling Dog.'
When he came, this Great Howling Dog would kill and eat all the people in a camp.
The old man divined that Great Howling Dog was running
toward them on its great dog trail leading across the frozen lake to the camp.[41]

In contrast, the following excerpt, from a 1960s translation of a Dunne-za (Beaver Indian) story of the Peace River district, shows how acculturation can colour the oral tradition. "All the People in This World Come From That Brother and Sister" is based on a English translation of a Dunne-za telling to an English speaker:

A long time ago there were just Indians in this Canada.
At that time all the animals knew how to talk.
Moose, Caribou, Beaver—
everything could talk just like people.
Life was really dangerous then.
The people had a hard time.
There was a big animal—*onli nachi*—
that used to kill the people, and everyone was afraid then.
That was before this new business.
Someone just like a bishop fixed everything up.
Now Indians know about God.[42]

Words such as "Canada," "bishop," and "God" reflect a Europeanized form of explanation.

Linguist Melville Jacobs claims that aboriginal oral narratives are more similar to Western dramatic poetry than to the "essayist prose into which they had so often been translated."[43] In discussing Athapaskan narratives, based on a study made at Fort Chipewyan, sociolinguists Ron and Suzanne Scollon suggest that everything between the narrator's pauses constitutes a line, usually less than one sentence. "As the narrative action increases," they write, "lines tend to shorten and the pace is slowed."[44] Lines form into verses, verses into stanzas, and stanzas into scenes, the largest unit of narrative organization. Oral narratives invite audience participation and interaction, creating a give and take of power, authority, and meaning.[45] Translation, then, is not merely an equation of one language with another, but the false equation of the expressive forms of an oral culture with the norms of a literate one.

This is evident in an early translation of aboriginal stories in Alberta by the North West Company trader, explorer, and mapmaker David Thompson. During the winter of 1787/88, Thompson recorded Piegan chief Saukamapee's accounts of the coming of horses to the Blackfoot (Siksika) and the smallpox epidemic of 1781. Thompson describes Saukamapee as a man of seventy-five or eighty years, tall, his face slightly marked by smallpox, and states that his account goes back to about 1730.[46] The editor of the book in which the account appears claims that since Thompson was "a fine storyteller himself," the tone of the story is probably substantially unaltered from the original narrative.[47] Yet this example from the text seems to dispute that claim:

> The Peeagans were always the frontier Tribe, and upon whom the Snake Indians made their attacks, these latter were very numerous, even without their allies, and the Peeagans had to send messengers among us to procure help. Two of them came to the camp of my father and I was then about his age (pointing to a Lad of about sixteen years) he promised to come and bring some of his people, the Nahathaways [Cree] with him, for I am myself of that people, and not of those with whom I am.[48]

What a contrast between this account and the contemporary Cree translation quoted earlier! This difference could represent a variation in oral forms as distinct as poetry and the novel. Or more likely, the difference results from the goals of the translator, with the older translation trying to be as English as possible for its European audience, while the contemporary one attempts to be as close to authentic native expression as possible.

Another example of overlaid cultural values is found in Alberta author Grant MacEwan's book *Portraits from the Plains* (1971). MacEwan attributes

SCAR-FACE.   55

Ki áisæmò Pɑχtsópisòɑχs ánis-
tsiu otɑ́kài: Nitákaχkài. Otánik-
aie: A´moiàuk nitsíkiatsis. Ki
omí nápi otánik: A´moiàuk matá-
piua nitáiakokoχkùyiχ´pi, ánnyaie
áiakauànistsiu. Otánik omí kipit-
áke: A´moiàuk naiáiua, notsǽm-
mokä̀´n, núnnatsis. Nepúsi àkoχ-
táukau. A`istæmátsis kitsíχ´kauau.
Ki ánnyaie kanistoχkòtoχpinan.
Otánik omí otɑ́kài: Napí, ákita-
pauop ómim áukskaie, kitákitsi-
nèpot. Aitotóeniki kitáuaχsìni,
noχkoχkókit ænnáχk akéuaχk.
Amói nitsíkiatsis kitákoχtaiki.
A´kitsitautò ænnáχk akéuaχk.
A´moi àsipis istsüiatapìksist. Anít:
Napí, ænnaχkauk kitoχkéman.
A´nistsiuaie: A´. Otánik otɑ́kài:
Nápistsàkit. A`utáχkoàiniki ksáχ-
kuma, istsápit. Itomátapinisò.
Aitotóaie annó ksáχkum. Omí
nitúmmo itoχkítaupiu. Moyìsts
mátsipiχ´tsiu.

Itsinóau.   Omá nínau amóm

of yours [not your own boy, but
Scar-face], this [will be called]
False-Morning-star.
    And after a long time False-
Morning-star said to his partner:
I shall go home. He was told
by him: Here is my whistle. And
he was told by the old man [the
Sun]: What the people will give
to me hereafter, they will do it
this way [the Sun says this after
having shown to the young man
how to make incense and to per-
form the sacrifice]. He was told
by the old woman: Here is my
cloak [of elk-skin], my hat, [and]
my wooden pin. In summer they
will have the medicine-lodge.
Show it to your tribe [how to
make the medicine-lodge]. And
then this is all, we have to give
you. He was told by his partner:
Partner, we shall go over there,
to that hole, I shall let you down.
When you arrive in your country,
give me that woman [that has
scorned you]. With this my whistle
you will whistle. Then that woman
will come [to you]. And this
sinew here, throw it into [the
fire]. Say [then to me]: Partner,
there goes your wife. He an-
swered him: Yes [I shall do just
as you told me]. He was told
by his partner: Shut your eyes.
When you feel the ground, [then]
open your eyes [literally: see].
Then he started down. He came
here on the ground. He sat there
on a butte. He was not far from
the lodges.
    He was seen. The chief said

A sample page from
C.C. Uhlenbeck, Original
Blackfoot Texts
(Amsterdam: Johannes
Müller, 1911). What is
striking about his text is the
amount of English required
to make the translated text
readable.

these stirring words to Crowfoot, the most famous of the late-nineteenth
century Blackfoot chiefs, as he lay dying:

A little while and I will be gone from among you. Whither, I cannot tell.
From nowhere we came: into nowhere we go. What is life? It is the flash of
a firefly in the night. It is the breath of a buffalo in the winter time. It is as
the little shadow that runs across the grass and loses itself in the sunset.[49]

MacEwan took the speech from an earlier book that hoped to confirm
Crowfoot's wisdom and visionary greatness—his regal nature. The earlier
author claimed his missionary father had witnessed this speech.[50]

C.C. Uhlenbeck, an early-twentieth century Dutch scholar of the Blackfoot language, attempted to capture a more accurate representation of Blackfoot language and consciousness. Uhlenbeck published a monograph containing a phonetic version of Blackfoot in one column and an English translation in the column next to it.

After spending three months living in northern Montana with the southern Peigans, he published the stories of NinoXkyaio (Bear-chief) and Ninaistaku (Mountain-chief), which were "communicated and explained" to him by Joseph Tatsey, a Blood living with the tribe.[51] Uhlenbeck says, "The English translation which accompanies the texts, though as literal as possible, does not suffice to obtain a grammatical understanding of all the words and forms contained in them."[52] What is striking about his text is the amount of English required to make the translated text readable. Hugh Dempsey says his Blackfoot wife found Uhlenbeck's translation accurate but felt it could not present the context of meaning, much of it unspoken, that linked the words into a narrative for its native audience.[53] Uhlenbeck's translation reveals how incompletely written English captures oral telling.

Uhlenbeck's attempt at linguistic accuracy contrasts sharply with the popular "renditions" effected by both earlier and later writers. Marius Barbeau, once revered as Canada's foremost anthropologist of the early twentieth century, published a popular book in the 1920s called *Indian Days in the Canadian Rockies*, which he claimed contained "true narratives of Indian lives substantially as reported from native sources."[54] An important source for Barbeau was George McLean (1871-1967), also known as Chief Walking Buffalo of the Bear's Paw Band of the Stoney. The following is McLean's English-language account of rock paintings in the Crowsnest Pass, as presented by Barbeau:

> There is a place on the Crowsnest Pass, along the mountain, where the cliff overhangs. Above the place where a man can reach, there are designs in paint in different colours. They are made like rainbows. And then there are buffaloes, and Indians on horses chasing them, and war dances shown on them, sun dances, pictures of them....There is also another place on High River where one sees such designs.[55]

Barbeau's translation aims to convey in a matter-of-fact tone subject matter that was anything but matter-of-fact to the Stoney. Chief Walking Buffalo's relationship to the "designs" is culturally sanitized in this representation.

The process of non-natives producing translations for English-language audiences continued into the late twentieth century. In 1977, Adolf Hungry Wolf, a German immigrant to Canada who has adopted native traditions and lifestyle, published *The Blood People*, in which he writes about the Blood and presents their stories. A story attributed to Jim White Calf, or Last Gun, is presented in English in Hungry Wolf's book with no indication of translation, as if these were the exact words in which White Calf recounted an incident he supposedly experienced in 1889:

> Calf Robe and I were sent up a hill as scouts during that day, and we soon spotted a lone rider coming our way. He looked to us like a scout, so we went down to distract him from finding our camp....We hurried back down to our party and all packed up and headed east, in case the scout came back with the Mounted Policeman.[56]

If the story was narrated in English to Hungry Wolf, it is one thing; if it was translated from Blackfoot, it is something else; if it was taken from some previous text, it is something else again. There is no indication of the story's original form, which potentially misleads readers about its authenticity.

All these narratives, from Thompson to Hungry Wolf, present aboriginal literary material for an English-language market. The work of scholars such as Uhlenbeck is more careful but is not widely available, so mainstream culture receives only the popular renditions, which simply reinforce its cultural biases. If Uhlenbeck's translation were widely available, its presentation of difference and acculturation might generate discomfort in the reader. Avoidance of the culturally unfamiliar may lead to misunderstanding, assimilation, and appropriation. However, there is a move toward cultural respect and authenticity among today's scholars.

The reworking of Leonard Bloomfield's *Sacred Stories of the Sweet Grass Cree*, a collection of traditional Cree stories originally published in 1930, is a case in point. Dictated on the Sweet Grass Reserve near Battleford,

6. HOW SWEET-GRASS BECAME CHIEF.

kâ-kisikâw-pîhtukâw.

(1) kayâs mitunih kisâyiniw âwakôw ukimâw. ôma nakiwatsihk ôtah wikiwak. kîtahtawâ kîkisâpâ utnâw misatimwah; uyahpitâw, âh-tâhtapit; sipwâhtâw, âh-papâmuhtât. mâkwâ âh-pimuhtât, ipatinâw wâpahtam, âh-âmatsiwâyit ayisiyiniwah, nâpâwah. âkwah kitâpamâw, kitâpâkan âh-kanawâpâkanâhikâyit, ayisiyiniw â-nanâkwâpamâyit. kiskâyimâw ayâhtsiyiniwah.¹ âkwah upâskisikan pîhtâsôw; môskistawâw âh-pimisiniyit. âkwah âh-kih-kiskâyihtahk aw ayâhtsiyiniw, nâhiyawah â-môskistâkut, tapasîw; â-sakâyik kutâskamôw. âkusi pâskiswâw nâhiyaw. namuya matwâwiw pâskisikan. âkutah â-sâskâmut, âkutaw uhtsi mâtâwisiwak nîsusâp iyâhtsiyiniwak. âkwah nâhiyaw âh-pâyakut môskistawâw, â-wîh-nôtinât, a-wîh-pâskiswât. tapasîwak ôki iyâhtsiyiniwak, âh-pâyakuwit âh-kustâtsik, âh-pâh-pâskisukuteik. kutak sakâw âkutah minah sâskâmôwak. âsay minah mâtâwisiwak, âh-pimipahtâteik. âkwah awa nâhiyaw âh-tâhtapit, âkutâ mîkiwâhpah, mitun â-mihtsâtisik nâhiyawak, âkutâ âh-itisahwât. iyâhtsiyiniw "âkutâ nika-pimâtisin", âh-itâyihtahk, namuya kiskâyihtam ayisiyiniwah nâhiyawah â-mihtsâtiyit âkutah k-âtuhtâtsik. iyikuhk âh-wâpamâtsik nâhiyawah, âkuyikuhk wayuniwak, âh-kîh-wâpamâtsik mihtsât nâhiyawah.

(2) âkwah pâyak awah nisusâp iyâhtsiyiniwah âh-nawaswâtât, â-sakâyik âyakô môskistamwak sîpîsis. âkutah pahkupâwak, âh-âsôwahahkik. âkutah nipîhk kôkîw pâyak ayâhtsiyiniw, âh-kâsôt, "namuya nika-wâpamik nâhiyaw", âh-itâyihtahk. kutakak ôkih tapasîwak pâyakusâp; kutak sakâw âkutâ sâskisiwak. âkutâ âkwah nâhiyawak wîhkwâskawâwak, tâpiskôts wâtihkân âh-usihtâteik iyâhtsiyiniwak, âh-nôtinâkâteik. âkwah ôki nâhiyawak kisiwâk âh-ituhtâtsik itah âh-ayâyit iyâhtsiyiniwah, âkwah âwaku kâ-papâ-nawaswâtât, âwaku nîkânuhtâw, tâpiskôts ayah simâkanis-ukimâw, âkwah ôkih ayâhtsiyiniwak kisiwâk âh-wâpamâteik nâhiyawah âkwah umah wâtihkân umah k-âyâtsik. âkwah ninisô² nâhiyawak âkutah nipawiwak wâtihkânihk teikih. âkwah pâyak nâhiyaw tâpiskôts umah mistik ôtah — âh-tâh-tahkamât môhkumân uhtsi ayâhtsiyiniwah; âyaku pâyak nâhiyaw kâ-tôtahk. âkusi âkwah kahkiyaw nâhiyawak pîhtukâwak wâtihkânihk, môhkumân âh-tahkunahkik, nâhiyawak ôhi ayâhtsiyiniwah âh-tâh-tahkamâtsik môhkumân uhtsi. nipahâwak; kahkiyaw nam âwiyak pimâtisiw pâyakusâp aniki ayâhtsiyiniwak. âkusi âkwah môhkumân uhtsi âh-manisamawâtsik, ustikwâniyiwah âh-manisamwâtsik nâhiyawak. âkusi puyôwak. ayis mâstsihwak; âyak uhtsi kâ-puyutsik. âkutaw

¹ In earlier texts I have noted the second vowel of this word as long; later I heard it predominantly as short.
² Word unknown to me; probably a mis-hearing.

6. HOW SWEET-GRASS BECAME CHIEF.

Coming-Day.

(1) In the time of the men of long ago he was chief. Here at Sweet-Grass they dwelt. One morning, he took a horse; he saddled it and mounted; he set out to roam. As he went along he saw someone climbing a hill, a man. He observed him, watching through a spy-glass, this man who was looking for people. He knew him for a Blackfoot. He loaded his gun and attacked him as he lay on the ground. When the Blackfoot perceived that a Cree was attacking him, he fled; he hid in the bushes. The Cree tried to shoot him, but the gun did not go off. From the place where he had fled into the woods, twelve Blackfoot came out upon the trail. The lone Cree attacked them, wanting to do battle and shoot them. The Blackfoot fled, fearing the one Cree who was shooting at them. They fled into another wood. Again they came forth in their course. But the Cree on his horse was driving them to where the Cree were many in their tents. The Blackfoot meanwhile, thinking, "In this direction I shall escape," did not know that there were many people, many Cree in the place to which they were going. When they saw the Cree, they turned, at the sight of the many Cree.

(2) Then, as the one one was pursuing the twelve Blackfoot, in a wooded place they made for a creek. They went into the water to cross. There one of the Blackfoot ducked under water to hide, thinking, "The Cree will not see me." The other eleven fled; they went into another wood. There the Cree surrounded them, the Blackfoot making a kind of trench as they fought. When the Cree went near to where the Blackfoot were, then he who had pursued them, he went in the lead, like an officer, and the Blackfoot saw the Cree come near the trench where they were. And the Cree stood there close to the pit. Then one Cree — holding it like this stick here — with his knife began to stab the Blackfoot; one Cree did this. Thereupon all the Cree began to enter the trench, knife in hand, stabbing one Blackfoot after another. They slew them; not one of those eleven Blackfoot was left alive. Then with their knives they scalped them; the Cree cut the scalps from their heads. Then they

3*

≡ *From Leonard Bloomfield,* Plains Cree Texts *(New York: G.E. Stechert & Co., 1934).*

Saskatchewan, these stories represent traditions that extend into north-central Alberta. The following example, from his bilingual 1934 edition, is Mrs. Coming-Day's story of a small-pox epidemic. Notice Bloomfield's application of conventional English sentence structure and paragraph form to the Cree text. Compare this to the 1981 rendering of the same text by linguists H.C. Wolfart and J.F. Carroll. Wolfart and Carroll assert that Bloomfield's translation "reflects the literary character of the Cree texts," but their own reproduction of the text is modified significantly by its placement on the page.[57] The words are similar, but the layout gives a sense of the narrative closer to the free oral style than the square block paragraphs reproduced in Bloomfield's original. In this case, the design speaks.

To bring aboriginal cultures into the history of Alberta writing, and to give them first place in that history, as this text does, opens up our literary imagination and roots Alberta literature in this place and in the cultures of those who first lived here. Native tradition forms the province's literary base. The failure to acknowledge this tradition for literature has created a certain impoverish-

kit-ôhpikiw; ka-wâpamik ôma ká-nanapotôkanêskátân;
'sîhkihp' kik-êsiyîhkátikwak; namoya ka-miyosin; osâm
kikisiwâhin ê-wîhtaman, ê-ôhkápiyan," itêw.

* * *

⁴⁹ êkosi êkoyikohk êwako átayôhkêwin.

(B)

ká-ksikáw-pîhtokêw:

¹ kayás mitoni kisêyiniw êwako okimâw. ² ôma
nakîwacîhk ôta wîkiwak. ³ kîtahtawê kîkisêpá otinêw
misatimwa; wiyahpitêw, ê-êhtapit; sipwêhtêw,
ê-papâmohtêt. ⁴ mêkwá ê-pimohtêt, ispatinâw wâpahtam,
ê-âmaciwêyit ayîsiyiniwa, nâpêwa. ⁵ êkwa kitápamêw,
kitápákan ê-kanawâpákanêhikêyit, ayîsiyiniwa
ê-nanátawápamáyit. ⁶ kiskêyimêw ayahciyiniwa. ⁷ êkwa
opáskisikan pîhtásôw; môskîstawêw ê-pimisiniyit. ⁸ êkwa
ê-kî-kiskêyihtahk awa ayahciyiniw, nêhiyawa
ê-môskîstátkot, tapasîw; ê-sakáyik kotêskamôw. ⁹ êkosi
páskiswêw nêhiyaw. ¹⁰ namoya matwêwiw páskisikan.
¹¹ êkota ê-êskámot, êkota ohci mátáwisiwak nîsosáp
ayahciyiniwak. ¹² êkwa nêhiyaw ê-pêyakot môskîstawêw,
ê-wî-nôtinît, ê-wî-páskiswát. ¹³ tapasîwak ôki
ayahciyiniwak, ê-pêyakoyit ê-kostácik, ê-pâ-páskisokocik.
¹⁴ kotak sakáw êkota mîna sêskámôwak. ¹⁵ âsay mîna
mátáwisiwak, ê-pimipahtácik. ¹⁶ êkwa awa nêhiyaw
ê-têhtapit, êkotê mîkiwáhpa, mitoni ê-mihcêticik
nêhiyawak, êkotê ê-itisahwât. ¹⁷ ayahciyiniw "êkotê
nika-pimátisin" ê-itêyihtahk, namoya kiskêyihtam
ayîsiyiniwa nêhiyawa ê-mihcêtiyit êkota k-êtohtécik.
¹⁸ iyikohk
ê-wâpamácik nêhiyawa, êkoyikohk wâyonîwak,
ê-kî-wâpamácik mihcêt nêhiyawa.

future time mortal man will grow up; he will see here on
you where I have kicked your rump crooked; 'Hell-Diver'
they will call you; you will not be handsome; too much
have you angered me by telling this and by opening your
eyes," he told him.

* * *

⁴⁹ And so this is the end of this sacred story.

(B) How Sweet-Grass Became Chief

Coming-Day:

¹ In the time of the men of long ago he was chief.
² Here at Sweet Grass they dwelt. ³ One morning, he
took a horse; he saddled it and mounted; he set out to
roam. ⁴ As he went along he saw someone climbing a hill,
a man. ⁵ He observed him, watching through a spyglass,
this man who was looking for people. ⁶ He knew him for
a Blackfoot. ⁷ He loaded his gun and attacked him as he
[the Blackfoot] lay on the ground. ⁸ When the Blackfoot
perceived that a Cree was attacking him, he fled; he hid
in the bushes. ⁹ The Cree tried to shoot him. ¹⁰ But the
gun did not go off. ¹¹ From the place where he had fled
into the woods, twelve Blackfoot came out upon the trail.
¹² The lone Cree attacked them, wanting to do battle and
shoot them. ¹³ The Blackfoot fled, fearing the one Cree
who was shooting at them. ¹⁴ They fled into another
wood. ¹⁵ Again they came forth in their course. ¹⁶ But the
Cree on his horse was driving them to where the Cree
were many in their tents. ¹⁷ The Blackfoot meanwhile,
thinking, "In this direction I shall escape," did not know
that there were many people, many Cree in the place to
which they were going. ¹⁸ When they saw the Cree, they
turned, at the sight of the many Cree.

From H.C. Wolfart and J.F. Carroll, Meet Cree: A Guide to the Language
(Edmonton: The University of Alberta Press, 1981). Used by permission.

ment. By ignoring our beginnings in the sacred and heroic of aboriginal
cultures, we severely limit our sense of literary identity. Cultural critic Derrick
de Kerchove believes the electronic universe we now inhabit is returning oral
values to dominance. "We are returning to an oral culture," he writes, "or,
more precisely, to an electronic oral culture."[58] If this observation proves valid,
Alberta's oral tradition can only have greater influence and importance for
everyone in Alberta.

To accept pictographs and winter counts as part of Alberta's literary
heritage is to treat them as texts, both sacred and secular. Of course, the argument can be made that this is an unfair appropriation of a creation that
belongs solely to one or another First Nation. This argument is often made for
exclusivity in aboriginal rights and cultural matters, and is a valid reaction to
the kind of exploitation and appropriation carried on earlier (from the
purchase or theft of sacred objects for museums to reputations and wealth
created by scholarly work).[59] The extent to which native peoples wish to share

their cultures with the dominant culture should be their decision alone. Given the history of European-aboriginal relations, it should not be surprising if this sharing remains restricted and limited. Nonetheless, the simple acknowledgement of the value and importance of Writing-on-Stone is sufficient to wrest Alberta literature from its imperial bondage to acknowledge its non-English, aboriginal literary roots.

Aboriginal texts may be considered part of Alberta literature, both in translation and in their original forms. But to appreciate them in their original forms is to be attentive to them outside books, where they are most alive and genuine. In their own voices, they are paramount. Just as Alberta's literary identity spans continents through immigrant cultures and overlaps with other national and imperial literatures, so too its literary culture shares its traditions with the aboriginal world. From the pictography of Writing-on-Stone through the syllabic alphabets created by the missionaries to the transliterations into European languages, the voices of aboriginal history in Alberta speak to us with differing understanding. It is not their speaking that is problematic—it is our listening.

2
Exploration
Literature

PHILOSOPHER REINER SCHURMANN claims, "As an epoch comes to an end, its principle withers away. The principle of an epoch gives it cohesion, a coherence which, for a time, holds unchallenged. At the end of an epoch, however, it becomes possible to question such coherence. In withering away, the supreme referent of an age becomes problematic."[1] The exploration and travel literature of Rupert's Land, the territory which encompassed present-day Alberta, reflects an epoch, a period of time with a certain unifying character or quality. Exploration literature was the voice of Alberta in 1800.

The epoch of exploration literature begins in 1754 with the travels of a Hudson's Bay Company clerk, Anthony Henday, and ends in 1869, when ownership of the area was transferred from the Hudson's Bay Company to the new country of Canada. During this period, cultures co-existed, clashed, and were transformed. It was through exploration literature, and then its outgrowth, travel literature, that the English language and its cultural heritage became the core of Alberta's literary identity, replacing the aboriginal voice.

European exploration culture initially shared the land with its native inhabitants, but at the same time worked to overthrow their cultures. First it undermined native cultures by importing the artifacts of the industrial age and the commercial assumptions of European capitalism. It later worked to eliminate these cultures altogether through the imperial mission of

Christianity, and, in the subsequent territorial period, the reserve system. Aboriginal cultures were not the only ones suppressed. Rooted in conquered Quebec, Francophone culture (whose contribution to exploration literature will be discussed in a later chapter) was also subordinated to the dominant English culture. The worldview of the English explorer that forms the core of this chapter began a cultural trajectory that lasted into the late twentieth century, when non-European forces again returned to the cultural stage in Alberta.

Alberta's exploration literature can be divided into three main periods. The early period (1754 to 1821) begins with Anthony Henday's travels to southern Alberta and ends with the amalgamation of the North West Company (N.W.C.) with the Hudson's Bay Company (H.B.C.) in 1821. The middle period runs from 1822 to 1850. This period reveals shifting aesthetic concerns, as well as a transition from the figure of the explorer to the persona of the traveller. The late period extends from 1851 to 1869 and marks the end of the epoch as the railways began their westward reach.

The writings of the exploration period brought a new consciousness to Alberta. They created an image of this place formed by a culture and an awareness rooted in a distant, non-Alberta reality. Schurmann writes, "the founding...decrees the original code that will remain in effect throughout that civilization."[2] Exploration literature established the primacy of European literature and consciousness in Alberta. But exploration literature was part of something larger, an expression of European imperial traditions, which meant that its relationship to the land was ambiguous: always valuing what was at home more than what was here, while exploiting what was here (from furs to "undiscovered lands") to gain status in "civilization." Exploration literature, for the most part, emphasized what was lacking in this place compared to its referent society. The narrative depended on the culture that sponsored it for value and validation. As a result, alienation and otherness characterize exploration literature.

With historical hindsight, we can see the period from 1754 to 1869 as the first stage of a long cultural transformation. The exploration stage was, in a literary sense, quite narrow, but it planted the seeds that, over a century and a half, flowered into a range of literary production. The aboriginal period was the basic thesis that gave identity to Alberta writing, while exploration literature was the antithesis that tried to negate it, setting in motion the fundamental dynamic of Alberta literary history as it sought to achieve a stable synthesis between the two world views.

Exploration literature was not only British and imperial; it was also a totally male literature. It was a literature of the first person singular, the individual achiever, and it was a literature that claimed ownership by naming. Exploration literature was an expression of the scientific mind, recorded in such objective terms as latitude, longitude, temperature, miles, dates, and times. Since most explorers were also traders, the language of this literature was laden as much with commercial interests as with scientific and political interests.

The world that the explorer "found" was treated in three distinct ways, all variants of the concept of "savage," which was used as a derogatory label. The people were not Christians, the flora and fauna were undomesticated, and the culture was primitive because it had not achieved writing and lacked technology.[3] The explorer's need to perceive savagery and cultural primitiveness in what was, for him, a new land was underpinned by his anxiety about the hostile, impenetrable other. The explorer asserted his belief in his inherent superiority by naming and claiming. He described the land in his own language, in terms that could be understood in the world he came from. This was a fundamental act of appropriation, both in political/legal terms and in terms of the imagination. In the act of appropriating this place and its peoples, the explorer attempted to contain the world around him. In *Images of the West,* historian Douglas Francis explains how the various stages of representation of the region in this period—wasteland, pristine wilderness, and source of imperial glory—served different needs and goals of the imperial imagination.[4]

When history enters a new phase, its literature echoes with a new sense of time, place, persons, and communities. The new literature restructures history by deconstructing what existed before and replacing it with the emerging cultural values and norms. Such is the history of this place that became Alberta. The native cultures that had existed here for centuries were displaced by the values and beliefs of first the imperial explorers and then the colonial settlers.

While the explorer felt himself a foreigner in a godforsaken hinterland, he also believed its strangeness must be controlled by making the unfamiliar into the familiar. It is the duality of being physically here yet elsewhere in one's mind that forms the essence of exploration literature—an existence bifurcated between the alien and the familiar.

The Early Period: 1754–1821

Victor Hopwood, writing in the *Literary History of Canada*, claims that "Our explorers and fur traders left much fair to excellent writing, although the bulk of what they produced is simply historical source material."[5] The issue of the literary value of these journals and books is important but problematic. Hopwood's observation implies that fur-trade journals are primarily historical sources, but some works, such as Alexander Mackenzie's popular narrative of reaching the Pacific Ocean over land, had literary pretensions and a large audience. The relative literary merit of the body of exploration literature must be left to the critics, but most of these works did little to further literary standards. Nevertheless, they are the shaky ground on which Alberta's English-language tradition has been constructed.

Anthony Henday and Matthew Cocking were the first Europeans to reach Alberta. Both were employees of the Hudson's Bay Company. Henday (also spelled "Hendey" and "Hendry") has been labelled (some would say incorrectly) a smuggler from the Isle of Wight who entered the Company's service in 1750 as a labourer and net-maker at York Factory on Hudson Bay. He left the Company in 1762, when he was not promoted after making his inland trek, and retired to England.

Four copies of Henday's journal are extant, including one sent to London in 1755 and a 1791 version.[6] Historian Glyndwr Williams concludes that either the earliest version or the later three are forgeries, because they are so different.[7] There is no evidence to indicate that any version is written in Henday's own hand. Williams says two versions, including the 1755 one, are in the hand of Andrew Graham, who was "Assistant writer" at York Factory on Hudson Bay.[8] The factor at York Factory added his comments and recommendations to the 1755 version when the journal was sent to London. Williams considers James Isham, the factor at York, an influence but believes Henday himself doctored the journal to make himself look more heroic. Later versions provide a different, more imperiled tone because Graham had access to Henday's notes and used them in the 1760s, after Henday's death, to produce a more accurate version of the journey.

This complex situation is explained by Ian MacLaren's four-stage theory of exploration writing. The first phase is the field note or log book entry; the second is the journal; the third, the draft manuscript; finally, the published work emerges.[9] Henday wrote the field notes; Graham and Isham then prepared the journal with Henday's collaboration. Graham later produced further versions without Henday's approval. Finally, L.J. Burpee published the journal in 1907 with his own editorial insertions.

Multiple authoring is normal for exploration literature. The following is an excerpt from version A, dealing with Henday's historic meeting with the Blackfoot. It may not accurately reflect his field notes, but it is how Henday wanted to be portrayed:

> we mett the Eaarchithinue [Blackfoot] men on horseback 40 in number they were out on a Scout from the main body, to see if we were Enemies, when they found us friends, Attickasish, Connawappa, and 2 more of our Leaders marched att the front about 4 Miles, where upon the top of a Hill I seed 200 tents....[10]

This account was the first prose "written" in English about Alberta. The European origins of Alberta writing are therefore the notes of a purported ex-smuggler and lowly labourer on a commercial reconnaissance for the Hudson's Bay Company. That it was a controversial reconnaissance at the time, resulting in several variant reports, only enhances the problematic nature of early exploration writing.

The next H.B.C. servant to write about Alberta was Matthew Cocking (1743-1799), whose journal of his travels in Blackfoot country in 1772/73 was edited and published by L.J. Burpee in 1908. Cocking was a clerk, of higher status than Henday, and was unsympathetic to the native people he met and travelled with. Historian Richard Glover describes Cocking's journals as "well-written...a sharp contrast to the intelligent but semi-literate production of Hearne."[11] The following excerpt is from Burpee's 1908 edition:

> Dec. 1 Tuesday. Our Archithinue friends came to us and pitched a small distance from us.... One of the Leaders talks the Asinepoet [Cree] language well, so that we shall understand each other, as my Leader understands it also. This tribe is named Powestir-Athinuewuck (i.e.) Water-fall Indians. There are 4 Tribes, or Nations, more, which are all Equestrian Indians, Viz.,

Mithco-Athinuwuck or Bloody Indians, Koskitow-Wathesitock or Blackfooted Indians,—Pegonow or Muddy-water Indians & Sassewuck or Woody Country Indians.[12]

Cocking's in-house journals were intended for a very different audience than Hearne's.

Samuel Hearne's work was titled *A Journey from Prince of Wales Fort in Hudson Bay to the Northern Ocean undertaken by order of the Hudson's Bay Co. for the discovery of copper mine; a northwest passage, etc. in the years 1769, 1770, 71 and 72.* It was not strictly a journal, but rather a record of his travels, prepared for a public reading audience. Hearne's book, including maps, appeared almost immediately in German, French, and Dutch translations. The appetite for exploration literature in Europe was immense, and works like Hearne's were much sought after. Ian MacLaren points out that Hearne's field notes are quite different from the published work, especially regarding the native peoples, who are belittled in the published work but not in the field notes.[13] Some historians have called Hearne's account "one of the best narratives of Canadian land exploration" because of its prose, factual detail, general sensibility in describing the traveller's experience, and overall sophistication.[14] Although Hearne's narrative does not belong to Alberta literature as such, as he only approached the northern boundary, it set the standard for subsequent writers.

The debate over the merits of exploration literature as writing has been ongoing. Travel and post journals were internal documents, intended to assist the H.B.C. in London in making decisions about trade possibilities in the interior. They were never meant for publication. When a contemporary historian describes works such as Hearne's as "exotic tales filled with hyperbole and even downright lies," the claim reflects a very recent postcolonial consciousness.[15] Contemporary critics of exploration literature tend to view it as fictionalized non-fiction, although there remain defenders of its heroic and empirical qualities. There is also debate about the intervention of editors, such as Dr. John Douglas, Bishop of Salisbury, who may have prepared Hearne's text for publication and who had a role in editing other exploration books. The Hudson's Bay Company staff who created the notes did not view themselves as writers. The only contemporary publication in book form in the eighteenth century of any of their writings was Hearne's, and his publisher used the editorial and writing talents of an established literary figure in order to create a saleable product.

Peter Fidler is a typical example of a H.B.C. writer whose work was not published until the twentieth century. Fidler (1769-1822) joined the Company as a labourer and quickly advanced. From 1790 to 1792, he was an assistant at Athabasca; in 1792/93, he journeyed from Buckingham House on the North Saskatchewan River as far south as what is now Fort Macleod. Here is his description of a chinook on February 17, 1793:

> a great flush of water came down the Red Deer river last night that ran with a pretty strong current over the ice. This is occasioned by warm weather at the Mountains melting the snow there.[16]

What is interesting about Fidler's journals is his use of phoneticized, English-language versions of the geographic descriptions provided by his native guides. In talking about what is now the Bow River, Fidler lists aboriginal names such as *As Kow seepee* and *Na ma Kay sis sa ta*. Fidler did not displace the aboriginal names by immediately naming and claiming places in English. At this very early stage of exploration, explorers depended on aboriginal culture for guidance and naming, suggesting a much more cooperative and equitable relationship than subsequently developed.

The English language was used not only in the field notes of the explorers and traders but also in the journals kept by trading post factors. The following extract is from a letter George Sutherland of Edmonton House wrote in 1797 to Peter Fidler:

> Edmonton House, February 17, '97
> Dear Sir, Several tribes of Indians have been in since my last, most of which have brought good trades which has reduced my trading goods very low, particularly guns, tobacco, kettles, knives and ball. I have therefore dispatched six men with twelve horses for what goods you can by any means spare, twine excepted....[17]

H.B.C. writing was understandably full of geographic and commercial concerns. And yet an example of early literary interests in Alberta can be found in the journals of Robert Seaborn Miles (1795-1870) for 1818/19, when he was posted at Fort Wedderburn on Lake Athabasca. In his journal, he records a letter saying, "With this you will receive the 2nd Vol. of Pliny...an author who is more generally or deservedly admired...."[18] He later requested and received two volumes of Shakespeare.

The North West Company, the H.B.C.'s Montreal-based rivals, produced both journals and books. Of the five N.W.C. writers that dealt with Alberta up to the period of amalgamation in 1821, two published books in their own period, while the H.B.C. men published none. Can the overpowering, centralized commercial bureaucracy of the H.B.C. account for this discrepancy? Likely. The Hudson's Bay men described their rivals as "pedlars," yet the pedlars turned out to be both more adventuresome explorers and better writers.

The five North West Company creators of exploration literature in the period prior to amalgamation are Cuthbert Grant (17?-1799), Duncan McGillivray (17?-1808), Alexander Mackenzie (1764-1820), David Thompson (1770-1857), and Daniel Harmon (1778-1843). Of these, the most important writer and explorer was Alexander Mackenzie. A slightly earlier journal was kept by Cuthbert Grant, father of the famous Métis leader of the mid-nineteenth century, also named Cuthbert Grant. Grant senior was second-in-command to Peter Pond, who explored northern Alberta in the 1770s and established a fort on the lower Athabasca River near what became Fort Chipewyan.[19] Grant's journal is the earliest North West Company post journal in existence.[20] The following excerpt describes his 1786 trip to Lake Athabasca via the Athabasca River:

> about 2 Oclock there Arrived three Achibawayans [Chipewyans] from above and a little afterwards L'homme de Castor arrived with 2 other Crees I Engaged the two Cadiens Le Doux La Prise Perault Laviolette & Janvier for three years....[21]

This listing of Québécois voyageurs suggests the ethnolinguistic cultural mix of the newly formed North West Company and indicates the strong French presence in northern Alberta.

Norwester and co-founder of Fort Chipewyan Alexander Mackenzie wrote the first popular book dealing with the area that became Alberta. In 1789, he travelled to the Arctic Ocean on the river that now bears his name; in

▤ *Sir Alexander Mackenzie,*
from a portrait by Lawrence.

1793, he crossed the Rocky Mountains and reached the Pacific Ocean. While at Athabasca, he had become acquainted with Peter Pond's erroneous theory of a great river linking Great Slave Lake with the Pacific: it led to the Arctic instead.

Mackenzie's book, titled *Voyages from Montreal in the River St. Lawrence through the Continent of North America to the Frozen and Pacific Oceans; in the Years 1789 and 1793. With a Preliminary Account of the Rise, Progress and Present State of the Fur Trade of that Country*, was published by Cadell and Davies in 1801. One commentator says that if Mackenzie had not published the book, he would not have attained the first rank of North American explorers (and a knight-hood).[22] First published in London in a quarter folio size of 412 pages, including a map titled "From Fort Chipewyan to the North Sea in 1789," the book received a second edition in 1802 and publication in Philadelphia that same year, followed by a New York edition. Foreign-language editions also appeared. It is reported that Napoleon himself ordered a translation to be made to assist with his military plans for North America, while Thomas Jefferson was so alarmed after reading Mackenzie's account that he dispatched the Lewis and Clark overland expedition to the Pacific.

Mackenzie had a literary assistant named William Combe, who edited his work, but the text is based on his own journals. An early literary sleuth, Franz Montgomery, claimed that William Combe, who had prepared other exploration literature for publication, ghost-wrote the *Voyages*, but it appears that Combe simply brought "Mackenzie's prose more in line with the standards prevailing in eighteenth-century polite literature."[23] Barbara Belyea concludes that "the hand of Combe lies heavy on Mackenzie's occasional description of land and weather...," but this does not invalidate Mackenzie's claim to authorship.[24] Victor Hopwood called Mackenzie's text "prosaic and repetitive" but important because of its story.[25]

Readers can judge for themselves. A fur trader by profession, Mackenzie wrote about a favourite primary resource, the beaver, in June, 1793:

> In no part of the North-West did I see so much beaver-work, within an equal distance, as in the course of this day. In some places they had cut down several acres of large poplars; and we saw also a great number of these active and sagacious animals. The time which these wonderful creatures allot for their labours, whether in erecting their curious habitation or providing food, is the whole of the interval between the setting and the rising sun."[26]

This account of beaver industriousness is similar to Samuel Hearne's 1795 account, in which he also glorifies beavers and their "towns." Ian MacLaren points out that the beaver trade drove early exploration writing. Since southern Alberta had few beaver, it attracted less exploration and description.[27] An aspect of this commercial orientation was the publication in Mackenzie's text of a ten-page dictionary with English in one column and two aboriginal languages in columns next to it. Trade depended on translation, and without the incentive of profit from trading, there would be no exploration. The single word translations reveal how the complex concepts of the aboriginal peoples were simplified for commercial expedience.

The great model for Mackenzie's book was the work of James Cook, whose published journals were immensely popular. The *Second Voyage* sold out its first printing in one day.[28] Cook insisted that his second book be published in his own prose rather than prettified, as the first book had been, by John Hawksworth. That volume had been criticized for being unscientific in its language, and the Royal Society was setting new standards for exploration texts. "Cook's insistence on the journal form and his own plain style made the difference between Cook and his predecessors," Barbara Belyea explains.[29]

Germaine Warkentin claims that, upon his return to Fort Chipewyan, Mackenzie "suffered a bad case of writer's block in attempting an account of his expeditions."[30] He enlisted the help of William Combe to revise the journals for publication when he returned to England in 1799. With the help of an assistant, Mackenzie created the book that now stands as the foundation of English-language non-fiction writing in Alberta.

The importance of contemporary book publication is evident in the case of David Thompson, a mapmaker and explorer who made a number of journeys through Alberta from 1787 to 1811. Thompson's narrative has been slow to take its place in the canon of exploration literature. His *Narrative of Explorations in Western Canada 1784–1812* was not published until 1916, while his Columbia River journals were only published in 1994.[31]

Thompson himself never completed his *Narrative*, which he rewrote between 1846 and 1851, because of the onset of blindness. Several drafts exist in addition to the original journals. One historian has said that "Thompson deserves...recognition for his work as a regional writer.... He is one of the first men whose writing conveys to the reader the [geographic] variations in regional character that are found within the Western Interior of Canada."[32] The following is an example of his accomplished treatment of the eastern slopes of the Rockies in 1800:

> Our view from the heights to the eastward was vast and unbounded; the eye had not the strength to discriminate its termination. To the westward, hills and rocks rose to our view covered with snow, here rising, there subsiding.... Never before did I behold so just, so perfect a resemblance to the waves of the ocean in the wintry storm....[33]

This lyric tone inaugurated Alberta's mountain literature as an aesthetic of glorification.

Thompson's critical view of native people can be found in his journals from June 6-30, 1801, when he attempted to cross the Rockies:

For a Guide to cross the Mountains, we had a Nathathaway Indian named the Rook, a Man so Timourous by Nature, of so wavering a Disposition, & withal so addicted to flattering & lying, as to make every Thing he said or did equivocal & doubtful.... Of his character Mr Duncan McGillivray was aware when he engaged him....[34]

Mackenzie's superior attitude is also found in the work of Thompson's colleague, Duncan McGillivray. McGillivray's journals were completed and published posthumously as *On the Origin and Progress of the North West Company* by his older brother, William McGillivray, a partner in the North West Company firm of McTavish and Frobisher.[35] The text was a defense of the liquor trade, in which McGillivray presented a jaundiced view of native people:

The love of Rum is their first inducement to industry; they undergo every hardship and fatigue to procure a Skinfull of this delicious beverage, and when a Nation becomes addicted to drinking, it affords a strong presumption that they will soon become excellent hunters."[36]

Books such as McGillivray's provide a mix of propaganda and corporate history. When he had travelled with Thompson along the Bow River corridor, McGillivray carried a copy of Captain George Vancouver's *Voyage of Discovery to the North Pacific Ocean* published in 1798.[37] This detail suggests how quickly such texts reached distant outposts, where they were important to further exploration.

The final Norwester to publish a book was Daniel Williams Harmon, who was born in New England during the American Revolutionary War. Harmon's 1820 book, *Journal of Voyages and Travels in the Interior of North America*, is described by Hopwood as lacking in "literary skill" and "heroic endeavour."[38] Harmon spent two years in Dunvegan, on the Peace River. In the 1950s, W. Kaye Lambe edited Harmon's journal and published it as *Sixteen Years in the Indian Country*. One of the prerequisites of writing in Harmon's day was some episode describing indigenous cannibalism, which gave

European society claim to moral superiority over "the heathen." Here is an entry from Harmon's journal (March 20, 1809), while he was stationed at Dunvegan:

> It is reported that one man killed his wife and child, in order to supply himself with food, who afterwards, himself starved to death...it is not infrequently the case, that, the surviving part of a band of Natives, subsist upon the flesh of their dead companions.... I know a woman, who, it is said ate of no less than fourteen of her friends and relations during one winter....[39]

In Lambe's edition, this section appears in square brackets with the explanation "The printed text added...," meaning it did not exist in Harmon's written manuscript. The passage was most likely added by the book's editor, Reverend Daniel Haskel of Burlington, Vermont, who claimed in his 1820 preface to have "written it wholly over."[40]

The interplay of clergyman editors like Haskel, liquor-selling traders like McGillivray, and fame-seeking explorers like Mackenzie produced an exploration literature full of self-importance and literary affectation. Through exploration literature, imperialism and commerce became a saga of European civilization braving the wilds of an unknown world and triumphing with musket, rum-barrel, sexton, and, of course, literacy.

Barbara Belyea points out that the fur-trade journals reflect a voluntary accommodation by these men through "the stages of encountering, accepting and adapting...."[41] The books made from these journals supported imperial goals with their emphasis on heroic, "civilizing" achievement in a hostile environment. By the time the rival Hudson's Bay and North West companies amalgamated in 1821, a new, Romantic view of nature was taking hold in Europe. This, combined with an increasing faith in technology brought about by the advent of the steam-engine, resulted in the gradual transformation of exploration literature into travel writing.

The Middle Period: 1822–1850

When the North West Company merged with the Hudson's Bay Company in 1821, Alberta writing entered the middle phase of the exploration period. The end of corporate rivalry and the stabilizing of commercial relations resulted in a broadening of writing interests. Travel literature began to emerge as a literary form, and the Christian missionary became a new voice in the land.

Botanist Thomas Drummond (1780?-1835) inaugurated the new phase in 1825 when he came to Alberta as assistant naturalist on Sir John Franklin's second overland exploration to the Arctic Ocean. Drummond travelled with the fur brigades to Jasper's House, where he spent a year collecting and cataloguing flora and fauna. His account of meeting a grizzly while picking floral specimens is a model for future accounts by bear-threatened hunters:

> ...I was surprised by hearing a sudden rush and then a harsh growl, just behind me; and on looking round, I beheld a large bear approaching towards me, and two young ones making off in a contrary direction as fast as possible. My astonishment was great.... She halted within two or three yards of me, growling and rearing herself on her hind feet.... Now was my time to fire: but judge of my alarm and mortification, when I found that my gun would not go off!... My only resource was to plant myself firm and stationary, in the hope of disabling the bear by a blow on her head with the butt end of my gun...when the dogs belonging to the brigade made their appearance....The horsemen were just behind....[42]

This passage contains the basic elements of the sporting genre: a surprise meeting, the misfiring gun, the imminent attack, then salvation. Drummond's "Sketch of a Journey to the Rocky Mountains and to the Columbia River in North America" appeared in W.J. Hooker's *Botanical Miscellany, Volume 1* in 1830.

Famed Arctic explorer Sir John Franklin published *Narrative of a Journey to the Shores of the Polar Sea In the Years 1819–20–21* in 1824 and *Narrative of a Second Expedition to the Shores of the Polar Sea, In the Years 1825, 1826, and 1827* in 1828. The latter contains the journals of Dr. John Richardson and Lieutenant George Back, parts of which deal with their journey through northern Alberta, although the focus of the journals is a more northerly locale. Franklin, Richardson, and Back were knighted, and Back published his own *Narrative of the Arctic Land Expedition to the Mouth of the Great Fish River and along the Shores of the Arctic Ocean in the Years 1833, 1834 and 1835* in 1836. While these books were classic exploration accounts, their primarily Arctic locale

suggests that areas like Alberta had moved beyond the exploration phase and were ready for settlement.

A more typical example of Alberta writing in this period involves John Rowand, chief trader at Edmonton House from 1824 to 1854. Rowand (1787-1854) began his career with the North West Company in 1803 and took charge at Edmonton after the merger. Under his watchful eye, Fort Edmonton became the major trade centre in Alberta, replacing Fort Chipewyan, because it served both northern and southern Alberta native peoples. He was also second-in-command of the H.B.C.'s Bow River Expedition of 1822, which sought unsuccessfully to establish forts in Blackfoot country.

Rowand figures prominently in various books by writers who passed through or spent time in Edmonton. One of these writers was Sir George Simpson (1786/7-1860), the Governor of the Hudson's Bay Company from 1820 to 1860. Simpson was a master of both travelling and travel writing. He made lengthy journeys throughout the region, consolidating and expanding H.B.C. operations, and he did so at great speed. His 1828 canoe trip from

Hudson Bay to the Pacific at Fort Vancouver on the Columbia River averaged a blistering eighty kilometres per day![43]

Simpson's 1847 book *Narrative of a Journey Round the World During the Years 1841 and 1842* is a highly gentrified account where wilderness gives way to landscape, ushering Alberta into the era of Victorian travel.[44] Europe was a pacified, pastoral, romanticized universe to its readers; in the new travel literature, the "unknown" universe of earlier narratives gave way to a "known" aesthetic. Ian MacLaren points out that "an aesthetic estimation of landscape as a structuring principle of narrative" is the best way of understanding the new sensibility, which Simpson incorporated in his published prose.[45]

One of his main companions on Simpson's round-the-world trip was the redoubtable John Rowand, who went as far as the Sandwich Islands (Hawaii) with Simpson before returning home. Alberta historian Jim MacGregor lightheartedly observes that in 1841 Rowand was the first "Albertan" to winter in Hawaii.[46] The trip could be considered a corporate holiday for Rowand if we accept Simpson's 1832 assessment of him:

> About 46 Years of Age. One of the most pushing bustling Men in the Service whose zeal and ambition in the discharge of his duty is unequalled, rendering him totally regardless of every personal Comfort and indulgence.... Has by his superior management realized more money for the concern than any three of his Colleagues since the Coalition [1821].[47]

If this is Simpson's observation of the European figure in the landscape, what about the landscape itself? Simpson wisely gave his audience what they wanted—the picturesque. What sold in the romanticized market were towering mountains and exotic species. Simpson's description of the continental divide captures the essential nineteenth-century quality—the sublime:

> ...while these feeders of two opposite oceans, murmuring over their beds of mossy stones as if to bid each other a long farewell, could hardly fail to attune our minds to the sublimity of the scene. (I, 119)[48]

MacLaren concludes that Simpson's *Narrative* "told generations of Britons... how the Northwest appeared to the eye of the seasoned British landscape

I will never leave Thee nor forsake Thee.

Ask and ye shall have, seek and ye shall find, knock and it shall be opened unto you.

*Let him that thinketh he standeth take heed lest he fall.

I am the way, the truth and the life.

---

* (Literally: He 'I stand upright' who thinks, shall be wary that he do not fall.)

[p. 14]

No man cometh unto the Father but by Me.

I will not leave Thee, I will come to you in trouble.

Can a woman forget her very own offspring, her suckling child, yes, she may forget, still I will not forget Thee.

See, I have written Thee down on the sole (sic) of my hand.

[p. 15]

— 19 —

Cree syllabics. From James Evans, Cree Syllabic Hymn Book *(Toronto: Bibliographical Society of Canada, 1954).*

tourist," in much the same way that Mackenzie's *Voyages* a half-century earlier had offered them the aesthetic of a threatening wilderness.[49]

As the world of exploration literature was evolving toward a gentrified travel literature, a new element appeared: the missionary account. Reflecting a

Protestant sensibility are the journals of Wesleyan Robert Terrell Rundle (1811–1896), stationed at Edmonton and Rocky Mountain House as Company chaplain and missionary. On the Catholic side are the books of itinerant American Jesuit Pierre-Jean de Smet (1801–1873), who crossed paths with Rundle. In fact, Gerald Hutchinson, who wrote the introduction to Rundle's journals, described the Rundle–de Smet relationship as "an extraordinary friendship," although de Smet never writes about it in his books.[50] Obviously, fraternizing with a Protestant was no way for a Jesuit to get a *nihil obstat*!

Rundle began his mission in 1840 as an agent of the Wesleyan Missionary Society that had been invited by Governor Simpson to begin missionary work on his territory; he started out as John Rowand's guest at Fort Edmonton. Rundle's journals, however, were not published until 1977. What is most interesting about the journals is his use of James Evan's Cree syllabics to name native converts. James Evans, a fellow Methodist and superintendent of the mission, had invented and published the new alphabet to facilitate communication, literacy, and conversion. Aboriginal peoples did not initially adapt well to this written language, because it was intended to serve the needs and interests of missionaries, not theirs. Syllabics were designed to bring literacy to an oral culture and to "civilize" its thinking, using the linear expression of the printed word. Using symbols to express common sounds in the Cree language, syllabics were a key tool in subjugating aboriginal cultures. This initial effort eventually gave way to the assimilationist ideology of the church schools, in which native languages were completely eradicated. Syllabics were most often used to produce hymn books, from which converts could sing unfamiliar Christian devotionals.

De Smet's 1847 book *Oregon Missions and Travels Over the Rocky Mountains in 1845-46* is a compilation of non-private letters, that is, letters intended for public consumption. A Jesuit of Belgian origin, de Smet worked in the United States as a missionary and became a U.S. citizen in 1833. In 1845/46, he travelled from Montana to Alberta to convert the Blackfoot. *Oregon Missions* is more than 400 pages in length, of which the Alberta part is but one chapter. In the introduction he writes:

From the distant solitudes of the Rocky Mountains in the midst of my mission among the Children of the Forests, I had the honor of addressing

to you [de Smet's religious superiors] most of the letters contained in the volume.[51]

De Smet had previously published a volume of letters in 1844; the 1847 book was a sequel.

De Smet's book was of immediate interest, and French, Italian, and German editions quickly appeared. It was published in revised form in both the 1860s and 1870s in a variety of languages. What made the book so popular was the Oregon boundary dispute between the U.S. and Great Britain in the 1840s, which resulted in the extension of the 49th parallel border to the Pacific. Any book with the word "Oregon" in it sold well, because the American public was agitated over the matter.

De Smet wrote in the romanticized style typical of his period. In describing a mountain scene on his journey to Rocky Mountain House, he enhances the view with a poetic quote, calling the peaks "Palaces where

Nature thrones, Sublimity in icy halls."[52] Sublime Nature and souls for the asking were the twin foci of his narrative. From the Alberta perspective, his comments on the province's resident personality, John Rowand, only add to the factor's reputation:

> I reached...Edmondton towards the close of the year. Its respectable commandant, the worthy Mr. Rowan, received me with all the tenderness of a father....[53]

John Rowand was a minor literary celebrity, not because he was a writer but because he was mentioned in so many books.

A year after de Smet's book appeared, Henry James Warre (1819-1898), a staff officer in the British Army, published *Sketches in North America and the Oregon Territory,* based on his 1845/46 trip to the West Coast on military reconnaissance. Warre's small book contains primarily his own lithographs with a brief text. His descriptions of the Blackfoot capture the "noble savage" concept popularized in the novels of James Fenimore Cooper. "I can imagine nothing more picturesque and more perfectly graceful," Warre writes, "than a Blackfoot Indian in his war costume, decorated with paint and feathers, floating wildly in the wind, as he caracolles on his small, but wonderfully active bard, in the full confidence of his glorious liberty...."[54] The sublime, the picturesque, and the noble were the key terms of European romanticism that became the standard vocabulary of North American literary imagery in this period. Yet when Warre penned his description of the Blackfoot warrior, he was already suggesting that warrior's demise.

The Late Period (1851-1869)

The first person other than fur-traders or missionaries to write about the Canadian West as a whole was artist Paul Kane (1810-1871), who came west in 1846. Kane's beautifully illustrated book *Wanderings of an Artist* was published in 1859. Kane was an Irishman from York, Ontario, who, after four years in Europe, returned to Canada to paint North American natives and scenery. He got the idea in the winter of 1842/43 from a London show by the celebrated American artist George Catlin. Catlin had published a bestselling book on

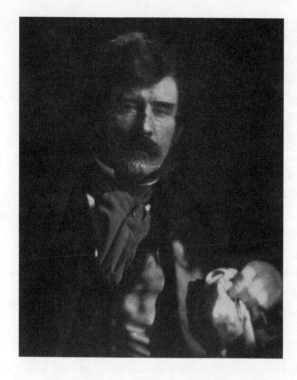

*Paul Kane, c. 1850.
Courtesy of I.S. MacLaren.*

North American aboriginal nations in 1841. Kane decided to do something similar for British North America.

Under the auspices of Sir George Simpson, Kane journeyed to the Pacific and back, spending about five months of his two-year journey in Alberta, primarily at Fort Edmonton, which he first visited in 1846. His description of the wedding of John Rowand Jr., son of the chief factor, held at the Fort, includes many familiar characters:

> On the 6th of January 1848, we had a wedding at Edmonton; the bride was the daughter of the gentleman in charge [Mr. John Harriott, who became chief factor in 1846], the bridegroom, Mr. Rowand, junior, who resided at Fort Pitt, a distance of 200 miles from the establishment. After the ceremony, which was performed by Rev. Mr. Rundell, the Methodist missionary, we spent a pleasant evening, feasting and dancing until midnight.[55]

Kane's narrative is full of such interesting anecdotes that provide a generally buoyant view of fur-trading life. Kane's goal had been to paint native life and western scenes, but he also kept a journal. In 1850, he petitioned the Legislative Assembly of Upper Canada for financial aid to publish his notes and pictures.[56] Funds were made available for the purchase of oil paintings based on his sketches but not to aid publication. Kane travelled to London in 1858 to get his book published and to supervise colour lithographic reproductions. He had to wait six months before the publisher agreed to do it.[57] The book sold 757 copies in the first month and was translated into Danish, French, and German.[58] It brought Kane money and fame.

As a combination of travel narrative and art, Kane's book is a classic of early Canadiana, but it is the art that has real historical and aesthetic value and not the writing, which is no better or worse than the genre in general. Ian MacLaren notes great discrepancies between "the field narrative" in Kane's own hand and the published text. He concludes the book was significantly edited and rewritten for publication, either through the efforts of Sir George Simpson, who had used two ghost-writers on his own book in the 1840s, or by unknown editors in Toronto.[59] MacLaren believes the imperialist attitude toward native people was the creation of these ghost-writers rather than Kane himself, whose notebooks contain no such prejudices.

The travel genre was well established by the mid-nineteenth century, with conventions all its own. Instead of the explorer's slogging "narratives" and "journeys," we have refined "sketches" and "wanderings." Exploration literature had been the major market for publishers for a century. With illustrations and fold-out maps, eighteenth-century exploration books were expensive, the preserve of the privileged. By the nineteenth century, more efficient print technology and increasing literacy among the middle classes meant the market for travel writing was greatly expanded. Travel literature was a combination of autobiography, documentary, and exotic sensationalism that appealed to the beliefs and curiosities of its readers. The presentation of a heroic human figure traversing a physical and social landscape none of his readers had visited is the core enticement of the travel genre. The land had been explored and claimed but moving across its roadless landscape still provided an emotional thrill for Victorian armchair travellers. While the exploration text was a tool for establishing empire and confirming the success of the scientific revolution, the travel book was a post-exploration entertainment and a revel in imperial triumph. The earlier exploration works were sold to a small but influential audience;[60] later travel writing appeared in large editions, eagerly bought up by the newly educated classes.[61]

The emerging reality of a post-fur trade west was heralded by the report of the Palliser Expedition of 1857-59, published in 1863. Among the report's journals were those of geologist Dr. James Hector (1834-1907), who provided some of the earliest sustained scientific observation about the geology of Alberta. The motivation for the expedition was the British government's desire to assess the region's potential for agriculture and settlement. John Palliser (1817-1887), the expedition leader, was a captain in the British army. He had been in the American West in 1847 to hunt buffalo, which he described in his immensely popular book *Solitary Rambles and Adventures of a Hunter in the Prairies* (1853). The Palliser Expedition report had no such popularity. Published by the Queen's Printer, *The Journals, Detailed Reports and Observations Relative to the Exploration of Captain Palliser of a Portion of British North America During the Years 1857, 1858, 1859 and 1860* was considered a publication of strictly official interest.

Germaine Warkentin describes the report as "a magnificently ironic elegy for a world which was about to die."[62] The poignancy one associates with the end of an era is expressed in this matter-of-fact statement found in the report, which foretold a tragic reality for the region:

> My intention had been to remain in my winter quarters in Edmonton... but owing to the great scarcity of provisions in Edmonton and the total absence of buffalo in that part of the country I was obliged to quit the fort and take my party southward to the plains in search of buffalo as fast as possible....[63]

The emerging post-fur trade world mapped and described by Palliser began to fill with non-fur trade voices. In 1862/63, Dr. Walter Butler Cheadle (1835-1910) and Viscount Milton (1839-1877) crossed from Fort Garry, Manitoba to the Pacific via Yellowhead Pass. In 1865, they published their account as *The North-West Passage by Land, being the Narrative of an expedition from the Atlantic to the Pacific, undertaken with the view of exploring a route across the Continent to British Columbia through British Territory, by one of the Northern Passes in the Rocky Mountains.*[64] It was popular enough to run through nine editions.[65] Although published under both their names, the book was the work of Dr. Cheadle alone.

Both men were in their twenties when they made the trip along with a shipboard acquaintance called Messiter. Financed and arranged by the travellers themselves, the trip prefigured the kind of aristocratic travel that was to become more common and certainly more comfortable in the late nineteenth century, especially after the completion of the C.P.R. in 1885. The party set out in June from Fort Edmonton to cross the Rockies on horse by way of the present-day Yellowhead Pass, west of Jasper.[66] On returning to England in 1864, Cheadle promptly rewrote "his lively journal into the more staid *North-West Passage by Land*."[67] Because of European interest in the American Civil War, Cheadle's North American account experienced good sales.

One of the last journeys made under the direction of the H.B.C. was undertaken by the Earl of Southesk. His book *Saskatchewan and the Rocky Mountains: A Diary and Narrative of Travel, Sport and Adventure, During a Journey Though the Hudson's Bay Company's Territories, in 1859 and 1860* was already an anachronism when it was published in 1875. Not only did the Earl carry the works of Shakespeare along with his portable table and camp stool, he also enjoyed the library at Fort Edmonton, where he read the works of Lewis and Clark, Harmon, and de Smet before heading into the mountains himself. The latter's literary style he judged as "exaggerated, forcible-feeble."[68]

Southesk started his journey in the company of seventy-one-year-old Sir George Simpson, who was making what was to be his last trip to Fort Garry from Upper Canada. At the start of his western adventure, the Earl also met Paul Kane in Toronto.[69] Southesk's was the last narrative of mountain travel to appear before the survey work for the C.P.R., and it is full of moralizing observations and bemusement at practices such as aboriginal polygamy and the business of Christianizing "the savages." The book ends with an appendix of essays on Hamlet and Macbeth, plus several pages of Cree syllabics. This mix of material forms an extreme example of what exploration literature had become in its late period.

A valuable commentary on this generation of travellers is provided first-hand by the mixed-blood guide and interpreter Peter Erasmus, who lived from 1833 to 1931, mostly in Alberta. In 1920, Erasmus was interviewed in Goodfish Lake (in east-central Alberta) by Henry Thompson for an Edmonton newspaper. The extensive interview took twelve days, but the newspaper refused to pay Thompson's five-dollar-per-day fee, so he took his material with him. Seven years later, he met Erasmus again and completed the old man's memoirs.[70] This work of oral history was published in the 1970s as *Buffalo Days and Nights*. It provides a salutary antidote to the pompous sensibilities of Victorian England and early colonial Canada. The following is Erasmus's heartfelt commentary on the native people, who faced an outbreak of smallpox in 1867, for which the only salvation was social isolation:

> It was a hopeless situation.... The Indians were doomed by the very qualities that were admirable: their loyalty to relatives; the sharing of their things with the band; their devotion and sympathy for any sick person; their continuous visiting of any ailing person, and kissing of children and women who met together even after a parting of a few day's duration. I knew that habits of lifetime could not be thrust aside, except by the bitterest of experience. The people of James Seenum's band practised far greater consideration of Christian sharing in their joys and pains than many white people of my later experience.[71]

Perhaps Erasmus's views had to wait for a more sympathetic time; they certainly did not fit the dominant perspective of native life in the 1920s.

Conclusion

The period from 1754 to 1869 belonged to the Hudson's Bay Company. It began with Anthony Henday's timid journey to an unknown region in which the aboriginal voice was strong and ended with the Earl of Southesk's pompous moralizing. In this period, the aboriginal voice was gradually silenced by British imperialism. The shaman's pictographs were replaced by the Bible of the European missionary, the warrior's winter count by the exploration journals of the trader and military officer. The oral tradition was overwhelmed by a new, literate, English-language tradition, whose highest expression was the book. This alien culture looked back to the metropolitan centres of Europe; its narratives were written out of and back to that European consciousness.

In the 125 years that this chapter covers, the persona of the explorer and fur-trader gave way to the persona of the privileged traveller, who in turn gave way to the persona of the tourist. With each European type came a different perspective on Alberta's landscape and peoples. In *Imperial Eyes: Travel Writing and Transculturation,* Mary Louise Pratt points out that the scientific and sentimental perspectives of this period were simply new forms of moral and political authority that replaced the older forms of travel narrative.[72] "Travel writing...," she writes, "is heavily organized in the service of...European literary history."[73] When we talk about the exploration literature phase of Alberta writing, we are also discussing an element of European literary history. The search for new commercial and political opportunities, the sense of scientific superiority, the romanticized aesthetic, and religious proselytizing are all products of European culture.

The great Canadian literary critic Northrop Frye observed that the oral tradition is by its collective nature anonymous, while the literate tradition tends toward individual authorship.[74] He claimed that the result is "the fetish of individual authorship."[75] Although individual authorship, in the case of exploration literature, often meant more than a single individual writer, Frye's observation distinguishes oral from literate culture. According to his schema of literary evolution, European Alberta can be said to have entered the literary world in the third phase of writing—the populist/domestic phase; while the oral, poetic phase, where he sees most world literatures beginning, occurred here only in aboriginal oral culture. It was this originating poetic voice that European culture overtook and rejected when it came to Alberta. What the imperial voice introduced was a literary heritage derived from European civilization, that is, literary colonialism.

Alberta's Eurocentric writing began as an imported, colonialized nonfiction, well advanced in its literary evolution. A well-developed, self-confident literary tradition has governed its sensibility ever since. Ian MacLaren asserts that "the art of writing is the formative imperial act."[76] Exploration and travel writing were acts of territorial, not cultural or linguistic, appropriation. In the drama of imperialism, the exploration text was an important way to take possession of the land, by transforming the unknown into the known. Yet the texts were often valued as much, if not more, for their maps as for their narrative. The standard use of ghost-writers and editors to shape and complete the notes and journals of explorers and travellers signals the hierarchy of hinterland-metropolis relations and the importance of the home culture to literary endeavour.

"The transmission of a text...informs and confirms the ideologies of the home culture," writes Ian MacLaren.[77] The heroic individual explorer in the service of company and empire fit the European sensibility of self-aggrandizement, as did the transformation of landscape into the sentimentally sublime world of the Romantic poets, for whom mountain tops were the literal peaks of aesthetic and mystic experience. Alberta, in the form of the Rockies, had the right landscape for the times. The transformation of the native peoples in the European narrative from strangers to be feared to a race to be pitied also fits evolving European sensibilities and power.

The voice of this era was constantly changing with European literary currents. That Alberta produced only insignificant fragments within that literary tradition is simply a sign of its hinterland status. The novels and poetry of that tradition were written elsewhere. Alberta's first expression of itself in English forms only a tiny part of a much wider English literary tradition—not a particularly grand beginning.

In the territorial period, emerging tensions, such as the struggle for self-government and the influx of settlers, would create new boundaries but also new possibilities for expression. British imperialism, the key factor in the Rupert's Land period, was now mediated through Canada, a British colony. Alberta writing was moving from resource-based imperialism to settler colonialism.

3

Territorial
Literature

...the first railroads revolutionized the contemporary experience of space and time. The railway did not create the modern consciousness of time, but in the course of the nineteenth century, it literally became the vehicle by which modern time-consciousness gripped the masses. The locomotive became the popular symbol of the dizzying mobilization of all life-conditions that was interpreted as progress.[1]

JURGEN HABERMAS

IN 1870, Rupert's Land, minus the province of Manitoba, was renamed the Northwest Territories. In 1882, Ottawa carved multiple districts out of this vast region. Alberta, named after Queen Victoria's fourth daughter (and wife of the Marquis of Lorne, Governor-General of British North America), was composed of the District of Athabasca in the north and the District of Alberta in the south. The railroad, which came to Alberta in the 1880s, turned Alberta from a fur-trade economy to an agrarian one; from the 1870 world in which aboriginal peoples outnumbered white settlers to the home of tens of thousands of white immigrants; from a representation dominated by exploration and travel literature to a colony in which a full range of Europeanized literature, from journalism to poetry, was produced. This chapter describes Alberta's transition from Hudson's Bay Company fiefdom to province.

During this transitional period, a number of literary elements appeared that had not previously existed in Alberta and did not come to fruition until after 1905. In this period, exploration and travel literature gave way to tourist literature; fiction made its first appearance; women writers were published; and writing in European languages other than English appeared. Yet non-fiction continued to dominate. Alberta still held exotic fantasies for reading audiences, but its strangeness was dissipated with each new book, as the British empire and its Canadian colony moulded Alberta into an agrarian hinterland filled with European and American colonists.

This chapter is divided into three sections. The first deals with the pre-railroad era from 1870 to 1884, which is a sparse literary period, reflecting a hiatus between the end of H.B.C. control and the coming of the C.P.R. The second deals with the core writing of the period between 1885 to 1904. The third announces the arrival of women writers and poetry in Alberta.

Before the Railroad: 1870-1884

The tradition of travel literature as overland journeying continued into the post-H.B.C. period in the writings of William Francis Butler (later Lieutenant-General, The Right Honourable Sir W.F. Butler, G.C.B.). Butler (1838-1910), an Irish-born career officer in the British Army, travelled to the Rockies in 1871 and again in 1872. From these travels came two very popular books, *The Great Lone Land*, published in London in 1872, and *The Wild North Land*, published in 1873. *The Great Lone Land* went through five printings in its first year and no doubt encouraged Butler to publish subsequent volumes. Butler wrote nearly twenty books during his career, all non-fiction except *Red Cloud: The Solitary Sioux* (London, 1882), a novel for younger readers. His autobiography was published posthumously in 1911. Butler spent only portions of three years in western Canada (1870-1873), followed by a brief trip in the fall of 1883, but from these short visits he produced two major travel books that capture the spirit of the territory just prior to the arrival of the railway. His books continued to be reprinted well into the twentieth century.[2]

W.F. Butler and his trusted husky, Cerf-vola, c. 1870. Courtesy of the Glenbow Archives, NA 249-27.

In his public persona, Butler was appropriately romantic about nature and the "wild West." The following excerpt from *The Great Lone Land* exemplifies his exuberant, almost melodramatic, style:

> The great ocean itself does not present more infinite variety than does this prairie-ocean.... In winter, a dazzling surface of purest snow; in early autumn, a vast expanse of grass and pale pink roses; in autumn too often a wild sea of raging fire. No ocean of water in the world can vie with its gorgeous sunsets; no solitude can equal the loneliness of a night-shadowed prairie; no one feels the stillness, and hears the silence, the wail of the prowling wolf makes the voice of solitude audible, the stars look down through infinite silence upon a silence almost as intense....[3]

As Butler approached Fort Edmonton he commented on how

the country maintained its rich and beautiful appearance....everywhere nature had written in unmistakable character the fertility of the soil over which we rode—everywhere the eye looked upon panoramas filled with the beauty of lake and winding river, and grassy slope and undulating woodland. The whole face of the country was indeed one vast park.[4]

Such pastoralism was eagerly consumed by the British reading audience of the day, as was Butler's sympathy for the "disappearing savage." Earlier in the book he had written angrily about the travesties of the white man, stating that "the countless deeds of perfidious robbery, of ruthless murder done by white savages out in these Western wilds never find the light of day."[5] Butler's angst over the misdeeds of white civilization and his grief for the decline of the noble savage hit a sympathetic note in industrialized Europe. In contrast, however, his private report to the Lieutenant-Governor of Manitoba about the situation in Alberta in 1871 expressed the less romantic thoughts of a military spy:

this Blackfeet nation forms a people of whom it may truly be said that they are against every man and that every man is against them.... Essentially a wild, lawless, erring race....[6]

Butler appealed to what he thought his audience wanted—be it the Lieutenant-Governor or London society.

In his autobiography, prepared almost forty years after these western journeys, Butler describes how he wrote *The Great Lone Land* in Ireland in late 1871 and early 1872, after a brief visit to the fighting around the Paris Commune. He candidly admits he returned to Alberta only because he had not been accepted for the expedition to find Livingstone in Africa. His travel was financed by profits from a chance oil investment in eastern Canada. While travelling, he was unaware of the success of his first book, as it had not been published when he left England. Only on the steamer home in September 1873 did he discover it was a bestseller. "I had the manuscript of another book of northern travel in my bag, nearly completed," he reported with pleasure on learning of his good literary fortune.[7] His second book was slimmer, weaker, and less popular. But the relative weakness of *The Wild North Land* did not stop others from jumping on the Butler bandwagon. For example, in 1879

American journalist H. M. Robinson published *The Great Fur Land*, a derivative work which used Butler and the writings of earlier travellers as the basis of its description.

Butler was deeply moved by the image of the west as the great lone land. In his autobiography, he says he was able during his 1883 trip to recapture some of the spirit (and eloquence) of an earlier time:

> One thing was still here unchanged: it was the twilight...where one could look again at some of the old sights, the great red sun going slowly down over the immense landscape, and leaving the western sky a vast half dome of rose-tipped wavelets from horizon to zenith. Scarce a sound but the splash of a wild duck...scarce a movement but the motion of a musquash swimming in the rainbow-coloured water, his head forming the beak of a bird-of-paradise, whose gorgeous wings and body plumage were the widening ripples that followed after.[8]

The aesthetic of glorious sunsets also serves as a metaphor for the dying of the great lone land itself, as it became the object of settlement, for which Butler was an advance scout.

If Butler represents the eager Victorian military officer evoking the distant reaches of the Empire as exotic landscape for his reading audience, then Reverend George M. Grant's 1873 book, *Ocean to Ocean: Sandford Fleming's Expedition Through Canada in 1872*, represents the spirit of indigenous Canadian expansionism and its vision of a transcontinental railway. Sandford Fleming was the chief engineer for the Canadian Pacific Railway, and Grant was the expedition's secretary. Grant suggests that Alberta's scenery was already ripe for exploitation through tourism:

> A good photographer would certainly make a name and perhaps a fortune, if he came up here and took views. At every step we longed for a camera.[9]

Other Canadian luminaries also wrote travel books, including the Honourable Peter Mitchell, a Canadian cabinet minister, who wrote *The West and North-West: Notes of a Holiday Trip* (1880), and John Douglas Argyll, Canada's Governor-General and the Marquis of Lorne, who wrote *Canadian Pictures* (1884). The latter book "helped fix the picture of Canada" for a wide readership in the east.[10] It emphasized the natural beauty of the west, a theme designed to encourage settlement—one of the key objectives of the government in Ottawa.

The Railway: 1885-1904: Tourists and Immigrants

European writing about Alberta had been inaugurated by exploration, but its interest was renewed with the coming of the railway. The railway turned travel into tourism. The key transformation in consciousness was the notion of travel in a straight line. Now the traveller was being carried in a fixed conveyance on a fixed schedule, more or less directly to his destination: one followed the rail line and not the meandering bends of rivers. Exploration literature had been caught up in the minutia of the journey itself. Now the destination, rather than the journey, became important. Although early train travel did describe passing scenery and life at the train stops, the trip itself was not central; what mattered was the arrival and what the tourist did or saw upon arriving.

The railway era was inaugurated by Alexander Stavely Hill's book *From Home to Home: Autumn Wanderings in the North-West in the Years 1881, 1882, 1883, 1884*. Hill (1825-1905) travelled west by steamer and train to the end of the line in Brandon, Manitoba in 1881, then switched to horse and wagon, went to Alberta, then south into Montana, where he took the Pacific Northern back to Chicago. The book is illustrated throughout with photos and ends with a foldout map of the C.P.R. and American railroads, with dashes for uncompleted sections. These may have been "autumnal wanderings," in the older sense of genteel journeys, but they also pointed to the advent of railway tourism.

Sir Sandford Fleming's book *England and Canada: A Summer Tour Between Old and New Westminster,* published in 1884, was the first account of exclusive railway travel to include Alberta. In this work, Fleming captures the spirit of the new age. His light tone indicates a new consciousness, where train travel was heralded as a triumph of time over space and comfort over hardship. Fleming travelled on a work train between Winnipeg and Calgary before the C.P.R. was completed. He mentions he had previously travelled from Fort Garry to within view of the Rocky Mountains in 1873. "The first journey," he writes for comparison, "occupied thirty-six days and the last about fifty-six hours!"[11] Such was the remarkable "progress" so beloved by Victorians.

The next two railway travel accounts came from passenger train trips a few years later. Morley Roberts (1857-1942) described his trip in *The Western Avernus, or Toil and Travels in Further North America*, published in 1887; Australian Stuart Cumberland's *The Queen's Highway: From Ocean to Ocean* was also published in London in 1887. Roberts captured typical Victorian sensibilities in his pithy descriptions of Calgary, aboriginal peoples, and the mountains:

> We came to Calgary, a flourishing and well-known town. Here numerous Blackfeet had their teepees.... I shook hands with two of this tribe, the most noble of the Indians....Ye two of the Indians who pass away, I salute you! *Vos moritures saluto!*
>
> ...
>
> But the untouched virgin peaks of snow, the rocky pinnacles where eagles sun themselves in swift and icy air, the dim and scented pine-woods, the haunt of bears, the gorges of glaciers, and the birthplace of rivers, these are sacred.[12]

When Roberts returned by C.P.R. in the 1920s, he saw the fruits of tourism in the "dream-castle" Banff Springs Hotel; he didn't like it one bit.[13]

Stuart Cumberland was working for a newspaper syndicate when he took the train across the prairies from Vancouver. He describes Banff as "the Yellowstone Park of Canada" and encourages "the passenger desirous of testing the medicinal qualities of its sulphuric baths, or of roaming amongst the natural beauties of the place, [to] get off at Banff station....Banff itself lies (or rather will be, for at present there are only a few log huts) in a romantic glen."[14] His promotional enthusiasm continues with this comment about Calgary:

> It is a pity that Calgary is passed so early in the morning, for it is one of the most—if not the most—beautifully situated towns in the whole of the North-west.[15]

Boosterism was born!

Nineteenth-century tourism and tourist writing were explored by Earl Pomeroy in his 1957 book *In Search of the Golden West: The Tourist in Western*

America. Here he lists the basic ingredients of tourism as created by North American trains: elegant hotels, Pullman cars, rejuvenating waters, fresh air (valued in soot-covered cities), and pristine wilderness. In contrast to the tourist in search of health, sport, and fun, the immigrant of the "colonial car," with its rough sleeping accommodations, saw train travel as a trial rather than respite. An early example of immigrant memoirs was A.J. Church's *Making a Start in Canada: Letters From Two Young Emigrants* (1889). Alfred John Church was a classics professor in London. His sixteen and eighteen-year-old sons took the train to Alberta, where they worked in ranching and eventually homesteaded. Church published their letters as a guide to other would-be English emigrants to the Canadian West. Here is the sons' lighthearted description of culinary delights on the "ranche":

Living here is of a somewhat simple nature; in fact, port, damper, and tea, damper, pork, and tea, and tea, damper, pork are the varieties in which we indulge....[16]

While the C.P.R. transformed Alberta into a new land of tourists, colonists, and advertising copy, another powerful element was seeking an equally formidable transformation of Alberta society—the missionary.

The Missionaries

Christian missionaries lived in an aboriginal universe and thus created literary material for indigenous use as well as for audiences outside Alberta. There were three major English-language missionary writers in the territorial period: Alfred Campbell Garrioch (1848-1934), John Maclean (1851-1928), and John McDougall (1842-1917). They were primarily non-fiction writers, but Garrioch and McDougall each produced a work of fiction later in life.

The Reverend Alfred Campbell Garrioch was born in Manitoba and ordained in the Church of England. He established the first Protestant mission at Fort Dunvegan in 1886. He also served at Fort Vermilion. Based on his knowledge of the Beaver language, Garrioch compiled an English-Cree-Beaver dictionary, published a *Manual of Devotion in the Beaver Indian Language* (1886) using syllabic characters, and translated the Gospel of St. Mark into Beaver (1886).

In the decade before his death, Garrioch published three other books, two of which dealt explicitly with Alberta. *The Far and Furry North: A Story of Life and Love and Travel in the Days of the Hudson's Bay Company* was a thinly fictionalized memoir of his years in the northwest, while *A Hatchet Mark in Duplicate* was his autobiography. In it, the chapter "Five Years at Dunvegan" recalls how he re-established the Anglican Mission "exactly a half-century after my grandfather re-established the trading post at Dunvegan."[17] One trilingual recollection of a penitent who came to him at Dunvegan in the 1880s suggests Garrioch's multicultural experience of early northern Alberta:

> I know that I am bad, and I am sorry for it; but I believe you when you say that Jesu *Nagha Tgha ma Chua*, the Son of our Father, can love me still, and I say, '*Merci, merci, sin-ih-te-ka*, thank you, thank you, I am pleased.'[18]

By the end of the territorial period, the educational acculturation of young native students in special residential schools was almost exclusively English; bilingual texts were no longer necessary. The new generation was taught enough English to be "saved" without translation.

John Maclean was a Methodist missionary among the Blood in southern Alberta from 1880 to 1889. He was well educated, with a doctorate from Wesleyan University (probably the first person with a Ph.D. to live in Alberta), and wrote extensively on the native peoples. His first book, *Lone Land Lights* (1882), was a collection of sermons and inspirational stories. In the explanatory letter at the beginning of the book, Maclean outlines the book's religious motivation and history:

> Most of the *Lone Land Lights* were first written to supply a lack of religious tracts in connection with my work. They were printed on printograph and distributed amongst the white settlers in the Bow River District.[19]

He wrote the book to raise money for his mission, using a title similar to Butler's popular 1870s book, *Great Lone Land*. Maclean acknowledges this borrowing in the introduction, referring to "the slopes of the Rocky Mountains and...adjoining valleys of the Great Lone Land...."[20]

Maclean published a major body of work, including *The Indians, Their Manners and Customs* (1889); *James Evans: Inventor of the Syllabic System of the Cree Language* (Toronto, 1890); *Canadian Savage Folk: The Native Tribes of Canada* (1896); and *The Warden of the Plains and Other Stories of Life in the Canadian North-west* (1896), a work of fiction. Maclean mined a good thing for all it was worth. He wrote several other books on the northwest after the turn of the century and ended his writing career with a biography of his fellow missionary, John McDougall, published in 1927 as *McDougall of Alberta*.

John McDougall was Maclean's contemporary, fellow Methodist missionary in Alberta, and friend. He was also a popular author in his own right, with almost a dozen books published between 1888 and 1908. Today, he is best known for his 1903 memoir, *In the Days of the Red River Rebellion*.[21] McDougall came west as a teenager in the company of his father, also a Methodist missionary, who had already worked with the Ojibway on Georgian Bay, Ontario. Because of this background, McDougall was fluent in several aboriginal languages.

He used this fluency to produce a *Cree Hymn Book* (1888) and, in conjunction with E.B. Glass, a *Primer and Language Lessons in English and Cree* (1890). McDougall also wrote a biography of his missionary father, *George Millward McDougall: The Pioneer, Patriot and Missionary* (1888), the first biography written in Alberta. The *Primer* was most likely the first English-language textbook developed for Alberta aboriginal use. It was designed for residential schools and had a page of English on the left and a page of Cree syllabics on the right. McDougall's approach to native assimilation is evident in the following excerpts:

Queen Victoria lives in England but has not yet visited Canada.... Often she visits the poor, and is very kind to them....

...

Dear Father and Mother

1. It is two years since I came here. At first I was lonesome but now, though I often think of you, I am glad I was sent here to learn English and to work....[22]

In the 1890s, McDougall turned to autobiography, publishing three volumes—*Forest, Lake, and Prairie: Twenty Years of Frontier Life in Western Canada 1842-62; Saddle, Sled and Snowshoe: Pioneering on the Saskatchewan in the Sixties;* and *Pathfinding on Plain and Prairie: Stirring Scenes of Life in the Canadian Northwest.*

The market for pioneering missionary autobiography set in the west was primarily Canadian, while the tourist and immigrant literature of this period was intended for an external market. As one historian explains, "tales of adventure and peril in remote lands peopled by strange 'primitive' races were enormously popular."[23] Missionary autobiography exploited people's fascination with the west and native peoples, and it clearly identified with "an ideal of progress" in which "civilization" was viewed as the goal of historical development.[24] McDougall appealed to this sentiment in *In The Days Of The Red River Rebellion*:

> Nine hundred and more miles we had travelled through a great farm, and not a farmer to break the virgin sod....Thousands of homesteads will dot the land we are passing in our day's journey, and which now is solitude sublime. This whole land is waiting....[25]

The missionary writers were highly conscious, both in their autobiographical writings and in their bilingual textbooks, of the transition from the fur-trade to the agrarian era. The purpose of their translation work was the assimilation of the native population into the new world order they were spearheading. Although short-lived, the development of bilingual texts was an important innovation in Alberta's cultural history. This approach would not reappear until the late twentieth century in native texts and study materials; today, students are being re-educated from English back into their native tongues.

The Mountaineers

While the missionaries recognized Alberta as the home of a major aboriginal population in their writings, mountaineers developed Alberta as a destination for mountain climbers and adventurers. The railway opened up the mountains to this activity. The originator of mountaineering writing in Alberta was an

Irish cleric, William Spotswood Green (1847-1918), whose 1890 book *Among the Selkirk Glaciers* included side trips into the Alberta Rockies at Lake Louise. His was the first book-length account of mountaineering in Canada and has been called "one of the most readable of all the narratives of mountain exploration ever published."[26] Green hiked from the railway into Lake Louise with his cousin Henry Swanzy. "I was quite unprepared for the full beauty of the scene," he writes. "Nothing of this kind could possibly surpass it...."[27] But for all their wonder at the beauty of nature, the mountaineers were quite unrestrained about their racial prejudices. During his stop in Calgary, Green made this observation about the native peoples he encountered:

we hope...real Christian feeling has made their ferocity, their love of torturing captives, and some of their more terrible vices impossible.[28]

Walter Dwight Wilcox (1869-1949), an American mountaineer and photographer who began climbing in the Rockies in 1893, followed Green's book with *Camping in the Canadian Rockies* (1896). Wilcox wrote with a delightful sense of humour, affecting the pose of a greenhorn in the mountains:

A crowd of business men of Banff, who usually take about 365 holidays each year, stands around to offer advice and watch the sport. Then the picturesque train of horses with their wild-looking drivers files out through the village streets under a fusillade of snap-shot cameras and the wondering gaze of new arrivals from the east.[29]

Like Green, Wilcox commented on the natives. He talks about McDougall's missionary work at Morley and describes the Stoneys as "a remarkable tribe" because "they are said to be great Bible readers."[30] By 1900, the "noble savage" of Butler's account thirty years earlier had become nothing more than a trope for Christian imperialism.

Camping in the Canadian Rockies was a large-format book, attractively printed on glossy paper, with an embossed, three-colour cover. It ran through several editions, including a revised and enlarged edition in 1900, and became the first major guide for climbers in the Alberta Rockies. The demand for guidebooks was increasing, as was the attraction of the area to mountaineers

in search of unexplored and unclimbed peaks. The thought of crisp, clean air and a healthy, outdoor lifestyle appealed to the middle and upper classes seeking to escape the soot of coal-heated cities.

Wilcox was followed by the English team of Hugh E.M. Stutfield (1858-1929) and J. Norman Collie (1859-1942), both of whom had published previously—Stutfield on travels in Morocco and Collie on climbing in the Himalayas. In 1898, Stutfield and Collie travelled along the north fork of the Saskatchewan river. This trip and others, including a failed attempt on the Columbia Icefield and a journey through Bow Pass in 1902, were described in their 1903 book *Climbs and Explorations in the Canadian Rockies*. The book contained fifty-one photographs taken by Collie, who was a pioneer of colour processes and the discoverer of neon. Like the other early mountaineers, Stutfield and Collie expressed grave concerns about the activities of native peoples. They complained that the Stoneys overhunted, saying unless these "untamable children of Nature" were held in check, there would not be enough "game for a tenth of their number."[31] The general negativity of mountaineers toward the native peoples is often ignored because it does not flatter the genre; it is, however, an important aspect of the writing, worthy of critical investigation.

The early flavour of mountaineering writing was captured by James Outram (1864-1925), whose 450-page book *In the Heart of the Canadian Rockies* (1905) provided a history of mountain exploration and climbing. Outram quotes Ruskin on the title page—"Mountains are the beginning and end of all natural scenery"—and the book recounts Outram's own experiences, including his 1902 climb of Mt. Forbes with Collie. To indicate how quickly mountaineering had progressed in less than twenty years, Outram observes that by 1904, "few peaks of the first magnitude and alpine difficulty remain unconquered by the ever advancing pioneer of mountaineering."[32] The formation of the Alpine Club of Canada in 1906 marked the beginning of popular climbing.

Through these books, Alberta's international reputation as a place of mountain adventure was solidified. The railway established the base camps for these ascents into trackless forests and snow-covered slopes. Alberta and mountain literature were now married, yielding a tradition of mountain books and guides that would continue through the twentieth century.

The Fiction-Writers

The period of territorial literature also witnessed the birth of fiction about Alberta. There were two kinds of novelists from this period. The first was the former North West Mounted Police (N.W.M.P.) officer turned novelist, who created popular fiction about the N.W.M.P.; the other was the gentleman author, who produced tales of pioneer adventure. The ex-N.W.M.P. writers were Henry Roger Pocock (1865-1941) and John Mackie (1862-1939), while the non-N.W.M.P. writers were William Alexander Fraser (1859-1933) and Ralph Connor (Charles William Gordon, 1860-1937).

Pocock dedicated his book *Tales of Western Life* to the N.W.M.P. It was a collection of short adventure stories, published in Ottawa in 1888, based on his experiences in the N.W.M.P. from 1884 to 1886. The writing is dense and ironic, with a strong psychological aspect. In 1896, Pocock published *Arctic Night*, another collection of short stories; only one of these is set in Alberta—

"The Arrest of Deerfoot." Pocock produced a third volume, *The Wolf Trail*, in 1923. The last third of this collection is set in southern Alberta in the mid-nineteenth century. *The Wolf Trail* is similar in style to Pocock's earlier works, with a sardonic tone and an interest in the absurd moments of life.

John Mackie preferred the novel to the short story and produced a half-dozen volumes between 1894 and 1904. Mackie served in the N.W.M.P. from 1888 to 1893, having emigrated from Australia. He later settled in Scotland, where he wrote romantic adventure stories set in the Canadian west. The first, *The Devil's Playground: A Story of the Wild North-West,* was published in New York in 1894 and is a love story. *Sinners Twain: A Romance of the Great Lone Land* was published in London in 1895 and has a N.W.M.P. hero. Like *The Devil's Playground*, this book is set in the Cypress Hills, where Mackie served. In the preface to *The Heart of the Prairie* (1899), Mackie states:

I lived for some years in that wild and fascinating portion of "The Great Lone Land" described in these pages as a mounted police officer in charge of that part of the frontier. So the cowboys, the mounted policemen, the Indians, and even the bears and the smugglers, are all old friends of mine.[33]

Mackie's *The Prodigal Son*, set on the South Saskatchewan river, was also published in 1899. A few years later, he published a historical romance about the Riel Rebellion—*The Rising of the Red Man*. Literary historian Dick Harrison asserts that Mackie "offers the beginnings of a view of the West as wide open mental spaces, which was the first view to become popular in fiction."[34] Although his novels have non-Mountie heroes and heroines, Mackie, along with Pocock, was a key proponent of the fictional Mountie.

William Alexander Fraser was born in Nova Scotia and worked in Alberta for six years. He wrote light comic adventures and had an irreverent approach to religious matters. His first book, *The Eye of a God and Other Tales of East and West* (1899), contained two Alberta stories about Father Lacombe. In 1904, Fraser published another collection, *Brave Heart*, which included one story set in southern Alberta's ranching country. A year earlier, he had published a novel, *The Blood Lilies*, which describes a frantic competition between a Catholic priest and a Presbyterian minister to officiate at the marriage of a Scots Presbyterian and a French Catholic.

Fraser also published a collection of juvenile fiction called *Mooswa and Others of the Boundaries*. In the introduction, he lends a bit of autobiographical insight into these animal stories:

This simple romance of a simple people, the furried dwellers of the Northern forests, came to me from time to time during the six summers I spent on the Athabasca and Saskatchewan Rivers in the far North-West of Canada.[35]

Fraser is the author of the first anthropomorphic animal literature set in Alberta. Animals as characters in a story with their own dialogue and personalities were a popular form of children's literature in his day, beginning with Ernest Seton Thompson's 1898 classic *Wild Animals*, and remain so today.[36]

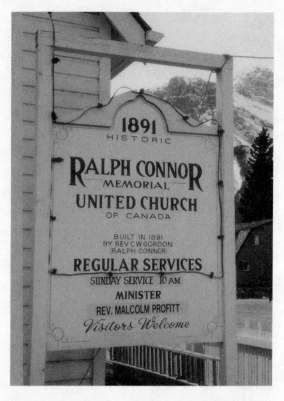

The church of Reverend C.W. Gordon, a.k.a. Ralph Connor, in Canmore, Alberta. Photo by George Melnyk.

Charles William Gordon, writing under the pen-name Ralph Connor, surpassed every one of the previous writers in output and popularity. He wrote two dozen novels about pioneer life in western Canada and made Canadian publishing history with the sheer volume of his sales. Connor was a Presbyterian clergyman who served as a missionary in Banff and Canmore from 1890 to 1893, then as the clerk of the presbytery in Calgary for a year before moving to Winnipeg, where he lived until his death in 1937. Although he spent only a brief time in Alberta, the majority of his novels are set here, a sign of the importance of Alberta to the popular imagination. In this chapter, only his early novels will be discussed.

Connor was in his late thirties when he embarked on a literary career as a way of raising money for the "home missions." He became Canada's best-selling author in the pre-World War One period. *Black Rock: A Tale of the Selkirks* was published in 1898; it had first appeared serially in Toronto's *Westminster* magazine. In the preface, Connor states that "the story of the book is true," and its popularity is attested to by the fact that a second printing

▤ *Ralph Connor's house in Banff. Courtesy of the Glenbow Archives, NA 841-22.*

appeared one month after the first.[37] *Black Rock* was followed by *The Sky Pilot: A Tale of the Foothills* (1899). In the preface to this book, Connor justifies supporting the "home missions":

> This is a story of the people of the Foothill Country, of those men of adventurous spirit...freed from all restraint of social law, denied the gentler influence of home and the sweet uplift of a good woman's face....[38]

This womanless frontier required moralizing tales of how "men" are saved. But the attitudes of the time also heralded the landscape as a purifying element. Later in the novel, he writes:

> Before us lay the hills, softly curving like the shoulders of great sleeping monsters, their tops still bright, but the separating valleys full of shadow. And there, far beyond them, up against the sky was the line of mountains—blue, purple and gold....[39]

The image of Alberta as a frontier was so powerful for both author and audience that Connor continued to locate much of his work here, including *The*

Prospector: A Tale of the Crow's Nest Pass (1904), *Corporal Cameron of the North West Mounted Police* (1912), and *The Patrol of the Sun Dance Trail* (1914).

Ralph Connor transferred the untamed identity of the native warrior to the figures of the miner, lumberjack, and rancher. Critic Frank Davey, drawing on Robert Kroetsch's essay "The Fear of Women in Prairie Fiction," divides the Connorian world by gender:

> *horse v. house*...in which male sexuality is founded on the rural—the horse, the cowboy, the coyote—and female sexuality on the walled and institutionalized space of the town....[40]

The first appearance of women writers in Alberta challenged this dichotomy.

Women Writers 1869-1904

The first woman to visit and write about Alberta in a book was Mrs. Arthur Spragge, whose *From Ontario to the Pacific by the C.P.R.* was published in 1887. Her book is a collection of articles from a Toronto magazine, written about her cross-Canada tour. Mrs. Spragge [Ellen Elizabeth *née* Cameron] was quick to adopt the romantic stereotype of Calgary as the home of cowboys and Indians. "At Calgary I had my first experience of the reality of Western life," she writes, "...a large body of Indians....A picturesque element of Calgary was the number of cowboys to be seen at all hours...."[41]

The railway brought other women writers to Alberta. Susan Agnes Macdonald (1836-1920) travelled across Canada with her husband, Prime Minister Sir John A. Macdonald, in 1886 and described her journey in *Murray's Magazine*. She was very taken with Banff and returned there to holiday for many years. Anne Mercier and Violet Watt co-authored two books with Alberta settings in the 1890s. *A Home in the Northwest: Being a Record of Experience* (1894) and *The Red House by the Rockies: A Tale of Riel's Rebellion* (1896) reflect the domestic themes alluded to previously. Mercier was a widely published English writer whose books were produced under the auspices of the Society for Promoting Christian Knowledge; it is uncertain whether either Mercier or Watt actually spent time in Alberta. These modest beginnings form the foundation upon which women would build a significant literary presence in the West after 1905.

Poetry

Alberta's only territorial poet was Lethbridge lawyer Charles F.P. Conybeare (1860-1927), who published a volume of poetry in England in 1902. *Vahnfried* is a large work of almost 200 pages, structured as an epic poem in four cantos ("The Forest," "The River," "The Plains," and "The Valley"), and its subject matter is Arthurian legend. Its *fin-de-siècle* sensibility blends heroic Wagnerian fantasy and French symbolism:

> The good-night uttered, Adimo retired
> And calm at heart, his brief devotion said,
> He seeks his couch, where drowsiness inspires
> The balmy rest that dreamy slumber shed
> In soothing haloes round his head.[42]

In 1907, Conybeare published his second volume of poetry, *Lyrics from the West*. This collection of individual poems clearly reveals Conybeare's imperial loyalty; "Mafeking" (the Boer War battlefield), is typical:

> Throned on the African plains,
> Crowned amidst thunder and flame,
> Blazoned in glory thy name,
> Long in our hearts shall remain
>   Mafeking.[43]

Conybeare was in his forties when these volumes appeared, and he seems not to have found the muse after that time. His work mixes contemporary European poetic trends with a hint of his local surroundings, but he always speaks to a reading audience far from Lethbridge. Unlike women's writing, which flourished after provincehood, poetry lagged far behind both fiction and non-fiction. Conybeare was not only the originator of English-language poetry in Alberta; he was also one of its few published practitioners up to World War One.

Conclusion

Unlike the image of many streams coming together to form a single river, the strong current of exploration non-fiction divided into numerous smaller streams in the territorial period, including popular fiction, juvenile fiction, biography, and textbooks, as well as the new genres of tourist and mountaineering literature.

A number of Alberta-specific motifs and stereotypes appeared: the fictional Mountie, the emphasis on "cowboys and Indians," the glories of mountain adventure, and indigenous animal stories for children. Many of these images were in vogue in the United States and Great Britain, and the Alberta locale lent itself to an approximation of the American "Wild West." This was, after all, the era of Buffalo Bill Cody's travelling road show, when frontier nostalgia was the rage across North America and Europe.

What is most significant in the territorial period is that Alberta became more than just a place writers recreated for a distant audience: there was now a local audience. Dick Harrison notes that the writers of the late nineteenth century "arrived with cultural baggage of their British or Ontario upbringing which they could not or would not unload"; but it is evident they pioneered genres and motifs that remain with us to this day.[44]

The fiction writers were, in Harrison's opinion, overly drawn to the "romantic, sentimental, and didactic," a weakness that can be easily understood if we recognize their need to assert civilizing police and missionary work on behalf of law, order, God, and country.[45] An overriding sense of "frontierism" dominates territorial writing, and it is clear that popular American and British conceptions of the Canadian West prized Alberta because it possessed all the imaginatively essential elements: cowboys, Indians, and Mounties.

The Americanized cowboy of southern Alberta exists in contrast with the older image of the backwoods Francophone of northern Alberta. Since the railway crossed Canada first through the south, it was this Americanized cultural icon that came to dominate. The railway split Alberta's literary culture in half in much the same way forest and prairie divided the province geographically; it was not until the C.N.R. was built thirty years later that northern Alberta began to reassert itself.

"Canadian Mounted Police in Action." The Mounties captured the imagination of the British and American reading public. Courtesy of the Glenbow Archives, NA 47-14, NA 2445-3, NA 1480-34.

*The real life of a Mountie
was rarely as glamorous as its
fictional counterpart. Courtesy
of the Glenbow Archives,
NA 513-40, NA 494-2.*

The exploitation and development of Alberta's identity as a frontier for adventure and salvation locked the province in a certain nostalgic mode, in which the heroic past lent its spirit to the present. By 1900, the urge to look back was as strong as the need to look ahead. If non-fiction represents civilization's self-glorification through historical rationalism, while fiction represents cultural myth and archetypal fantasy, both mythologies coexisted in Alberta in the territorial period.

A new era, dominated by fiction-writing and strongly influenced by the success of new women writers, was just on the horizon. With the end of the territorial period, Alberta writing found a new direction, its mythical identity augmented by new sensibilities, carried by the Pullman coaches and colonist cars of the C.P.R.

4

Provincial
Literature

ON SEPTEMBER I, 1905, Alberta became a
province of Canada, with Edmonton as its capital. Alberta's literary history
entered a new stage: that of a provincial literature, with all the nuances that
designation carries. Becoming a province helped to solidify Alberta's literary
and cultural identity, both for a local, provincial audience and a wider, national
and international one.

This chapter deals with the increasing strength of an indigenous Albertan
identity as it emerged to displace the work of the traveller and the tourist, the
literary personae who had dominated the territorial period. For the first time,
Alberta was to become associated with major Canadian literary figures, such
as Nellie McClung, Robert Stead, and Arthur Stringer, but at this early stage,
it was more a sense of place than a literary ethos.

This chapter reaches across two eras and three genres. The first period
extends from 1905 to the end of the First World War; the second covers 1919
to 1929. Alberta was represented in several kinds of non-fiction, in fiction for
both adults and children, and in poetry. The geographic divisions of the
province—the soaring mountains versus the rolling prairies and the forested
north versus the grassland south—fostered economic and, therefore, cultural
divisions. Economically, Alberta was identified with wheat and cattle. The
figure of the ethnic farmer of the parkland dominated Edmonton and vicinity,
while the English rancher and the American dryland farmer personified
Calgary and the south.

Sociologically, Alberta was dominated by the small farmer whose life was built around his homestead. The thousands of immigrants from Europe and the United States who flocked to Alberta each year were attracted not to the cities but to the free farmland provided by the government. This overwhelming rural context gave birth to a political era commonly referred to as the age of agrarian populism. Agrarian populism led to the formation of political entities like the United Farmers of Alberta, who formed the government in 1921, and laid the foundations for other radical political organizations, such as the Social Credit Party and the Co-operative Commonwealth Federation (C.C.F.) in the 1930s.

The literature of this era was primarily agrarian realism and romanticism. The romance of the west hung on from the territorial period, especially in the N.W.M.P. novel, but a trend toward realism tried to deal with serious social issues in both fiction and non-fiction. Romanticism, with its optimistic sense of the human condition, matched the upward, "boom" cycle of the new regional economy, while realism matched the downward, "bust" cycle. Agrarian populism was fueled by utopian optimism and hope for a better future, as well by anger at the structural injustices of Alberta's present. Farmers felt they were victims of the railways, the grain elevator companies, and pro-Ontario federal policies. They sought to empower themselves as producers through homegrown political movements.

Literary trends in Alberta continued to reflect the imported tastes of eastern Canada, the United States, and Britain. In general, Alberta maintained its earlier role as an imaginary frontier for foreign readers, but at the same time, it began to create a new identity, based on the settler's reality.

Non-fiction: 1905-1919

The imperial tourist tradition that was a hallmark of the territorial period spilled over into the early twentieth century in some minor work by the renowned British writer Rudyard Kipling. Kipling had first passed through Canada in 1892 on his honeymoon, an account of which was published as *From Sea to Sea* (1899). In 1907, he made another trip, resulting in the small volume *Letters to the Family*, which was originally a series of articles in *Collier's* magazine. In this book, Kipling recounts the joys of imperial travel, reminding

🎵 *Mary T.S. Schäffer (second from left) at camp in the Rockies. Courtesy of the Glenbow Archives, NA 529-8.*

readers that "these mountains are only ten days from London."[1] Kipling puts his best descriptive foot forward in this treatment of the mountains:

> There are many local gods on the road through the Rockies: old bold mountains that have parted with every shred of verdure and stand wrapped in sheets of wrinkled silver rock, over which the sight travels slowly as in delirium; mad, horned mountains, wreathed with dancing mists; low-browed and bent-shouldered figures of the wayside, sitting in meditation beneath a burden of glacier-ice that thickens every year....[2]

Kipling also took a liking to the town of Medicine Hat, whose name he thought most appropriate. When in 1910 there was an attempt to change the name, Kipling wrote a letter in its defense.[3]

Travellers' fascination with the Rockies and the mountaineering life was reflected in the work of Mary Townsend Sharples Schäffer (1861-1939), whose *Old Indian Trails* was published in 1911.[4] In 1908, Schäffer and several companions explored the Maligne Lake area in what is now Jasper National Park. She had visited the Canadian Rockies as early as 1889 with her first husband, botanist Charles Schäffer, and had also illustrated Stewardson Brown's book *Alpine Flora of the Canadian Rocky Mountains*. Schäffer's literary style is chatty and unpretentious and carries a certain historical sentiment:

> Opposite lay all that remained of Henry House, an old North-west Fur Trading Company's post...the site was close to the water's edge, directly opposite the mouth of the Maligne. As I looked across at those silent sentinels, back came the pictures of bygone days...when the beaver pelt was currency, when the Indians gathered there to trade....[5]

A widow when she made the trip with Mary Adams of Boston, Schäffer later married her guide, William Warren, and settled in Banff.

Historian Douglas Francis describes this era as one of intense propaganda for western settlement. The west is portrayed as an "agrarian paradise," a kind of pastoral utopia in which everyone prospers.[6] Frank Yeigh was such a writer. Yeigh (1860-1935) wrote about southern Alberta in *Through the Heart of Canada* (1911), a nationalistic account of his time on the prairies. He represents Alberta as "the great ranching province of Canada" and Calgary as the home of the most "virile representation of humanity" in the country. Calgary was growing rich, he boasted, from the millions of ungulates "dining off the succulent grasses a bountiful Nature has there provided."[7]

Not all non-fiction writers were such Alberta boosters. John Burgon Bickerseth (1888-1978) was a lay Anglican missionary in the area northwest of Edmonton. In *The Land of Open Doors: Being Letters from Western Canada 1911-13* (1914), he wrote this delightful description of a scene at one of the lumber camps he visited:

> On my left were a group of men gathered round a grindstone putting a good edge on their axes: on the right were a group of French Canadians talking and laughing with many gesticulations; round a table in the middle

were gathered a number of men gambling; and at the far end a square dance was in full swing. Two fiddlers were playing a jig, beating time with their feet, another fellow was calling the dance at the top of his voice, and a number of huge lumberjacks were hopping around like so many ballet-girls.[8]

Bickerseth was an Oxford graduate who served in the Alberta missions for two years. He returned briefly after World War One to lecture at the University of Alberta before settling down as warden of Hart House at the University of Toronto. He retired to England after World War Two.

Several other pre-War non-fiction writers spent only a short time in Alberta. One of these was Stanley Washburn (1878-1950), whose *Trails, Trappers and Tenderfeet in the New Empire of Western Canada* (1912) describes the author's travels by packhorse in the Rockies and the Yellowhead Pass just prior to the construction of the Grand Trunk Pacific Railroad. This excerpt captures Washburn's delight in internal rhyme:

Some game I have shot and some fish I have caught. Many rivers have I forded and some have I swum. Vast peace have I enjoyed, and many hardships and some risks have been encountered and overcome....[9]

The book is written in the popular genre of "roughing it" campfire adventures, with the reader identifying with the "tenderfoot" author.

Quebec City journalist Frank Carrel (1870-1940) prepared a guide to Alberta for immigrants, *Canada's West and Farther West* (1911). A chronicle of the author's month-long travels on a circle-tour of Alberta, the book is filled with photos and spontaneous impressions. Carrel was quick to point out that "the town [Calgary] had a very much more Western air about it than Edmonton."[10]

In contrast to Carrel's rather plain account, *The New North: Being Some Account of a Woman's Journey through Canada to the Arctic* (1909) by Agnes Deans Cameron (1863-1912) is a pleasure to read even today. In 1908, this American and her niece decided to journey from Chicago to the Arctic. They travelled north through Alberta after arriving in Calgary by train. Cameron reports that her port of departure for the Mackenzie River, Athabasca Landing, "...is part of the British Empire. But English is at a discount here; Cree and French and a mixture of these are spoken on all sides."[11] Cameron includes Cree syllabics in her text, as well as excerpts from early fur-trade diaries that she examined at Fort Chipewyan. On returning to Edmonton, via the Peace River and Lesser Slave Lake, she commented on Alberta's recent provincehood:

> Alberta has been a full-fledged Province of Canada for barely three years, and, coming out of the wilds we sit on the back benches and see her open the doors of her First Provincial University.[12]

Another woman traveller of the period was Scottish social writer Elizabeth B. Mitchell (1880-1980). Her book *In Western Canada Before the War: A Study of Communities* (1915) was set primarily in Saskatchewan but also deals with Edmonton and vicinity. Mitchell contrasts the gender egalitarianism of the frontier with the strict roles back home:

> Of all delightful things about the West, perhaps the most delightful is that one escapes from all the modern strain and dislocation in the relations between men and women. There is no division of interest here, no idea of men losing what women gain.[13]

She was firm in her belief that "the burden of Empire-making most truly rests on the prairie woman."[14]

A well-known literary traveller was British poet Rupert Brooke (1887-1915), who visited Alberta in 1913, two years before he was killed in the War. His *Letters From America*, published posthumously, is composed of material sent home to be published in the *Westminister Gazette*. Brooke's sense of humour is evident in this all-too-recognizable situation:

> It is imperative to praise Edmonton in Edmonton. But it is sudden death to praise it in Calgary... I travelled from Edmonton to Calgary in the company of a citizen of Edmonton and a citizen of Calgary. Hour after hour they disputed....[15]

In 1968, his friend Geoffrey Keynes published a selection of Brooke's private letters, one of which was written in the King George Hotel, Calgary (in Edmonton he had stayed at the King Edward). Brooke's candour reflects his imperial attitudes toward life in the hinterlands:

> I average two reporters a day, who ask me my opinion on every subject under the sun....What's really wrong with these damned Canadians is that at bottom they believe...that war is impossible....They live a thousand miles from the sea, and make an iniquitous living by gambling in real estate....[16]

A lesser-known diarist was Edmund Morris, an Ontario artist whose father, Alexander Morris, was a former Lieutenant-Governor of Manitoba and the Northwest Territories. Morris came to Alberta on an Ontario government commission to paint the surviving chiefs from the treaty period. His diaries provide a glimpse of Peter Erasmus, who had worked as an interpreter for his father when he was Treaty Commissioner:

> Peter Erasmus, my father's old interpreter, & Dick Bad Boy drove down to see me.... Peter says in 1857 they started for Battleford, travelling a month, and all the way passed through vast herds of buffalo which opened apart to let the red river carts pass through....[17]

As a Canadian with genuine links to the West, Morris possessed a sense of historical continuity which travellers to the region, such as Rupert Brooke, did not.

American ethnologist Walter McClintock (1870-1949) turned to the Old West in his book *The Old North Trail; or Life, Legends and Religion of the Blackfeet Indians* (1910). The book is set on the Alberta-Montana border, and the Alberta section contains a fine account of Peigan chief Brings-Down-the-Sun's view of aboriginal life thirty years after the treaties:

> The white race have always cheated and deceived us. They have deprived us of our country. Now they are trying to take away our religion by putting a stop to the ceremonial sacred to the Sun [Sundance].[18]

He quotes Brings-Down-the-Sun's descriptions of various birds using transliterated Blackfoot:

Gertrude Balmer Watt, c. 1910. Courtesy of the University of Alberta Archives.

When the Isik-o-ka-e (black breast or chestnut collared longspin) is flying, he sings "Kiowa-kinix-apis-is-tsis-ta-kits-itope," "Spread out your blanket and I will light upon it."[19]

McClintock's work communicates a sense of Alberta's deeply rooted aboriginal culture. This attitude contrasts sharply with the journalistic accounts and boom-and-bust stories of the Alberta newcomers, whether short-term travellers or long-term settlers.

The settler viewpoint is captured by two male writers from Calgary and four women writers from Edmonton. John Roderick Craig's *Ranching with Lords and Commons; or Twenty Years on the Range* was published in 1903. It is an anecdotal autobiography of the first years of open-range ranching in southern Alberta in the 1880s. Craig (1837-1930) was involved in the Oxley Ranch, organized in 1882, and was also a promoter of ranching south of Calgary.

Leroy Victor Kelly (1880-1956) provides a more historical account in *The Range Men: The Story of the Ranchers and Indians of Alberta.* The book is illustrated with numerous photos, including one photo of the first black woman in Alberta (1870s), as well as photos of native people and ranchers. The book ends with a description of the 1912 Calgary Stampede, which leads Kelly to conclude that "the day of the open range was a thing of the past...."[20]

Of the four women writers, two were journalists in Edmonton and two were established authors. Gertrude Balmer Watt (1882-1963) settled in Edmonton in 1905, where she edited a weekly paper, *Edmonton Saturday News,* and was one of the founders of the Canadian Women's Press Club. Watt published two books through the firm that published the weekly newspaper. In 1907, selected writings from *Edmonton Saturday News* were published as *A Woman in the West;* a year later, selections from the *News* and its sister weekly, *The Alberta Homesteader*, were published as *Town and Trail.* The following experience was typical in her profession: "I was having dinner with eight men recently (shockingly Western isn't it and I the only woman!)...."[21]

Katherine Hughes (1876-1925) joined the *Edmonton Bulletin* in 1906, after several years on the editorial staff of the *Montreal Star.* A devout Catholic,

Hughes' first book was *Archbishop O'Brien, Man and Churchman* (1906), the biography of her late uncle. Two years later, she spent a year as the provincial archivist, then was seconded to be private secretary to the Premier; during this period she wrote *Father Lacombe: The Black-robe Voyageur* (1911). This was the first biography of the great Alberta missionary; it was reprinted in 1914 and 1920.[22] In Hughes' biography, "Lacombe emerges in all his contradictions as missionary and colonizer...simple churchman and wily old politician."[23] The biography is long (467 pages) and filled with recollections and anecdotes about Lacombe's life, dramatized with dialogue. A French-language biography appeared several years later, but Hughes' pioneering biography was the standard until it was updated the 1970s by James MacGregor.

Hughes was also well known as the founder of the Catholic Women's League. After the publication of the biography and the founding of the League, Hughes travelled to London to work for the Alberta government. She returned to Canada during World War One to write an official biography of Sir William Van Horne, the builder of the C.P.R. However, the published book, *The Life and Work of Sir William Van Horne*, based on her typescript, was attributed to Walter Vaughan (1865-1922) because the Van Horne family did not want to be associated with a known supporter of Irish independence.[24]

Nellie McClung (1873-1951), the most famous Canadian novelist of this period, moved to Edmonton from Manitoba in 1914. McClung published two autobiographical volumes after she left Alberta, but she wrote one book of creative non-fiction while living in the province. *The Next of Kin or Those Who Wait and Wonder* (1917) is a series of essays describing the homefront during the World War One, containing such morally toned chapter headings as "The Orphan," "The War-Mother," and "The Slacker." The book calls for the "conscription of wealth" to match the conscription of men.[25]

Emily Gowan Ferguson Murphy (1868-1933) moved to Edmonton in 1907 and published four non-fiction books between 1910 and 1922. Her writing career had started in Manitoba, where she wrote for the *Winnipeg Telegram*. Her first book, *Janey Canuck in the West,* was a national bestseller. It is an autobiographical account of her move from Toronto to Manitoba to Edmonton. The book is full of sentimental, melodramatic writing that appealed to the nation's sense of frontier utopianism. She describes the North Saskatchewan at Edmonton as a river of "golden sands, and anyone may garner the grains for the mere sifting of them," while the city itself "stretches like a dream city.

▤ *Emily Murphy (right) with Emeline Pankhurst, 1918. Courtesy of the City of Edmonton Archives, EA 10-1985.*

Edmonton is Queen of the Northland."[26] In 1912, she published a book of travel and homestead writing, *Open Trails,* under her *nom-de-plume,* Janey Canuck. Two years later, another book of sketches of frontier life appeared, titled *Seeds of Pine.*

Murphy was appointed a Police Magistrate and Judge of the Juvenile Court in Edmonton, and she was prominent in women's legal issues, including the famous "Persons Case," in which she and four other women successfully appealed to the Privy Council to declare women legally "persons." Her last non-fiction book in this period was *The Black Candle* (1922), a tract against drug addiction with chapters on cocaine and "marahuana," as well as photos of drug addicts. In her preface, Murphy says she seeks to expose the evils of drug addiction while endeavouring not to offend "the sensibilities of the readers."[27] The book had a wide readership and put Murphy's name before the English-reading public across North America and abroad.

Writers continued to pass through Alberta, either on the lecture circuit or for holidays. For example, Sir Arthur Conan Doyle published *Memories and Adventures* (1924), in which he describes his visit to the Rocky Mountains and Jasper in 1914, complete with stops in Calgary and Edmonton. This kind of tourist observation was no longer formative in Alberta writing, however. It belonged to another era.

Historical writing about Alberta made its debut in the work of Archibald Oswald MacRae (1869-1963). MacRae was principal of Western Canada College in Calgary when his *History of the Province of Alberta* (1912) was published in two weighty volumes. The *History* was published by "a syndicate," called the Western Canada History Co., and contained a history of the province along with numerous biographical profiles and photographs of provincial dignitaries. The two volumes totalled more than 1,000 large, glossy pages! This huge work attempted to establish Alberta as a milieu of accomplishment through which the province's elite might define itself.

Another aspect of the Alberta identity that developed at this time was anti-Ottawa sentiment. A. Bromley Moore's book *Canada and Her Colonies; or, Home Rule for Alberta* (1911) voiced a common complaint: Alberta's lack of control over public lands, a domain the federal government had retained for itself in granting Alberta provincehood in 1905.

Non-fiction writing up to the 1920s was a mixture of travel writing and observations about pioneer life whether on ranches, on farms, or in cities. What is significant is the women writers who came to lead the genre after provincehood. Their journalistic experience provided the writing skills for biographies and autobiographies, which have remained an important aspect of Alberta letters. The emerging era of agrarian populism gave women a major role in non-fiction writing.

Fiction: 1905-1918

Provincehood also inaugurated a heightened fictional and poetic identity for Alberta. While the territorial period had been dominated by outside writers, this period had a better balance of Albertan and non-Albertan writers. Fiction was being written with increasing frequency, an important development in the literary culture.

In 1905, American writer Abbe Carter Goodloe released a collection of stories called *At the Foot of the Rockies*. Goodloe (1867-19?) had spent the summer of 1904 at Fort Macleod, and the stories are based on his observations. "The tales of this book," he writes in the preface, "reflect some of the phases of that life we saw about us in that isolated little Police detachment in Alberta, and which was, in miniature, the life of the whole vast country. For there were to be found three factors which make life in the Territories what it is: the British soldier, the Indian, and the settler."[28] By British soldier, Goodloe meant the N.W.M.P. officer. This triad, for Goodloe, represented the essence of Alberta society.

Catherine E. Hayes (*née* Simpson), writing under the pseudonym Mary Markwell, produced a small book titled *Aweena: An Indian Story of a Christmas Tryst in the Early Days* (1906). Hayes (1856-1945) came west in 1879 and served as the Legislative librarian of the Northwest Territories from 1891 to 1898 before settling in Winnipeg, where her book was published. It is uncertain whether she ever visited Alberta in the 1890s, where her story is set.

Another woman writer was Ada B. Teetgen, whose novel *A White Passion* was published in both Toronto and London in 1913. The book was written to raise funds for a municipal hospital in Finlay, Alberta, where Teetgen lived and where her story of homesteading hardship is set (fictionalized as Islay, Alberta).

A more accomplished novelist than either of these women was Isabel M. Paterson (*née* Bowler). Born in Ontario, Paterson spent her childhood on a ranch in southern Alberta. She worked in Calgary, and went on to work as a journalist in British Columbia and the United States. Two of her early novels are set in Alberta. *The Shadow Riders* (1916) is set in Calgary and involves a romantic tale interwoven with urban business interests. *The Magpie's Nest*, published the following year, features Hope Fielding, a young woman who endures various vicissitudes and careers but eventually returns to Alberta. Paterson's work is refreshing in that it offers an urban image of Alberta, beyond the fantastic world of the N.W.M.P., Indians, and settlers.

The Mountie theme, however, was simply too lucrative for most writers to avoid. Ralph Selwood Kendall wrote police adventure novels based on his experiences in the N.W.M.P. He wrote *Benton of the Royal Mounted* in 1918 and *The Luck of the Mounted* in 1920.[29] *Benton* was dedicated to "My Old Comrades, present and ex-members of the R.N.W.M. Police," a detail that doubtlessly added to the book's authenticity in readers' eyes.

■ *Ralph S. Kendall. Courtesy of the Glenbow Archives, NA 1265-1.*

Dick Harrison points out that the American image of the Mountie as "U.S. Marshals in red tunics" was taken up by Canadian writers like Kendall.[30] This simply furthered the popular image of the province as a land of wide open spaces and American-style Western adventure. A good example of a writer who exploited these images was American James Oliver Curwood (1878-1927), who wrote both Mountie westerns and outdoor adventure stories. Curwood wrote a large number of novels, with total sales in the millions. For a few years, he was paid by the Canadian government to write about the northwest as a publicity agent, and he made pack trips into Alberta's mountains, as well as visiting parts of northern Canada. *Philip Steele of the Royal Northwest Mounted Police* (1911) is typical of his Mountie writing, while *The Grizzly King, A Romance of the Wild* (1916) is representative of his hunting adventure stories:

James Oliver Curwood hunting grizzlies in British Columbia in 1913. Courtesy of Bentley Historical Library, University of Michigan.

The big grizzly was perhaps six hundred yards up the slope, and pretty close to three hundred yards from the nearest point reached by the gully.

Bruce spoke in a whisper now.

"You go up an' do the stalkin', Jimmy," he said. "That bear's goin' to do one of two things if you miss or only wound 'im—one o' three, mebbe: he's going to investigate *you*, or he's going up over the break, or he's coming down in the valley—this way. We can't keep 'im from goin' over the break, an' if he tackles you—just summerset it down the gully. You can beat 'im out. He's most apt to come this way if you don't get 'im, so I'll wait here. Good luck to you, Jimmy!"[31]

While this excerpt describes one of Curwood's experiences in the B.C. Rockies, it could just as easily have been set in Alberta. One of his numerous western romances, *The Flaming Forest* (1923), is set in northern Alberta, beginning at Athabasca Landing. Its hero is a N.W.M.P. officer, whom Curwood describes as "a worshipper at the shrine of God's country."[32] The massive audience for Curwood's work led to numerous Hollywood movies being made from his novels.[33]

English novelist Harold Bindloss spent some time travelling through western Canada in the late nineteenth century, prior to becoming a journalist and popular writer. Bindloss (1866-1945) set some of his romantic adventure novels in Alberta, including *The Mistress of Bonaventure* (1907); *Winston of the Prairie* (1907); *The Impostor* (1908); *Lorimer of the North-west* (1909); *Ranching for Sylvia* (1913); and *Pine Creek Ranch* (1926). Bindloss published more than sixty novels in forty-three years of writing, and his Alberta novels are heavy with N.W.M.P. characters. Harrison comments that Bindloss' stories appealed to his audience's identification with "English adventures in a strange land," because his audience was mainly British.[34]

The western action tale set in Alberta was also heavily promoted by three other writers of the period: Hulbert Footner (1879-1944), Robert Leighton (1859-1934), and William Lacey Amy (?-1962). Hulbert Footner was born in Ontario but spent most of his life in the United States. Although Footner may never have visited the province, he set two of his early novels in what can loosely be considered Alberta: *Two on the Trail: A Story of the Far Northwest* (1911) and *Jack Chanty: A Story of Athabasca* (1913). *Jack Chanty* was illustrated with stills from the motion picture of the same name.

Robert Leighton was a British journalist, critic, and author of juvenile adventure stories, a number of which were set in Alberta, including *Woolly of the Wilds: A Story of Pluck and Adventure in North-West Canada* (190?) and *Rattlesnake Ranch: A Story of Adventure in the Great Northwest* (1912).

But it was William Amy, writing under the pseudonym of Luke Allan, who developed the most successful series of Alberta-set western action novels. His string of novels, many featuring the character Blue Pete, spanned four decades (1913 to 1954). He had been born in Ontario but came west briefly. For a time, he was owner of the *Medicine Hat Times*, before moving to Toronto to earn his living as a writer. Allan's first novel was *The Blue Wolf: A Tale of the Cypress Hills*, published in 1913. It was more substantial than his Blue Pete series, which began in 1921 with *Blue Pete, Half Breed: A Story of the Cowboy West* and continued until 1954 with fourteen more titles, including *The Return of Blue Pete* (1922) and *Blue Pete: Horse Thief* (1938). Allan also wrote another half-dozen related western action novels, with titles such as *The Lone Trail*

(1922) and *The Westerner* (1924). His books were published in Canada, the United States, and Great Britain.

The lines between the mass fiction of pulp novels, juvenile adventure literature, and action western were often blurred in the era before there was a radio in every home; recreational reading was the primary form of literate entertainment. Popular genres sold millions upon millions of books over the decades. Alberta-set adventures were so common that any writer could adopt the style and find a ready market. English writer Bessie Marchant (Mrs. J.A. Comfort, 1862-1941) wrote more than 150 books for younger audiences, several of which were set in Alberta, including *Athabasca Bill: A Tale of the Far West* (1906) and *Daughter of the Ranges: A Story of Western Canada* (1906). Her books were widely read in Canada (Emily Murphy mentions being influenced by them), but whether Marchant actually visited Alberta is uncertain. What is crucial is that Alberta as a locale was popular with English-speaking audiences—in Canada, the United States, and Britain—and attracted writers from all three countries. Several generations of readers were raised on this popular literature.

In contrast to the foreign writers who used Alberta as an imaginary locale, three important literary figures in this period rightfully called Alberta their home. Arthur Stringer (1874-1950), Robert Stead (1880-1959), and Nellie McClung (1873-1951) were the heavyweights of Alberta fiction prior to 1919, and their writings had both a national and international audience.

Arthur Stringer was best known for his trilogy of novels, *The Prairie Wife* (1915), *The Prairie Mother* (1920), and *The Prairie Child* (1922). The three novels were then collected into a single volume and published in 1922 as *Prairie Stories*. Described in the *Literary History of Canada* as "probably [the] most fully professional of all the Canadian writers of the period," in his day Stringer ranked with Charles G.D. Roberts and Gilbert Parker for popular appeal.[35] Stringer, Ontario-born and Oxford-educated, came to Alberta in 1913, when he was in his thirties. Prior to coming to Alberta, he had a successful career in New York as a journalist and poet. He lasted less than two years here as a rancher, but out of that brief experience he produced his most memorable writing. The *Prairie* trilogy describes the experiences of a New England woman coming to an Alberta ranch as a young bride. As early as 1941, critics recognized Stringer's achievement:

From it dates the gradual displacement of the romantic prairie novel with its "bad men" and red-coated mounties by the novel of the West as it is. With the possible exception of Robert Stead, Stringer was almost the first fiction writer to portray a West that...found an even greater charm for the reader in the human appeal of its characters and the actualness of its backgrounds.[36]

Stringer's trilogy inaugurated the struggle against agrarian romanticism. He had learned the craft of realism while writing urban journalism and crime novels in New York. In the early thirties, he returned to his prairie setting with *The Mud Lark*, whose straightforward style is characteristically Stringer's:

...the metropolis of Elk Crossing didn't strike me as very inspiring. It was like a great many other prairie towns I'd seen from my coach-window, a row of wooden-front shops along a main street lined with untidy-looking motorcars....[37]

In the earlier trilogy, Stringer displayed a more poetic style, a good command of dialogue, a talent for female characterization, and a sympathy for human drama. He was a stylish writer with solid descriptive powers, who gave a more accurate reflection of Alberta in the agrarian period than the ubiquitous Mountie story.

Robert Stead was a more prolific writer than Stringer. He published both fiction and poetry about Alberta. Ontario-born but Manitoba-raised, Stead was a newspaper man and public relations writer. He worked for the *Morning Albertan* in Calgary and chose the foothills as an important locale in most of his novels. *The Bail Jumper* was published in 1914, followed by *The Homesteaders* in 1916 and *The Cow Puncher* in 1918. Stead had a marvellous ear for local slang, as seen in this excerpt from *The Cow Puncher*:

He reasoned with his horse as he rode. 'Taint no use, you ol' slop-eye; a fellow can't get the bede if he ain't got the fillin'; cooked meals an' decent chuck. I could plug 'em six out o' six—you know that; you flop-ears....[38]

In the 1920s, while living in Ottawa, Stead published four more novels, of which only *Dennison Grant: A Novel of Today* (1920) (retitled *Zen of the Y.D.: A*

Novel of the Foothills in England) is set in Alberta. Historian Howard Palmer claims, "Stead idealized the pioneer farmer as the soul of the nation."[39] This was especially true in his Manitoba-set masterpiece *Grain,* published in 1926. In contrast to Stringer's realism, Stead was a major contributor to pastoral romanticism, according to Dick Harrison. "Stead gives us the romance of pioneering," he writes, "in terms of the infinite, the eternal, and the ineffable; traditionally the terms and concerns of romance."[40] But Harrison sees Stead moving toward realism in works such as *Grain* and *The Smoking Flax* (1924). The passage quoted above from *The Cow Puncher,* while reminiscent of the dialogue in American action westerns, also captures the slang Stead would have heard routinely. His romanticism is infused with a certain realism, and his work possesses a dualistic or transitional quality. Although Stead's prose has not become a classic of Alberta literature, it ranks high in literary achievement and certainly provided an accurate reflection of agrarian society's values and aspirations. (This accomplishment will become more evident when discussing his contribution as a poet later in this chapter.)

Of the triumvirate of major pre-World War One novelists, Nellie McClung has been the most analyzed in recent years, primarily because of her role as a suffragist and advocate of women's rights. Born Nellie Letitia

Mooney in 1873 in Ontario, McClung moved to Manitoba in 1880, then to Edmonton in 1914. By the time she arrived in Edmonton, she had a national reputation as a feminist activist and fiction writer, having already published three books—*Sowing Seeds in Danny* (1908), its sequel *The Second Chance* (1910), and a collection of stories, *Black Creek Stopping House and Other Stories* (1912). McClung lived in Alberta from 1914 to 1932, when she retired to British Columbia.

In her 1979 book *Our Nell,* Candace Savage describes McClung as "celebrated and controversial."[41] McClung was forty-one when she arrived in Alberta, and she published four novels while living here: *Three Times and Out* (1918), *Purple Springs* (1921), *When Christmas Crossed the Peace* (1923), and *Painted Fires* (1925). After her retirement to Victoria, she published two nonfiction autobiographical volumes: *Clearing in the West* (1935), which described her Ontario and Manitoba years, and *The Stream Runs Fast* (1945), which dealt with Alberta and British Columbia.

In *Purple Springs*, which completes her Manitoba trilogy, McClung promotes two major themes: women's suffrage and temperance. As a political activist for both the vote for women and Christian temperance, she used her fiction to advance her viewpoint. Randi R. Warne is convinced there is only a very thin line between ideology and fiction in McClung's life and work:

> Throughout McClung's life, literature and public speaking were two sides of the same coin, novels become speeches, just as speeches, such as those collected in *In Times Like These*, became so well known as books that their original context is largely forgotten. These speeches, many of which were given in churches and church halls, reinforce the notion of literature as pulpit....[42]

McClung also published three collections of her short stories, which had originally appeared in magazines like *Maclean's* and *Toronto Star Weekly: All We Like Sheep* (1926), *Be Good to Yourself* (1930), and *Flowers for the Living* (1931). She also called her wartime essays, *The Next of Kin or Those Who Wait and Wonder* (1917), a collection of "short stories," which confirms Warne's assessment.[43] McClung served as a Liberal MLA in Alberta from 1921 to 1926, but remained an active writer, producing three novels during this time, even after moving to Calgary in 1923 and commuting to Edmonton during sessions of the Legislature.

McClung was able to devote more time to writing after her 1926 defeat, often writing a story per week for magazines, but never wrote another novel.[44] Feminist critics Mary Hallet and Marilyn Davis conclude that "mainstream literary critics have often dismissed her fiction as effete romanticism, when, in fact, the essential thrust of her writing was anti-romantic."[45] They blame this misreading on patriarchal critics and believe McClung should occupy a significant place in the canon of Canadian women's literature, because she helped to sensitize readers to social problems of patriarchal society.[46]

One commentator notes that McClung's "considerable literary output has been confined to oblivion."[47] The same can be said for most of her fellow writers of the period. Literary tastes change, historical sensibilities evolve, and new ideologies come to the fore. Very few writers survive their own generation's interest, especially bestsellers like McClung. Even so, McClung's work belongs in the upper echelons of Alberta's literary culture in this period (for content if not for style). When considered alongside her historic status as the leading feminist in western Canada—culminating in her participation in the "Persons Case" of 1928, with fellow writer Emily Murphy—McClung's writing should be remembered and discussed well into the future.

The works of Stringer, Stead, and McClung were popular and widely read but slipped from literary view as times changed. Alberta had yet to produce a work of fiction that would be read and studied for decades to come.

Poetry 1905–1919

Robert Stead was an important contributor to Alberta poetry with his pro-imperial book *Kitchener and Other Poems* (1917). Stead had authored two earlier collections while living in Manitoba: *The Empire Builders and Other Poems* (1908) and *Prairie-Born and Other Poems* (1911). In "The Homesteader," published in *Kitchener,* Stead wrote about the world of the new farm pioneer:

Far away from the din of the city
    I dwell on the prairie alone,
With no one to praise or to pity,
    And all the broad earth for my own[.][48]

By combining the forces of romanticism and realism, Stead was able to appeal to a wide audience.

Stead had been preceded as a poet by a long-time resident in southern Alberta, Rhoda Sivell. Sivell (1875?-1962) was a ranch wife who lived north of Medicine Hat after 1899. Her book *Voices From the Range* was published in 1911 by the T. Eaton Company in a 101-page edition; the 1912 Briggs edition was pared down to forty-three pages, while another, unidentified 1912 edition had eighty-eight pages.[49] The poem "Little Joe" is typical of Sivell's voice:

> Just a little ranch shack
>   by the river's bank,
> Trees all growing round it—
>   Let me stop and think—
> Standing in the doorway
>   Was a halfbreed child;
> Only four was little Joe;
> Clean, though dark and wild.[50]

Sivell's language is clean, almost sparse, and its sensibility is tied closely to a simple narrative. Her verse appeals to the contemporary ear more than Stead's lines do.

Three other books of poetry were published by Alberta-based authors in this period. Harwood Steele, son of Sir Samuel Steele of the N.W.M.P., published a volume of juvenile patriotic verse in London in 1914. Titled *Cleared for Action,* it was a song of rhyming couplets full of praise for the British navy. The other two were published by Robert T. Anderson of Edmonton. The first, *Old Timers and Other Poems,* was published in Edmonton in 1909 by the Edmonton Printing and Publishing Co. The second, *Canadian Born and Other Poems,* was published in 1913 by Esdale Press, also of Edmonton. One or both volumes may have been published for the author; his last book of poetry, *Troopers in France* (1932), certainly was. Despite this possibility, these volumes represent the first poetry actually published in the province and provide a northern sensibility to balance the southern ranch poetry of Sivell and dryland farming poetry of Stead. They also capture the ethnic flavour of Edmonton and its local history. *Canadian Born and Other Poems* has sections such as "Scottish Canadian Poems" and "French Canadian

▤ *William Irvine. Courtesy of
the Glenbow Archives,
NA 5123-1.*

Poems," and one poem, "The Protest of the North," was written about heated contemporary debates such as "the rejection of the Great Waterways Railway Bill by a majority of the Alberta legislature."[51]

Poetry was published extensively in newspapers and periodicals, but its appearance in volume form was sparse. Most poetry came from southern Alberta poets, whose themes had a greater audience. Styles ranged from the sing-song rhymes of Steele to the minimalism of Sivell. This variety reflects the formative state of Alberta poetry up to 1919. Sporadic in its composition and self-conscious about its imperial loyalty and agrarian virtues, Alberta poetry was only beginning to find its voice at the conclusion of World War One.

Non-fiction: 1919–1929

The 1920s saw a major decline in non-fiction writing in Alberta. There are only seven authors of non-fiction in the 1920s, while there are twice as many fiction writers. Perhaps Canadian readers began to prefer fiction, because, in

the twenties, the novel reached a dominance in Alberta it has never relin-
quished.

The new decade in non-fiction began with a book by the radical Alberta
politician William Irvine (1885-1962). *The Farmers in Politics* (1920) described
the idea of "group government," a concept championed by Alberta's indigenous political movement, the United Farmers of Alberta. Irvine came to
Calgary in 1916 as a Unitarian minister. He was later elected a Member of
Parliament in the 1920s, and in the 1930s became identified with the C.C.F.
and socialism.

In 1916, Irvine started a bi-weekly newspaper called *The Nutcracker*, which
later became the *Alberta Non-Partisan* and finally *The Western Independent*, the
official publication of the United Farmers of Alberta. He wrote political
pamphlets and booklets in the 1930s and 1940s, but his only other non-fiction
volume (aside from a self-published political testament *cum* autobiography late
in life) was *Co-operative Government,* published in 1930. Irvine was the founder
of Alberta political writing and precursor of the many other Albertan political
figures who have produced ideological tracts and political memoirs

throughout the century. His other literary work involved two anti-capitalist agitprop plays: *The Brains We Trust* (1935) and *You Can't Do That* (1936). Anthony Mardiros, Irvine's biographer, says the purpose of Irvine's books was "to explain and assist" the political movements he supported.[52]

Another well-known figure of the time was Bob Edwards (1864-1922), editor of *The Eye-Opener*. A Calgarian like Irvine, Edwards is probably the most famous of Alberta journalists. In 1902, he launched a weekly paper in High River but soon moved it to Calgary. His newspaper had a large circulation (18,500), almost half of it outside Calgary.[53]

The most common adjective used to describe Edwards is "irascible."[54] He had a vitriolic wit and was known both provincially and nationally for his biting humour. He seemed to fear no one. In 1920 and 1921, he published books titled *Bob Edwards Summer Annual* with Musson in Toronto. These paperbacks, of less than 100 pages each, reprinted material from his columns. Their publication by a national publisher reflected his reputation as a humourist. This pithy observation was common fare for Edwards:

> At 16 a romantic girl expects to marry a prince who will drink wine from her slipper; ten years later she probably grabs a chap who drinks suds out of a can.[55]

In 1921, Edwards was elected to the provincial legislature, but served only one year before his death. Grant MacEwan published a biography of Edwards, *Eye Opener Bob: The Story of Bob Edwards* (1957), in which he made this observation about Edwards' literary talents:

> One of the great misfortunes is that a man with his talent for creativeness did not devote himself to the writing of Canadian novels or something else which would have made a lasting contribution to Canada's living literature.[56]

Edwards was master of the paragraph rather than the page, and his scathing journalism gave pleasure to many.

Louise Rourke wrote *The Land of the Frozen Tide: An Account of the Life of the Author for Two Years at Fort Chipewyan* (1928), her "impressions of the country, gained during the two years spent at this historic post."[57] Rourke wrote in the hope that "at no great distant time a white woman's sojourn at Fort Chipewyan will not be considered with the romantic interest which may be attached to it at the present time."[58] She comments,

> Many books have been written about the North; some by those who have actually spent many years there, gaining first-hand knowledge of the life; and others by people who have made the summer trip to "The Land of the Midnight Sun" for the purpose of obtaining "copy." I believe there are few women contributors to the literature of the North who have actually lived beyond the reach of railroad and telegraph lines and become familiar with the country in all seasons. [59]

Rourke's book is a historical survey of the north country, written in an "authentic" voice for the interested outsider, including discussions of local customs, the seasons, and the native population.

Herbert E. Church (1868-19?), whose letters from Alberta had been published in London in the 1890s as *Making a Start in Canada: Letters from Two Young Emigrants*, produced a modest memoir in 1929 titled *An Emigrant in the Canadian Northwest*. This volume covered his experience horse ranching with his brother at Sheep Creek, south of Calgary, from 1888 to 1897, and described his life on the west coast after his brother's death. Church concluded the British were "the best pioneer settlers known."[60]

James Nevin Wallace (1870-1941) produced a small fur-trade history, *The Wintering Partners on the Peace* (1929), about the North West Company in northern Alberta and British Columbia. Wallace was a surveyor for the 1905 boundary between Alberta and British Columbia, and lived in Calgary until 1925, when he moved to Ottawa. He retired in the 1930s to live in Bowness, outside of Calgary.

Following in the footsteps of Archibald MacRae's 1912 history of Alberta was John Blue's three-volume *Alberta Past and Present* (1924). Blue (1874-1945) was the Provincial Librarian when he prepared the book, and he followed MacRae's format: large volumes printed on glossy paper, with history ranging from the missions to mining in the first volume, and biographical sketches and formal photographs of noteworthy Albertans in the other two. The project totalled 1400 pages.

The most interesting of the non-fiction writers was Buffalo Child Long Lance (1890-1932), an impostor who wrote *Long Lance*, a purported autobiog-

▤ *Buffalo Child Long Lance
(Sylvester C. Long), c. 1920.
Courtesy of the Glenbow
Archives, NA 177-1.*

raphy and history of the native peoples of Alberta and Saskatchewan. His real
name was Sylvester C. Long. Long was born in North Carolina of mixed
parentage. After World War One, he became a journalist in western Canada,
including a stint at the *Calgary Herald*. Long committed suicide in 1932.

Alberta historian Donald Smith concludes that "to lead a full life, Sylvester
Long was forced by a vicious racial system to conceal his true identity."[61] He
was able to use his appearance to portray himself as the "noble redman," invent
a Blackfoot identity, and, with his journalist writing skills, put together a book
that sold well. It was not until Donald Smith published *Long Lance: The True
Story of an Impostor* (1982) that Sylvester Long's true identity was revealed. Like
Grey Owl, Long was "one of the most famous Indians of his day."[62]

This eclectic mix of non-fiction interests, ranging from history to humour
to political tracts, replaced the travel and exploration literature of earlier eras
and opened up a wider area of endeavour for non-fiction.

Fiction: 1919-1929

Fiction in this period fell into three broad categories: adventure and western writing, female romance, and agrarian realism, with the latter being the dominant genre. The popular adventure novel, predictably, centred on Mounties. It had three practitioners: George S. Surrey, Laurie York Erskine, and Harwood E.R. Steele.

George Surrey wrote two novels—*An Outlaw of the Plains* (1922) and *The Shack in the Coulee* (1930). The latter reads autobiographically, while the former is a typical wild west story. Laurie Erskine (1894-19?) developed a N.W.M.P. character named Renfrew and wrote numerous Renfrew police adventures, including *Renfrew of the Royal Mounted* (1922), *Renfrew's Long Trail* (1933), *Renfrew Rides the Range* (1935), *Renfrew in the Valley of Vanished Men* (1936), and *Renfrew Flies Again* (1942). These books were written primarily for the male juvenile fiction market. Erskine travelled extensively in North America and could very well have visited Alberta in his travels.

The most prolific of the Mountie writers was Harwood Steele, son of Sir Samuel Steele. Steele (1897-1978) was born in Fort Macleod but spent only his childhood in Alberta. He was a soldier and journalist, as well as the author of numerous Mounted Police stories beginning in 1923 and continuing until the 1960s. He lived most of his adult life in Quebec and Ontario.

Steele began writing professionally in 1914, at age seventeen, with the publication of a book of poetry in London, but his novel *Spirit-of-Iron (Manitou-pewabic): An Authentic Novel of the North-west Mounted Police* (1923) launched his literary career. He explains his approach in the foreword to the book as "an attempt to present fact in the form of romantic fiction...," against "ignorant writers of the 'red love, two-gun' variety." He hopes to show "the marvellous devotion to duty, the high idealism, the splendid efficiency which have made the Mounted Police famous, than any to be derived from these inaccurate romances."[63] Steele maintained this theme throughout his books, always emphasizing that he was an accurate researcher with privileged insider information (although one would not be remiss in thinking of him as a glorifier of and apologist for the Police and its male paramilitary ethos). Steele spent time in the North for the federal government and wrote a northern Mountie novel titled *The Ninth Circle* (1927), but he returned to western Mountie stories after World War Two with works such as *To Effect An Arrest*

(1947) and *Ghosts Returning* (1950). In later years, his books were written for the juvenile fiction market.

As Alberta had its Indian impostors in non-fiction, so it had a cowboy impostor in fiction. The Quebec-born and raised Ernest Dufault (1892–1942), better known as Will James, the popular American writer of westerns in the 1920s and 1930s, wrote twenty-four books, all of them feeding the American public's seemingly unquenchable thirst for western adventure full of gunfights, tough sheriffs, mean stagecoach robbers, marauding Indians, cattle rustlers, and saloons. He spent three years (1907 to 1910) as a cowboy on ranches in Saskatchewan and Alberta, and out of those few years styled himself an American cowboy writer. His first book, *Cowboys North and South* (1924), a collection of his magazine stories, established the charade that was his persona:

> What I've wrote in this book is without the help of the dictionary or any course in story writing.... Me, never being to school and having to pick up what I know in grammar from old magazines and saddle catalogues.... I was born and raised in the cow country.[64]

James illustrated his books with his own pencil drawings of cowboy life, such as roping and branding cattle. He went on to Hollywood fame and renown in the American world of the pulp western genre.

If southern Alberta produced major figures in adventure romance, northern Alberta produced some fictional curiosities, including writer Paul A. W. Wallace (1892–1967), who taught at the University of Alberta from 1919 to 1921. From this experience he created *Baptiste Larocque: Legends of French Canada*, a collection of short stories. Wallace's French-Canadian characters speak in accented English, like blacks in many southern novels:

> Den w'at happen nex', eh? We devil (dats him) he was shout, "She cheat me, by t'onder!" An *pouf.*[65]

The French element of northern Alberta's multicultural identity was as important as the English remittance man and the cowboy ranch was to southern Alberta—and, obviously, just as stereotyped.

Three women novelists wrote books with female heroines in this period. Irene Roy produced a single novel, *Junette or Are Women Just To One Another*

(1919), which she most likely paid to publish. Charlotte Gordon (1880-1929) is listed as the author of *Red Gold: A true story of an Englishwoman's development in the West* (1928). The book was a romantic treatment, emphasizing soft, feminine refinement:

> As she lay, lost in reverie, there came floating through the air the sweet, low music of the bell...it seemed as if the soft, delicate air through which it passed had a rarefying influence upon the sound itself, and had mellowed its tones into a strain throbbing with peace....[66]

The last of these romantic novelists was Flos Jewell Williams (1893-19?), the most accomplished of the three.

Williams came to Calgary in 1915 and published four novels between 1925 and 1950. Her first novel, *The Judgment of Solomon* (1925), featured a male hero in a love story. It was followed a year later by *New Furrows: A Story of the Alberta Foothills*. *New Furrows* was the story of a Belgian immigrant woman's life in southwestern Alberta. The 300-page novel has the familiar romantic, idyllic tone:

> Marie paused at the edge of the meadow, gazing with beauty-brooding blue eyes at the little stream creeping sleepily along its boundary.[67]

In 1930, Williams published *Broken Gods*. Her final book was *Fold Home* (1950), set in Calgary and the Turner Valley ranch district. The jacket for the latter book describes the Ontario-born Williams as "a full-fledged Albertan by the time she stepped onto the station platform," so well had she taken up western stylings.

The agrarian theme was taken up more realistically by three male and two female novelists of varying ability. Augustus Bridle (1869-1952) was an Ontario writer who lived in Edmonton and area for a few years. *Hansen: A Novel of Canadianization* (1924) is set partly in Edmonton before and after the turn of the century. It tells the story of a new Canadian who runs for election to the Alberta legislature. Bridle states in his introduction that the novel "contains many characters, all but two or three of whom are taken from life...."[68]

Charles Walter Peterson (1868-1944) founded the *Farm and Ranch Review* in Calgary in 1905. *Fruits of the Earth: A Story of the Canadian Prairies* (1928) is a didactic work of sentimental fiction about farming in southern Alberta. (By the time Peterson published this novel, he owned 25,000 acres.) Peterson claimed it was a forthright treatment of immigration and colonization, but the slipjacket of the novel with a nude female figure rising sun-like out of a field of golden wheat, representing agrarian bounty, bespeaks Peterson's promotional talents more than his literary gifts. In fact, Peterson, as an agricultural and ranch journal editor, wrote numerous polemical publications on such topics as Social Credit, the railways, and drought.

Another male contributor to this period was an American writer, Harold Loeb (1891-1979), whose third novel, *Tumbling Mustard* (1929), was set in frontier Medicine Hat. In a 1970s afterword to another novel, Loeb explains that he actually began work on *Tumbling Mustard* while travelling in Palestine and Jordan after living in Berlin and Paris.[69]

The two women novelists of the period, Laura Goodman Salverson (1890-1970) and Winnifred Eaton Babcock Reeve (1879-1954) were much more important to Alberta letters. Both women produced large bodies of fictional work and can be considered major writers of the decade.

Critic Edward McCourt describes Laura Salverson's first novel, *The Viking Heart* (1923), as "the most popular novel in Canadian literature based on a mass migration movement...."[70] Salverson was the daughter of Icelandic immigrants, and her novel dealt with the Icelandic migration to Manitoba in the 1870s. Although claiming to be a realistic treatment, the novel has strong romantic overtones. In her autobiography, *Confessions of an Immigrant's Daughter,* Salverson tells of her move to Edmonton and how she began the novel:

> Back in Edmonton [after World War One], I hired a second-hand typewriter, bought a kitchen table and some Manila papers and shut myself up in a slice of a room to draw up the skeleton of the story.[71]

She went on to show the manuscript, which had been typed up by her husband, to Nellie McClung, who "assured me the story was good."[72] After the manuscript was completed, Salverson moved to Calgary, where she was living when the book was published.[73]

The Viking Heart is considered her best work, although she did publish other novels, mostly historic romances. *When Sparrows Fall* (1925) was her second novel; it was written in Calgary and dedicated to Nellie McClung, who was clearly her literary mentor. *Lord of the Silver Dragon* (1927), *Johann Lind* (1928), and *The Dove* (1933) followed quickly, suggesting what a large audience existed for her work. In 1937, her novel *The Dark Weavers* won the Governor General's award for fiction, but by this time Salverson had left Alberta.[74]

In addition to novels, Salverson also published a volume of poetry, *Wayside Gleams* (1925). She moved around western Canada a great deal because of her husband's railway and communication work, and her poems were written in a variety of prairie settings. Their general tone is captured in this excerpt from "Ad Finem":

> Dark, and the moon's fair glow
> > Falls on the sea;
> Love and a far-off dream
> > Beckon to me.[75]

Salverson was a major figure in literary circles in Calgary after her novels appeared in the 1920s and played an active role in local literary culture.

An equally interesting Calgarian was Winnifred Eaton Babcock Reeve, who published two novels about Alberta in the 1920s, although she had published numerous others prior to her move to Alberta. She was born in Montreal to Chinese and English parents, and grew up in a large, impoverished family. She moved to New York, married, and began writing under the pseudonym Onoto Watanna. *A Japanese Nightingale* (1901) was the first of a dozen romance novels.

Babcock was her first husband's name, and Reeve was that of her second husband, whom she married during World War One and with whom she moved to the Cochrane area to ranch in 1917. The move to Alberta interrupted her writing career, which she did not resume until 1922, when she published her Japanese romance, *Sunny San*. She wrote this novel in Calgary after leaving her husband and the ranch.

Her next novel was a major departure from her previous work. *Cattle* (1923) is written with almost journalistic plainness, although the story tends toward the melodramatic. The novel is set in Alberta. "In a country like

Alberta," she writes, "...we do not scrutinize too closely the visitor or the past of the stranger in our midst. Alberta is in a way, a land of sanctuary...."[76]

Watanna wrote a second novel with an Alberta ranch theme, *His Royal Nibs* (1925), but by the time it was released, she was back in New York, working for Universal Pictures as a scenario writer. She moved to Hollywood and worked for Universal and MGM until 1931, when she was reconciled with her husband and returned to Calgary.

Watanna published no further novels. During her professional life in Alberta, however, she became acquainted with fellow writers and took a leading role in the establishment of the Canadian Author's Association.[77] Like Salverson, Watanna was a local literary personality. The inscription on a copy of her novel *Cattle* in the Margaret P. Hess Collection of the University of Calgary library suggests Watanna's literary status:

> To Lady Lougheed—a picturesque and delightful personality
> with the regard of the author.
>
> > Onoto Watanna
> > Calgary, December 22, 1922
>
> The world is just as a person's heart makes it.

One other novelist of this period deserves mention: Franco-Albertan writer Georges Bugnet (who will be discussed in more detail in chapter six because he wrote in French). Bugnet's 1924 novel *Nipsya* was published in English under the same title in 1929. Bugnet (1879-1981) lived in a rural area northeast of Edmonton, having come to Alberta from France in 1905. *Nipsya,* the Cree name of the novel's Métis heroine, deals with the west of the Riel period and is written from a Métis perspective. It is written in a refreshingly unadorned and straightforward style, although its French and Catholic references give some of the dialogue an old-fashioned air. Constance Davies Woodrow's 1929 translation captures some tender, powerful moments, such as this speech by Nipsya's lover:

> Nipsya, there is but one law for every living thing, and that is that it must fulfill its destiny. Do you see those withered reeds over there? In the summer, countless water-lilies grow around them and fish is plentiful here. The reeds, by their very withering, accomplish something...In the spring, they will decay, but the decayed matter will produce new life. If the reeds did not give themselves that way, both the water-lilies and the fish would disappear....[78]

Although this translation did not bring him fame, Bugnet represents one of the few French-language writers from Alberta whose work has also appeared in English.[79]

Conclusion

A notable feature of this period was the lack of poetry books in the decade from 1919 to 1929. Only Laura Goodman Salverson published a volume of poetry. Compared to the large number of non-fiction and fiction books, this was a regrettable gap. In the whole period, only a half-dozen poets published books.

At the same time, important figures in Canadian poetry, such as Charles G.D. Roberts, Bliss Carman, Duncan Campbell Scott, Pauline Johnson, and Robert Service, were coming to the fore. The reason for the poetic paucity in Alberta may lie in the roughness of pioneering culture, which saw poetry as a genteel craft unsuited to the demands of a founding society. Economic growth, social issues, and the creation of a viable community with fundamental institutions were the priorities of the day. This slow start for poetry in Alberta was to have a damaging effect on the art for decades to come.

A second notable feature was the surge of women writers after 1905. Women writers dominated fiction by the 1920s. Writers from Nellie McClung to Laura Goodman Salverson produced a body of literature that opened up the province to a sensibility removed from the adventure and action-oriented male imagination. Agrarian settlement brought a large number of women to the province, and their presence made a difference to literary culture. They expanded the range of the dominant narrative and produced a different Alberta voice.

Nostalgia for the frontier of the imagination continued to play an important role in literary culture, especially in popular Mountie adventure and crime novels, but this nostalgia was balanced by an increasing maturity that sought to express the issues facing Alberta. Because of these changes in the quarter-century from 1905 to 1929, Alberta was in a position to make a major leap forward in its literary culture when the Depression struck.

5

Depression
and War

BY 1930, ALBERTA WRITERS, such as Stead, McClung, and Murphy, had national reputations. Alberta finally had an indigenous writing voice. But Alberta's confidence had been shattered: first by the Depression, then by a long period of drought. The agrarian economy collapsed. Class divisions became sharper as people turned to utopian solutions. Non-fiction writing rebounded in this bleak atmosphere, while fiction introduced a new generation of writers, whose work captured the mood of the times. In 1939, the Second World War replaced this desperate utopianism with patriotic enthusiasm. Initially, war seemed a brief distraction from the perpetual struggle of agrarian life. People did not realize, at the time, that it marked the end of an era.

Non-fiction: 1930-1945

Non-fiction writing in this period brought several new kinds of writing to the province. Scholarship, essay, and nature writing began to appear alongside the work of journalists and memoirists.

Alberta's first native-born scholar was George F.G. Stanley, who was born in Calgary in 1907, schooled in the city, and granted his Bachelor of Arts degree from the University of Alberta in Edmonton. At age twenty-two, he went to Oxford as a Rhodes Scholar, eventually earning his D.Phil. with a

E.A. Corbett. Courtesy of
the University of Alberta
Archives.

thesis on the Riel Rebellions, published as *The Birth of Western Canada: A
History of the Riel Rebellions* (1936).

British historian A.J.P. Taylor reviewed Stanley's book in the *Manchester
Guardian*, calling it "an important contribution to Canadian history...well
worth reading as a fascinating and admirably told story...."[1] Stanley became a
military historian and wrote a number books on Canadian military topics. In
1982, he was named Lieutenant-Governor of New Brunswick, which experience he described in his eighteenth book, *The Role of the Lieutenant-Governor*,
published in 1992. (Stanley had gone to New Brunswick in 1936 to take an
academic teaching position.) In a brief reminiscence of his time in Alberta and
the writing of *The Birth of Canada*, Stanley recalls that when his thesis advisor
at Oxford suggested he write the book, he remembered

old "Grannie" Rose of Lethbridge tell of her experiences in Battleford
during the "seige" by the Cree.... I had listened to stories by old Colonel

James Walker of the early days of the Mounted Police.... I had known half-breeds among my school mates in Calgary and remembered the old Métisse, Lady Lougheed, whose summer cottage on the road to Banff Springs Hotel was not far from our own. While other boys were reading Henty's *With Wolfe in Canada*, I was reading Ralph Connor's *The Doctor, The Foreigner*, and *Corporal Cameron*.... No historical subject could have pleased me more.[2]

Clearly, his early scholarship was framed by his Alberta roots.[3]

While George Stanley left Alberta for the Maritimes, Edward Annand Corbett (1887-1964) came to Alberta from the Maritimes to become the University's Director of Extension. Corbett wrote a number of books dealing with Alberta. In 1934, he published two books, *Blackfoot Trails* and *McQueen of Edmonton*. The former dealt with the history and legends of the Blackfoot, while the latter was a biography of David G. McQueen, who served as a Presbyterian minister in Edmonton from 1887 to 1931. Corbett wrote two other biographies—*Father, God Bless Him* (1953), a memoir of his father and of his own youth, and *Henry Marshall Tory, Beloved Canadian* (1954), a biography of the first president of the University of Alberta. Corbett's last book was a collection of essays on Alberta education and adult learning, *We Have With Us Tonight* (1957). Corbett was not a great writer, but he provided valuable historical material on life in Alberta from the turn of the century until World War Two. His affection for people, his interest in religious matters, and his devotion to further education made him a central figure in the development of Alberta's early cultural and educational institutions, such as CKUA radio and the Banff School of Fine Arts.

The most curious of the scholars was Robert E. Gard (1910-1992), an American specialist in folk drama. In 1942, Gard became director of the summer folk-playwriting program at the Banff School of Fine Arts; a year later, he helped to establish the Alberta Folklore and Local History Project at the University of Alberta. His work collecting Alberta folklore material had two results. The first was a book, *Johnny Chinook: Tall Tales and True from the Canadian West* (1945); the second was a short-lived periodical, *The Alberta Folklore Quarterly* (1945-46). *Johnny Chinook* is a collection of stories from four geographic areas of Alberta: short grass country, foothills country, park-belt country, and Peace River country. The author's foreword states, "the writing of this book was undertaken for the people of Alberta...to perhaps encourage other writers to use the fine materials of the West."[4] In one story about Bob Edwards, Gard brings his light touch to a discussion of Senator Lougheed's role in the legal battle between Lord Strathcona and the feisty Bob Edwards:

> The wire [to Senator Lougheed] said: "Begin civil and criminal actions at once!" and named the culprit and mentioned the battery of legal talent in London standing by ready to back the Senator up.... Senator Lougheed, wise in the ways of the West, knew that if action were brought against Edwards, it would end in a downright farce.... Senator Lougheed finally succeeded in persuading Lord Strathcona to call off his dogs. The legal side of the affair ended but the West is still laughing.[5]

Gard left Alberta in 1945, and the *Alberta Folklore Quarterly* shut down the following year. Gard left behind an introduction to popular Alberta culture that has yet to be surpassed or updated. When he wrote about his Alberta experience a decade later, Gard said:

> In Alberta I deepened my feeling for place and, I think, became more sensitive to elements in regional life—elements which can make any region unique, a place of distinctive flavour.[6]

Stanley, Corbett, and Gard developed the interest in compiling Alberta's history initiated by Archibald MacRae and John Blue in the two previous decades. After only a quarter-century of provincehood, there was a strong attachment to the province's past and a sense of distinctness.

Scottish novelist Frederick John Niven (1878-1944) wrote a non-fiction book that touched on Alberta. *Canada West* was published in 1930. This scene from Banff in the 1920s communicates powerfully:

> I recalled walking round the mezzanine floor at Banff Springs Hotel to the dining-room, and hearing music played in such a way that it pinched the heart. Who was playing, and where? And then between two pillars I saw the musician: somebody's chauffeur, by his uniform, a negro (his ebony face as black as the ebony of the piano), who had found that instrument in the alcove and was expressing himself on it, rapt and lost....[7]

Niven did not spend much time in Alberta, although he visited and wrote about the place. He exalted the Alberta mountains in *Colour in the Canadian Rockies* (1937), a travelogue Niven co-wrote with artist Walter J. Phillips, who provided water-colour illustrations and black-and-white etchings. Niven finally settled in British Columbia.

A long-term resident of Alberta was Edmund Kemper Broadus (1876–1936), who came to the province in 1908 from Harvard to establish the English department at the University of Alberta. Broadus published a variety of textbooks for English students, including one of Canadian prose and poetry he co-edited with his wife, but his major contribution to Alberta letters is *Saturday and Sunday* (1935), a collection of anecdotal essays. In his foreword to the book, Broadus judges his early essays as "a little overwrought—'tenderfoot' impressions, at which a real pioneer would tolerantly smile."[8] He explains that these essays were "a week-end diversion, a Saturday-Sunday interlude."[9] Broadus wrote with a low-key sense of humour, as is suggested in his description of the birth of the province's first university: "In an attic, then, with a president, a faculty of four, and a student-body of forty-five, University of Alberta began its work. It was a curious little family."[10]

One of Broadus' students in the 1920s was Lovat Dickson, who later played an important role in Alberta letters. Dickson (1902-1987) took his English degree at the University of Alberta, and went on to become a publisher in London with his own imprint, eventually returning to Canada to work with the publishing firm of Macmillan in Toronto and to write. In the late 1930s, Dickson wrote several books on Grey Owl, the great Canadian naturalist and impostor, having become acquainted with him through his publication of Grey Owl's book, *Pilgrim of the Wild*. In the first volume of his autobiography, *The Ante-Room*, which covers the period to 1929, when he left Edmonton for London, Dickson recalls Broadus chewing him out as a student. "Who in God's name," Broadus raved, "told you that you can write?"[11] Obviously, someone had, because Dickson wrote occasional editorial columns for the *Edmonton Journal*. In 1971, he published an essay in *The Globe Magazine* about his literary life in Edmonton:

> I used to finish my copy late at night, and walk across the High Level bridge to deliver it to the *Journal* office. The frozen river, the frozen night, the crunch of my Arctic boots on the stiff, rutted snow, the stars cold in the deep of the sky; and in the northwest the aurora borealis turning green at this midnight hour, leaping like a snake at the supper sky, and falling back to flicker and pulsate before trying again....[12]

Dickson had an real talent for both creative non-fiction and journalism. He published one novel, *Out of the West Land* (1944), but it was a long, overdrawn love story about an English aristocrat and an impoverished University of Alberta student vying for the hand of a local maiden. Dickson's main contribution to Alberta letters, however, was as a publisher of a number of Alberta writers, discussed later in this chapter, who found in him a valuable resource in London, when the province itself had no real trade book publishers.

Matthew Halton, a professional journalist, wrote a memoir, *Ten Years to Alamein,* in 1944, just before the end of the War. Halton (1904-1956) was from Pincher Creek, where his father and uncles had homesteaded in 1902. He had been a foreign correspondent before the War for the *Toronto Star,* then a war correspondent for the C.B.C. The following is Halton's perfectly acceptable contribution to the war-writing genre, where he describes the North Africa campaign against Rommel:

> I went down and ordered beer. It was one of life's pleasanter moments. I had been to Tobruk. I had come out of Tobruk. I felt I was taking some small part in the great events of our times. Now we were out of danger— and I had a cold drink. Ahead were Alexandria and Cairo; asparagus and sausage to eat at Le Petit Coin de France; letters from home; clean sheets; and friends.[13]

Prior to the War, another kind of memoir was popular. Five memoirs of pioneer life were published by an equal number of authors, none of whom matched Halton's sparse but effective prose. The first was John D. Higinbotham's *When the West Was Young* (1933). Higinbotham (1864-1961) was a pioneer druggist at Fort Macleod, who served as postmaster in Lethbridge from 1886 to 1910. His memoir is prosaic but full of anecdotal information about southern Alberta, based on Higinbotham's own experiences. The work is large (over 300 pages) and ends with an account of Higinbotham's trip up the Mackenzie River to the Arctic. Higinbotham later self-published a chap-book, *Foothill and Prairie Memories* (1948), poems he had written prior to 1900.

A more eccentric autobiography is John James Rouse's *Pioneer Work in Canada: Practically Presented* (1935). Rouse (1869-19?) was a Protestant minister who spent a few years after the turn of the century in Edmonton, then settled in Calgary in 1921. The book, filled with biblical quotations, portrays Rouse's life as an itinerant minister, preaching across the province, often in revivalist tents. The book was published in Scotland in 1935, and is of interest as an expression of Christian fundamentalism, an important element of Alberta's social history in the first half of the twentieth century.

William Griesbach, another pioneer figure, was a military man. Griesbach (1878-1945) fought in the Boer War, became an alderman in Edmonton at the age of twenty-seven, and was elected mayor two years later, in 1907.[14] After World War One, he was appointed to the Senate as a Conservative; during World War Two, he was appointed Inspector-General of Western Canadian Forces. His memoir, *I Remember*, was published posthumously in 1946. Griesbach's writing is light and entertaining, and a significant portion of the book deals with his life in Edmonton and Alberta. His pages are full of colourful recollections of people from the city at the turn of the century.

More interesting from a literary point of view than either of these writers were two women writers of the period. The first was Dr. Mary Percy Jackson (1904-), who was a medical doctor in the Peace River district. Her letters, written to family in the United Kingdom, were published in 1933 as *On the Last Frontier: Pioneering in the Peace River Block*.[15] Janice Dickin-McGinnis notes that Dr. Jackson's book is valuable because it provides a unique woman's perspective on the pioneer culture of the Peace country in the 1920s.[16] The following is an example of cultural clashes Dr. Jackson experienced:

I've got three men dying of TB and a couple of sick children and an old woman of 80 with heart failure and that's about all. The old lady is booked for the next world, I'm afraid, and there's little I can do. She is Ukrainian, doesn't speak or understand any English and is an *obstinate* old woman.

All these Central and Eastern Europeans go to bed in their clothes.... Now this old woman was wearing sundry cotton and woolen vests, a marvellously hand-embroidered linen blouse and a thick cloth skirt. Well, she's pretty bad and...I didn't want her to get bed sores to add to her troubles, so I told her grand-daughter she was to give her just a cotton or woolen nightgown. However, the old woman wouldn't hear of it. Told them to tell me to go away and stop bothering her![17]

Dr. Jackson received an honourary doctorate from the University of Alberta in the 1970s and continues to live in the Peace district.

The other woman writer was Kathleen (Redman) Strange (1896-1968), whose book *With the West In Her Eyes: The Story of a Modern Pioneer* was published in 1937. Strange and her husband, Henry, won the world wheat championship in Chicago in 1923, and her memoir deals with the eleven years that they farmed in Alberta, from 1919 to 1930. In the memoir, Strange recalls their reward for winning the championship was "the magnificent sum of fifteen dollars," all of which she spent on postage to answer the thousand or so letters they received because of the publicity.[18] The success of her book led her and her husband to write a further memoir, *Never A Dull Moment* (1941).

Alberta's agrarian society was in crisis during the Depression. It needed to affirm its pioneering values, to see itself as a successful product of hard work, inventiveness, and solid social values, all of which came under siege with the drought and poverty of the 1930s. Most of the non-fiction work of the period referred to more positive times, when the sense of achievement, of creating a civilized society and settling the land and making it productive, was the core of the Alberta identity. These books assured Albertans that all their work had not been lost in bankruptcy and dust.

Alongside this beleaguered agrarian sensibility, a distinctive, non-agrarian, mountain voice developed. Building on the popularity of the work of the Saskatchewan writer Grey Owl, other writers adopted the naturalist perspective. Mountaineer Conrad Kain's (1883-1934) posthumous autobiography, *Where the Clouds Can Go*, was prepared by his climbing companion J. Monroe Thorington, who first wrote about mountaineering in the Rockies in the 1920s. But the major contributor to Alberta's naturalist genre was Dan McCowan (1882-1956), who came from Scotland to settle in Banff 1911. He became a well-known lecturer, photographer, writer, and broadcaster. In 1936, McCowan published *Animals of the Canadian Rockies*, which he re-issued in an expanded edition in 1950. The book had such anthropomorphic chapter headings as "Rip Van Winkle of the Rockies" (marmot) and "The Outlaw" (grey wolf). *A Naturalist in Canada* (1941 with a second, enlarged edition in 1946) and *Outdoors with a Camera in Canada* (1945) followed. McCowan also prepared several books after the Second World War: *Hill-top Tales* (1948), *Tidewater to Timberline* (1951), and *Upland Trails* (1955). In *Hill-top Tales* and its sequel, *Upland Trails,* McCowan told a variety of stories about the people, animals, and places of the foothills and mountains of western Canada.

McCowan used a combination of anecdotal history and personal observation to create his popular, knowledgeable, and often humorous approach to nature. *A Naturalist in Canada* draws upon his C.B.C. radio broadcasts; they read well as conversational storytelling. The following clever juxtaposition is exemplary of his reverence of nature:

In Calgary on a torrid day in July, I heard an aeroplane droning in the sky and stepped to the curb the better to catch a glimpse of the machine as it circled over the city.

Looking upwards I saw not only the plane but also two splendid eagles, etched cleanly against a large white cloud. I forgot all about the stuttering machine of the airman and was oblivious to the earthbound traffic flowing noisily past. The birds in lofty splendour entranced me with their effortless movements and I watched till my eyes tired....[19]

McCowan was one of the first Albertans to use the media in a multi-faceted way, creating books for a market that had been primed by his lecture tours and radio broadcasts.

Fiction: 1930-1945

Fewer fiction writers published in this period than non-fiction writers. The writers who came into their own in the 1910s and 1920s continued to produce, but the work of new writers lacked the critical mass achieved by the previous generation. The Mountie motif retained its hold on the imagination, as did agrarian fiction, but there were also new developments—animal adventure stories, historical novels, and mountain fiction.

Robert (Bob) Dyker, an ex-N.W.M.P. officer, published a fictionalized autobiography titled *Get Your Man: An Autobiography of the North-west Mounted* (1934). It was based on his seven years of service between 1907 and 1914, one year of which he spent in Edmonton. Dyker's storytelling style involved the intermingling of autobiographical narrative with constructed dialogue. He makes this bizarre and racist observation about crime in Alberta:

Most of the large towns in Western Canada have one particular foreign element which dominates all the other nationalities.... In Regina it was Swedish.... In Winnipeg German.... And I believe I can safely say that in Edmonton the dominating element was negro....[20]

This is probably the first (and likely the last) time anyone claimed that blacks were the dominant criminal element in Edmonton in the agrarian period.

Thankfully, other writers who appeared in the thirties were somewhat more accurate in their treatment of Alberta. Norman M. Plummer published two novels set in Alberta. The first, *The Goad: A Human Story of the last great west in the early part of the twentieth century based mainly on facts* (1930), is a story of pioneering agricultural life in southern Alberta and the Peace River country. The second, *The Long Arm* (1939), is a juvenile crime novel, set in the early part of the century, about a Mountie hero who goes back to England to fight in World War One. Not much is known about Plummer, other than that he was of English descent, but he may have spent some time in Alberta (probably Calgary), because he claims his novels are based on personal experience.

Another English writer, Mrs. K.H. Gwynn, writing as Ursula Leigh, produced two novels set in Alberta. *Give Me My Robe* (1934) and *Chinook* (n.d.) both take place in the early-twentieth century ranching country of southern Alberta and feature female protagonists. Whether Mrs. Gwynn ever visited Alberta is uncertain.

An English-born writer who was clearly rooted in southern Alberta was Wilfred Eggleston (1901-1986), whose family settled on a homestead near Manyberries in 1909. Eggleston was a teacher with the Golden Prairie School District at Bull's Head Butte in the early 1920s. He later attended Queen's University, became a journalist in Toronto, and served in the Press Gallery in Ottawa. Eggleston said of his departure, "In leaving Alberta for the East I sensed that I was drawing closer to the literary heart of English-speaking Canada."[21] In 1927, he realized his literary aspirations by self-publishing a collection of poetry, *Prairie Moonlight and Other Lyrics*. He later published a novel, *The High Plains* (1938). The novel was based on the life of his parents and their family and is dedicated to "The Pioneers Who Settled in 'Palliser Triangle' My Parents Among them." Forty years later, he published *Prairie Symphony*, a sequel to *The High Plains*. Eggleston wrote a few journalistic non-fiction works, but, other than his 1980 memoir *Literary Friends*, they did not deal with Alberta. Eggleston's career in journalism drew him away from fiction writing, and he left only the two novels.

Ronald Ross Annett (1895-1988), a very successful magazine short-story writer, began his career in 1938. Annett was the principal at Consort School when *The Saturday Evening Post* published his first short story, paying him a handsome $500 (almost half what the local school district was paying for a full year of teaching). He published thirteen stories with the *Post* between 1938 and 1942, collected as *Especially Babe* (1942).[22]

The *Babe* stories centred on a female child called Babe, her older brother, Little Joe, and their father, Big Joe, a family trying to make ends meet on a Depression farm. The stories had simple, homely dialogue and happy endings, comforting words for such uncertain times. A healthy, steady income (the *Post's* circulation was 6 million at this time) allowed Annett to quit teaching and live from his writing. He kept producing stories for the *Post* until 1962, when the magazine closed. By then Annett was earning $2,500 per story, producing about five per year. In all, he published more than seventy *Babe* stories.

Annett's stories represent an Americanized Alberta, featuring folksy language and simple characters. They provided innocent entertainment for a vast North American audience. Like his fellow Alberta writer John Patrick Gillese, who also published numerous short stories in a similar style, Annett was able to earn a much better living from his popular writing than from agricultural or educational pursuits. During the terrible troubles of the Depression and War, popular humour was greatly appreciated.

One other fiction writer using the agrarian theme was Eva Bruce, who lived for several decades in Alberta before moving to British Columbia. Bruce published one melodramatic novel, *Call Her Rosie* (1942), involving a teen heroine, an alcoholic father, and a stallion.

The animal story genre was new to Alberta in the 1930s. In 1932, Gray McClintock, a writer and broadcaster from Albany, New York, published *The Wolves at Cooking Lake and Other Stories*, a book based on his broadcasts. The studies included a mix of animal, aboriginal, and N.W.M.P. tales set in Alberta.

A more significant contribution was made by Kenneth Conibear, a writer raised in the Northwest Territories but educated in Alberta. Conibear (1907-) published a collection of animal stories, *North Land Footprints; or, Lives on Little Bent Tree Lake,* with Lovat Dickson in 1936. Conibear was raised in Fort Smith, several miles north of the Alberta border. He went to high school in Edmonton and attended the University of Alberta, where he was selected Alberta Rhodes Scholar in 1931. He spent three years in England, where he wrote his first book. He approached Dickson, who remembered him from the University of Alberta's student newspaper, *The Gateway*, where Conibear had served as editor.[23] The animal stories did not sell well, although one reviewer called Conibear "the Kipling of the North."[24] Conibear's next book, *Northward to Eden* (1939), was set in northern Alberta during the 1920s.[25] His final book, *Husky* (1940), was co-written with his brother, Frank, the inventor of the humane Conibear trap. Unfortunately, the ship carrying the books was torpedoed and his other books were destroyed in wartime bombing.[26] Conibear returned to the Northwest Territories in 1938 and did not publish after 1940. He is one of the now-forgotten writers whom Alberta nurtured in the 1930s.

Another new genre introduced into Alberta letters at this time was the historical novel. Laura Goodman Salverson, already an established novelist, published a few historical novels with Viking themes in this period. But William George Hardy launched the genre in a major way in the 1930s. Hardy (1895–1979) was a classicist who taught at the University of Alberta from 1920 to 1964. He took time from his scholarly pursuits to publish several historical novels dealing with the Biblical era, pharaonic Egypt, and ancient Rome. His first novel, *Father Abraham*, was published by Lovat Dickson in 1935.[27] Hardy's historical style can be seen in this descriptive example from *Father Abraham*:

> The slopes were gentle with acacias and with drooping willows. By the white-walled villages ran rills of sparkling water. From the houses the whiteskinned Mitanni women, strong of thigh and deep of bosom, eyes

blue as ice of their ancient northern home, put cupped hands to broad foreheads to watch them pass.[28]

Hardy examined Roman times in *Turn Back the River* (1938), then prepared a fictional life of Moses in *All the Trumpets Sounded* (1942). He took a literary detour in 1951 with a novel about World War Two, but returned to his Roman theme a few years later with *The City of Libertines* (1957). Hardy was particularly interested in Caesar and his final novel, *The Scarlet Mantle* (1978), published a year before his death, deals with the first part of Caesar's life. He was preparing a sequel (working title "The Bloodied Toga"), but died before finishing it. Hardy thought of his novels as a popular way to bring the lives of famous historical figures, whose biographies were ordinarily the preserve of specialists, to a wider audience. He succeeded.

Hardy was strongly committed to his literary career, which began in 1928, when *Maclean's* magazine serialized his novel, *Son of Eli*. Hardy was three times president of the Canadian Authors Association, and was a prolific writer of short stories, a number of them anthologized. His involvement in the literary community in Edmonton and Alberta was extensive, and he developed many contacts in his role as editor-in-chief of the *Alberta Golden Jubilee Anthology* (1955) and *Alberta: A Natural History* (1971). Hardy belonged to a new generation of writers, who made Alberta their permanent literary home.

The writer whose fiction has endured the longest is Howard O'Hagan, whose 1939 novel *Tay John* is a true Alberta classic. Of all the fiction published in the 1930s, only this novel remains in print to this day. O'Hagan (1902-1982) was born in Lethbridge but was raised in the Yellowhead Pass region of the Rockies. His father was a doctor based in Jasper. O'Hagan studied Law at McGill University in Montreal, but he returned to the Rockies, where he made a career as a guide. He was thirty-seven when *Tay John* was published. Michael Ondaajte writes of the novel:

> Howard O'Hagan's *Tay John* was one of the first novels to chart important motifs that have become crucial to the work of later western writers like Robert Kroetsch and Rudy Wiebe. O'Hagan's mythic realism seems...much more apt as a way of portraying the west and much of this country....[29]

Ondaajte confirms that *Tay John* remains an important source of contemporary fictional sensibility. The novel is set in the 1880s in the Yellowhead Pass area:

> The wind, studded with snow, was blowing from the north. The pinto horse, waiting, tied to a poplar, was cold. Mounted, he bucked, and Tay John, left arm lifted high for balance, saw his black Stenson hat, jarred from his head, fall to the ground....Tay John did not turn. He jogged off across the clearing, merging with the curtain of snow, becoming less a man than a movement. He did not leave so much as he disappeared from view, his proportions whittled by mist and distance. He left his hat discarded where it had fallen. He renounced it entirely.[30]

O'Hagan was also an accomplished short story-writer. His stories were collected as *Wilderness Men* (1958) and *The Woman Who Got on at Jasper Station and Other Stories* (1963).[31] The interaction between nature and humanity that characterizes his work is evident in this excerpt from "The Woman Who Got on at Jasper Station":

> She had sat with her back against a log and watched the waves of the lake roll in. The little waves, like the sky, were grey and she listened to each one as it dissolved with a whisper into the grey sand at her feet. Above the waves, a migrating flock of small, black birds, wheeled and dipped and twittered, like a handful of music notes thrown up against the lowering sky.[32]

In recognition of O'Hagan's talent as a short-story writer, the Writers Guild of Alberta named its short fiction award in his honour.

Poetry: 1930–1945

The only Alberta poet to publish during the 1930s was Sara E. Carsley, whose *Alchemy and Other Poems* was published in 1935. Carsley was originally from Northern Ireland, and she taught Latin at Central High School in Calgary. She was a romantic poet, who wrote in a rather dated style. In "Quia Multum Amavit," the speaker prays to God:

Lord, often I, a graceless knave,
   Have snatched, unshamed in haste and greed,
Too much of all the joys You gave
   To meet our need.[33]

Carsley also published a small chapbook of poetry titled *The Artisan* with Ryerson in 1941; it appeared in an edition of 250.

The difficulty of publishing poetry in this period caused local poets to take matters into their own hands. In 1930, the Edmonton Branch of the Canadian Authors Association sponsored a poetry competition "to inspire Canadian writers to make use of the vast wealth of western Canadian material which lies before them."[34] *The Alberta Poetry Yearbook,* and the contest associated with it, continued for over half a century, making it one of the longest-running poetry publications in the country.

Emily Murphy wrote the foreword to the first volume, pleading that "our land must not be songless."[35] The tenth anniversary issue (1939/40) featured contributors from across Canada, including Sara Carsley. In later years, poems were divided into various categories such as "lyrics," "humorous verse," and "juveniles," with first, second, and third prizes awarded in each category.[36]

The use of contests to promote Alberta writers may have been inspired by the agricultural fairs with their contests, prizes, and awards that were popular in western Canada. The introduction of such competitions was a prelude to a major use of this form of promotion much later, in the 1970s.

The major breakthrough for Alberta poetry came in 1942, when Earle Birney's *David and Other Poems,* for which Birney received the Governor-General's Award for poetry, was published by Ryerson. Birney was only the second Albertan, after Laura Salverson, to receive a Governor-General's Award.

Birney (1904-1995) was born in Calgary before Alberta became a province. He spent the first few years of his life on a farm near Lacombe, then his family moved to Banff, where he lived and went to school until 1922 (except for a couple of years in British Columbia). In 1922, Birney went to study at the University of British Columbia. He never returned to Alberta as a resident, going on first to graduate school at the University of Toronto, then teaching at the University of British Columbia. Birney published his second book of poems, *Now Is Time*, in 1945 and again won the Governor-General's award for poetry. Birney belonged to the new generation of Canadian poets, like

Raymond Souster, Louis Dudek, and Dorothy Livesay, for whom their Canadian experience and everyday language were paramount. Birney was the strongest and most modern voice that Alberta produced before 1945, and he went on to become a major twentieth-century Canadian poet.

Birney's classic poem "David" is set in the mountains of Birney's youth. Its narrative style is a welcome change from the standard versifying of the time:

> I will not remember how nor why I could twist
> Up the wind-devilled peak, and down through the chimney's
> empty Horror, and over the traverse alone. I remember
> Only the pounding fear I would stumble on It
> When I came to the grave-cold maw of the
> bergschrund...reeling.[37]

At the end of the poem, David, badly injured in a fall, is put of his misery by his climbing companion.

In the 1940s, Birney was still writing about his Alberta experiences, including an elegy to Banff mountaineer Conrad Kain. Birney was the first

Alberta-born poet to contribute a major body of poetic work to the Canadian canon, and his assumption into the pantheon of poetic greats at mid-century both broadened his national identity and narrowed its Alberta component. When Northrop Frye reviewed *Trial of a City and Other Verse* (1952), he called Birney one of Canada's two leading poets, the other being E.J. Pratt.[38] George Woodcock, the editor of *Canadian Literature*, described Birney as "a humanising landscapist," a quality that may well have come from his Alberta experience.[39] Poet A.J.M. Smith called Birney a practitioner of "heroic narrative."[40] By the mid-1960s Birney was considered Canada's leading poet, just as a new generation was beginning to appear.

As poetry editor of *Canadian Forum* from 1936 to 1940, Birney was in touch with leading Canadian poets and helped to formulate a distinctive Canadian poetics. The difficulty of developing such poetics at the time is evident from the small number of works that were published in 1942, the year Birney won his first Governor-General's award. Fewer than twenty books of poetry appeared that year, aside from a handful of chapbooks published by Ryerson in small editions. In exasperation, Birney wrote that Canada's "most celebrated and most read" poet, E.J. Pratt, did not have one book that sold "as widely as any of a score of cheap, highly touted and already forgotten 'Canadian Novels' appearing in the last ten years."[41] This sentiment was shared by many Canadian poets of the day, including those from Alberta.

In a tribute to Birney upon his death in September 1995, the *Calgary Herald* called him the "Grand Old Man of Canadian Poetry" and quoted his biographer, Elspeth Cameron, who feels "his sense of space, both intellectual and physical, is very western."[42] Ironically, the last time Birney visited his birthplace, Calgary, was in 1983, at age seventy-nine. In *Spreading Time* (1980), his collection of writings on Canadian poetry, Birney remembered how writers with an Alberta experience, such as Nellie McClung and Ralph Connor, were popular in his home when he was growing up in Alberta. From them he learned it was possible to write about one's own locale with honesty and still be a success.

▤ *Elsie Park Gowan, c. 1970.*
Courtesy of the City of
Edmonton Archives,
EA 282-01.

Drama: 1930–1945

The 1930s were a very difficult period both economically and socially. Throughout North America, populism and other forms of radicalism arose in response to widespread human misery. Theatre was particularly influenced by these populist movements, because it provided an arena where popular education and political propaganda could be enacted before large audiences. Alberta's contribution to these movements was two indigenous playwrights, Elsie Park Gowan (1906–) and Gwen Pharis Ringwood (1910-1984), who together set the foundations for playwriting in Alberta.

Elsie Park Gowan (*née* Young) moved to Edmonton from Scotland in 1912. She earned her Bachelor of Arts degree from the University of Alberta in 1930 and was active in the Edmonton theatre scene through the early part of the decade. Gowan's first published play was *The Royal Touch* (1935). She had earlier received recognition for her plays in a playwriting competition funded by the Carnegie Foundation and administered by the University of Alberta. Gowan was a witty writer with strong socialist and pacifist beliefs, whose scripts often had historical themes. Her plays were performed by Edmonton's Little Theatre, an amateur company, and by the Co-operative Commonwealth Youth Movement. She also collaborated (uncredited) with C.C.F. member William Irvine on an agitprop play, *You Can't Do That* (1936), and she wrote a full-length comedy, *The Last Caveman* (1937). In 1942, she won a Canadian Drama award in recognition of her significant contribution to Canadian drama.

Gowan wrote prolifically for the stage into the 1940s, by which time she was also writing scripts for radio, something she continued into the late 1950s.[43] Her focus on radio plays suggests both the large audiences for such plays at the time and the constant demand for material; radio plays were an important part of mass entertainment prior to the popularity of television. One of her many scripts is *One Who Looks At the Stars*, a play about nineteenth-century artist Paul Kane, which appeared in the 1955 *Alberta Golden Jubilee Anthology*. The play was first broadcast on Edmonton station CJCA, then was rebroadcast on the C.B.C.'s Western Network. Gowan scholar Moira Day feels Gowan treated ethnic minorities and French-Canadians with sympathy in her work, perhaps because of her early experience as a rural school teacher.[44] Gowan also believed adamantly in social justice for women, as seen in *Back to the Kitchen, Woman* (1941) and *Breeches from Bond Street* (1947).

In a reminiscence of her days as a playwright, Gowan describes what motivated her work:

> The playwright wants an audience. He wants a good production. He wants to be paid. And he wants a creative adventure in partnership with other artists in the living theatre.[45]

Gowan drew literary material from her life in Edmonton, stating, "The characters in 'The Last Caveman' are all people my husband and I have observed on the shores of Lake Wabamum, where we have a cottage."[46] In her later years, Gowan taught English at Ross Sheppard High School in Edmonton, and in 1982 she was recognized by the University of Alberta, her *alma mater*, with an honourary doctorate. As a pioneer playwright, Gowan created a strong sense of Alberta society within the dramatic medium.

≣ *Gwen Pharis Ringwood and others at a tea party. Emily Murphy is third from the left in the front row; Ringwood sits second from the right. Courtesy of the University of Alberta Archives.*

Elsie Park Gowan's reputation was overshadowed by her lifelong friend and colleague, Gwen Pharis Ringwood, whom Moira Day has described as "the definitive prairie playwright of her generation."[47] Ringwood was born in Washington state in 1910 and moved with her family to a farm near Lethbridge in 1913. The family moved back to Montana in 1926, then returned to Magrath in 1929. Ringwood received her Bachelor of Arts degree from the University of Alberta in 1934 and was appointed the registrar of the Banff School of Fine Arts. From there, she took a Master's degree in drama at the University of North Carolina in 1939, then continued her playwriting career in Alberta, Saskatchewan, and, after 1953, British Columbia.

Ringwood's first published play was *Still Stands the House* (1939), the most performed one-act play in Canadian theatre.[48] This work won first prize for a Canadian play at the Dominion Drama Festival. *Dark Harvest: A Tragedy of the*

Canadian Prairie followed in 1945. In later years, Ringwood also wrote juvenile fiction. Her coming-of-age novel *Younger Brother*, set in southern Alberta and dealing with white-aboriginal relations, appeared in 1959. Fellow Albertan playwright George Ryga comments, "her characters and stories took on the qualities of the climate and landscape in which they were placed."[49] Several years before her death, Ringwood was honoured for her achievement with honourary doctorates from both the University of Lethbridge and the University of Victoria; she had already been awarded the Governor-General's Medal for outstanding service in the development of Canadian drama in 1941.[50]

Geraldine Anthony believes Ringwood "fashioned a rich body of folk and regional literature" with a great variety of memorable Alberta characters.[51] *The Oxford Companion to Canadian Theatre* also notes Ringwood's use of local characters, especially when Robert Gard of the Alberta Folklore and Local History Project commissioned her to write local history plays like *Jack and the Joker*, which dramatized the life of Bob Edwards, and *Stampede*, about black cowboy and rancher John Ware.

Like Gowan, Ringwood also wrote a number of radio plays, but she was less active in this genre than Gowan.[52] Moira Day compares their work, describing Ringwood's approach as "a celebration of the things of the spirit that gave significance, richness and dignity to the most arid, tragic and commonplace situations," while Gowan's response was "an angry, impatient demand that [conditions] be changed where they inhibited human growth and progress."[53] Gowan's reputation suffered because of her political orientation and her divided focus between radio and the stage; Ringwood's was strengthened because of her humanistic, universal approach. The image of rural Alberta was strong in Ringwood, while the urban sensibility of Alberta was strong in Gowan. Yet, together, these playwrights established the base for Alberta drama, which has continued to expand, making the province a major source of dramatic talent in the later twentieth century.

Conclusion

In this period, authors concentrated on documenting Alberta's pioneer past, both in scholarly work and in high-quality fiction. The essay came into its own in the 1930s with the writings of Broadus and Corbett. But the introduction of naturalist writings by McCowan still stands as the most popular literary product of the time. Fiction explored several new genres, in Hardy's historical novels and Conibear's animal stories. In poetry, Earle Birney brought modern idiom to Alberta. And, at last, indigenous drama appeared with the works of Elsie Park Gowan and Gwen Pharis Ringwood.

During the Depression and the War, Alberta's literary repertoire and reputation grew immensely—not bad for fifteen difficult years.

6

Francophone and Other Literatures

1820–1945

ALTHOUGH THE ENGLISH LANGUAGE has dominated Alberta writing for two centuries, other languages have been used in Alberta. The English tradition has produced the largest number of Alberta writers and has drawn strength from the steady rise of English as a great imperial language, but other European languages deserve recognition for their more modest, yet significant, contribution. Writers in languages other than English drew their literary values and traditions from their linguistic backgrounds, just as English-language writing took its values from English culture. Although European in origin, these literatures differed from the dominant English voice.

This chapter deals with that difference and how it has influenced Alberta's literary identity to 1945. Theoretically, these writers could have been discussed in previous chapters. But Alberta's literary history is not simply a matter of chronology. To include a French-language writer of the 1870s in the chapter on territorial literature would subordinate his work to the English tradition, a tradition to which he did not belong. Each language has its own cultural traditions out of which and for which its writers produce works. Non-English writers had their own literary models, issues, and heroes, and those traditions are best respected by dealing with them as a single continuum. How this distinctiveness and cultural integrity should be related to the dominant

English narrative is a key issue. All minority voices face the challenge of subordination, while the dominant voice is in turn challenged by the minority literature that shares its space and time.

A variety of European languages were used for writing in and about Alberta, including French, Ukrainian, Icelandic, German, Polish, and Danish. Except for French, which pre-dated the massive agrarian settlement of the West, European languages appeared in Alberta with the opening of the province to settlement after the completion of the C.P.R. in 1885. These other literatures were the writings of agrarian immigration. In non-fiction, they describe the agricultural life and potential of the region, while in fiction and poetry, they express the immigrant's view of settlement, beginning with unbridled optimism and ending with bitter disappointment.

The French Tradition

French literature is the oldest European literary tradition in Alberta after English. Because of historical circumstances, this tradition has proven to be a minor one, producing less than ten percent of Alberta's writers. Nevertheless, French literature from Alberta is the most important colonial literature after English because it covers the full historical range from exploration to territorial to provincial writing, which the other languages discussed in this chapter do not. Although the number of French writers is small and is divided between writers born in Québec and those born in France, the quality of the work is high.

When New France fell to the British in 1759, French explorers and traders had not yet reached Alberta. Québécois trader Nicolas Jeremie (1669-1732) published a 1720 account of his life at York Factory on Hudson Bay from 1694 to 1714 and contributed to a 1732 French-language book published in Amsterdam (*Recueil de Voyages au Nord* edited by Jean Frederic Bernard); but this early material centred on trade through the Hudson's Bay Company and the French/English battles over its forts. Jeremie's scope did not reach beyond the Bay. At this relatively early stage, Europe had not penetrated the territory that would become Alberta.

With the British conquest of Canada, English control of Québec meant the only travellers and traders who produced accounts of the northwest region in the late eighteenth century were either Hudson's Bay Company employees from Scotland and England or Norwesters from Montréal, who were primarily English-speaking. The French-speaking *coureur de bois* was usually illiterate. The ethnic and class system of English domination that developed in Québec after 1760 conspired against the early development of a vital French-language literature.

The first example of French-language exploration literature about Alberta was published in Montréal in 1820, about two decades after Alexander Mackenzie's book. *Relation d'un voyage à la côte du Nord-ouest de l'Amèrique septentrionale dans les années 1810, 1811, 1812, 1813 et 1814* (An Account of a Voyage to the Northwest Coast of North America in the Years 1810, 1811, 1812, 1813, and 1814) was written by Gabriel Franchère (1786-1863); the original edition had 284 pages, only a small number of which dealt with Alberta. Franchère was a Québec-born trader who worked at Fort Astor on the Columbia River for American fur-trader John Jacob Astor. At the time, the War of 1812-14 was raging on Canada's eastern boundary, and the situation at far-away Fort Astor was tense. In 1814, Franchère travelled east by canoe with a group of Norwesters via the Columbia, Athabasca, and North Saskatchewan rivers, all the way to Montréal.

Franchère eventually set up business in the United States, and in 1854, because of American interest in the Oregon territory, his book was translated into English by American writer Jebediah Vincent Huntington and published in New York.[1] The Alberta section describes Franchère's rapid progress through the northern part of the province, typical of the speed with which the fur brigades travelled. It was the first account about Alberta written and published in French.[2]

As late as 1898, the French-speaking population of Alberta was composed of only about 500 families, centred around Edmonton and neighbouring towns. French-speaking travellers from either Québec or France tended to be missionaries.[3] Up to the 1830s, England forbade French visitors entry to Canada. Because of its own internal difficulties and with the interference of British hegemony, France lost interest in its Canadian colony for much of the nineteenth century, and the Québécois themselves began to develop a native literary tradition only after 1840. These factors, in addition to the English domination of commerce in the Alberta territory, meant French writing in Alberta was severely disadvantaged. In *History of French-Canadian Literature,* literary critic Gerard Tougas comments,

> For generations the little French-Canadian population lived almost
> entirely withdrawn unto itself....A few young people were able to go to
> France to study. French books arrived in Québec very irregularly by way of
> London.[4]

French-Canadian culture was tied to the classical education system of
Québec. The Catholic clergy sought to produce lawyers, clerics, and politi-
cians to serve the Québécois community. In the west, the furthest reaches of
the literate French world in the nineteenth century was St. Boniface,
Manitoba, which was and remains a prairie focus of French-Canadian culture.
With a powerful religious establishment of both priests and nuns, its own
bishop, college, and hospital, and the political traditions of Louis Riel and a
strong, French-speaking Métis identity, St. Boniface and the surrounding
French-speaking communities became a distant outpost of French Canada. If
any place in the west was capable of producing a French-language literature,
Manitoba was the natural locale.

However, through the missionary activity of Québec and French clergy, Alberta was able to make a major contribution to French-Canadian letters, far out of proportion to its small population. The first of these was Catholic missionary Père Albert Lacombe, who is remembered as one of the great men of nineteenth-century Alberta life. Lacombe (1827-1916) was a Québec-born Oblate who came west in 1852 as a newly ordained priest. He spent his first years in Manitoba but later moved to Lac Sainte Anne, near Edmonton. In 1863, Lacombe founded the mission at St. Albert. In 1872, after twenty years in the west, he returned to Manitoba, then to Montréal, where he published a number of works.

Lacombe's writing was primarily as a translator, grammarian, and developer of textbooks and dictionaries. His *Dictionnaire et grammaire de la langue crise* (Dictionary and Grammar of the Cree Language) was published in 1872 as a booklet. This was surpassed two years later by his monumental *Dictionnaire de la langue des Cris* (Dictionary of the Cree Language), a 700-page tome; a 190-page grammar, *Grammaire de la langue des Cris* (Cree Grammar), was published the same year. In 1874, Lacombe published the New Testament in Cree syllabics and, in 1875, a Cree-language version of the Catholic catechism. In 1880, he produced a 382-page book of prayers in Saulteux, followed a year later by an abridged catechism in Saulteux. Six years later, the same prayers were published in Cree, as was a reader in English and Blackfoot. Between 1872 and 1886, Lacombe produced almost a dozen large, bilingual works in French-Cree, French-Saulteux, and English-Blackfoot. No other Christian missionary created such an extensive body of work; looking at these works today, one is overwhelmed and humbled by the extent of his achievement.

The drive to Catholicize the aboriginal population was strong in French-Canadian culture. Men of letters, like Lacombe, created these works to train and assist other clergy in their missionary work. Robert Choquette claims that for the missionary activity to succeed, "the first priority was to learn the aboriginal languages...."[5] Expertise in aboriginal languages was a considerable advantage in the conquest of souls.

Lacombe died in 1916 in Midnapore, south of Calgary, where he lived out his final years. The year he died, a French-language biography of Lacombe was published in Montréal. *Le Père Lacombe, "l'homme au bon coeur," après ses mémoires et souvenirs* was written anonymously by "une soeur de la Providence." The Sisters of Providence was a prominent French-speaking

▤ *Emile Grouard as a young priest. Provincial Archives of Alberta, OB 3044.*

order of nuns. If the author was an Alberta nun, she must be counted as the first (and only) French woman writer in Alberta up to World War Two. The text is a 578-page glorification of Lacombe, typically concerned with his saintliness and service to the community; Lacombe himself wrote a 1914 foreword to the biography.

Lacombe has been installed in the pantheon of great Albertans because of his achievements as a missionary and peacemaker among native peoples. He is remembered through the French biography and through two English-language biographies—the first, *Father Lacombe: The Black-Robe Voyageur* (1911), by Edmonton resident Katherine Hughes and the second, *Father Lacombe* (1975), by popular historian James MacGregor. MacGregor did not make much of Lacombe's career as a linguist, although he mentions that in 1879 Lacombe travelled to Rome "where he presented a copy of his Cree-English [?] dictionary to the pope."[6] Given Lacombe's active missionary life, it is natural to focus on his historical role, rather than literary accomplishments; but his extensive work as a translator, linguist, and writer of textbooks and catechisms in aboriginal languages makes Lacombe one of the most significant cultural players in Alberta's nineteenth-century literary history.

A contemporary of Lacombe was Oblate missionary Émile Grouard (1840–1931), who arrived in the Peace River-Athabasca district in 1862. Grouard brought the first printing press to Alberta in the 1870s; it was installed at the Oblate Mission at Lac La Biche. In 1878, Grouard printed Oblate Henri Faraud's paraphrase of the Bible in Chipewyan. (The book had originally been published in Paris by the Oblates two years earlier.) Faraud (1823–1890) served on Lake Athabasca from 1849 to 1858, after which time he spent two years at Dunvegan and was Grouard's predecessor as bishop of Athabasca-Mackenzie. In 1883, Grouard printed the Roman Catholic liturgy in Cree syllabics, followed in 1887 by *Prières, cantiques et catechisme en langue montagnaise ou chipewyan* (Prayers, Canticles and Catechism in the Montagnais or Chipewyan Language) and the same book in Cree syllabics in 1894.

In 1922, Grouard's memoirs of life in northern Alberta, *Souvenirs de mes soixante ans d'apostolat des l'Athabaska-Mackenzie* (Recollections of My Sixty-Year Mission in the Athabasca-Mackenzie), were published in Winnipeg by newspaper publisher La Liberté. In his memoirs, Grouard describes his determined struggle to learn aboriginal languages:

Je continuai l'étude et la pratique du montagnais sans relâche. Papier et crayon à la main à chaque mot ou phrase que je ne comprenais pas, j'arrêtais mon interlocuteur....[7]

I continue my study and practice of Montagnais without respite. With paper and pen in hand for each word or phrase I do not understand, I would stop my speaker....

What Lacombe did for southern and central Alberta, Grouard did in a lesser way for the northern part of the province.

Two other contemporary writers in French were both from France and produced books for a European French audience. Charles Benoist (?–1895), a French naval officer, visited western Canada in the 1890s. Following Charles' premature death, Benoist's father published a small book in 1895, based on his son's notes. *Les Français et le Nord-Ouest Canadien* (The French People of the Canadian Northwest) describes the region including Alberta with an eye to its potential for colonization. In his introduction, the elder Benoist informs his countrymen that his son found "dans sa population...les caracteres de Français energiques, independants et catholiques..." (in this population...an energetic French character, self-reliant, and faithful).[8] Benoist notes that, as recently as 1870, the French-speaking peoples of the prairies were in the majority, and he encourages settlement either in Manitoba's Red River valley or around Edmonton.[9]

Jules Marie Armand de Curville, a vice-admiral in the French navy, toured Canada in 1891 and published his account in 1898. Its purpose was also to promote French colonization. The vice-admiral entered Canada from Vancouver, having taken a steamship from Japan, and travelled east by rail. De Curville describes the west as a land for the taking. *Le Canada et les intérêts Français* (Canada and the Interests of France) is a mixture of geographical and agricultural information, to which de Curville added a glorification of French-Canadian history on the North American continent.[10]

Jean Lionnet, another French writer, continued the practice of colonization writings in 1908, when he published *Chez les Français du Canada* (French-Canadian Homes). This 120-page volume surveys French settlements in western Canada. Such texts were intended to keep the French presence alive and vital in western Canada by encouraging new emigration from France.

One such immigrant was André Borel, who came from the French cantons of Switzerland to homestead near Bassano, about 150 kilometres east of Calgary, from 1913 to 1917. Borel produced two books after returning to Europe to fight in World War One. The first, *Croquis du Far-West canadien: gens, bêtes, choses, travaux* (Sketches of the Canadian Far West: People, Animals, Property, and Work), was a non-fiction account of his homesteading experience, published in 1928. The second, *Le Robinson de la Red Deer* (Robinson of Red Deer), an autobiographical novel based on the same experience, was published in 1930. The non-fiction work provides insight into early Alberta immigrant life, with such headings as "The Women of the West" and "The Bison," as well as a description of the cycle of the seasons an immigrant would experience. The novel describes the life of a Swiss immigrant named Fancey, using a similar form.

Louis-Frédéric Rouquette (1884-1926) published his *L'épopée blanche* (White Epic) in 1926. This French journalist and novelist travelled to western Canada in 1925/26 and produced "une série de tableaux" about the French communities of western Canada; he died shortly after spending a few months in Edmonton. Rouquette was ostensibly in the west to witness the investiture of eighty-four-year-old Mgr. Grouard with the Legion of Honour from the French government for his service to the French community of Alberta. Rouquette flamboyantly describes Grouard as "a pure incarnation of the genius of France."[11] The book contains forewords by two cardinals and lauds the work of the Oblates in the west. *The Oxford Companion to Canadian Literature* calls Rouquette a "vivid writer," and his book about Alberta missionaries is full of exaggerated prose and flattery.[12]

One Catholic missionary who visited Edmonton, although he spent most of his life in northern British Columbia and St. Boniface, was Adrien Gabriel Morice. Morice (1859-1938) produced a vast body of writing, from aboriginal-language dictionaries to histories of the Catholic Church in the west, much of which he published himself. His *Edmonton et l'Alberta français: Impressions et statistiques* (Edmonton and French Alberta: Observations and Statistics) was published by Le Courier newspaper publisher of Edmonton in 1914. Morice prepared the forty-page booklet after attending a French-speakers congress in Edmonton that year. It contains his own lengthy essay about Francophone history and life in the city and surrounding districts, numerous photographs of French institutions in the city, and ads from local French businesses. This volume represents the kind of journalistic enterprise that kept the French community in Alberta alive. In 1931, another Oblate, Jules Le Chevalier, wrote *Esquisse sur l'origine et les premiers développements de Calgary 1883-1930* (A Sketch of the Origins and Early Development of Calgary 1883-1930), a similar production paid for by merchant advertising and filled with photographs of French-founded institutions such as the Holy Cross Hospital.

Another missionary, Jean-Baptiste Morin (1852-1911), produced numerous pamphlets promoting French settlement in the west.[13] The journal he kept as a Catholic cleric among Franco-Albertans was published in 1984 as *Journal d'un missionaire-colonisateur 1890-1897* by the Salon d'histoire in Edmonton.

The most outstanding French-language writer in Alberta up to World War Two was Georges Bugnet (1879-1981), whose longevity matched his literary

Georges Bugnet (1879 - 1981)

Georges Bugnet at Rich Valley Plantation, 1966.

An author, horticulturalist, editor and activist, Georges Bugnet contributed greatly to the Franco-Albertan community, the Canadian literary scene and the field of botany.

In 1904, Bugnet emigrated from France with his wife, and later homesteaded in Rich Valley. While pursuing his literary work, he created a plantation with cuttings from prairie experimental farms, Siberia, Alaska, the Orient and northern Europe, and developed hardy species which survived Alberta's winters. Bugnet's works received recognition before his death.

Écrivain, horticulteur, journaliste et activiste, Georges Bugnet a grandement contribué à la communauté

franco-albertaine, à la scène littéraire canadienne et à la botanique.

Émigré de France avec sa femme en 1904, Bugnet s'établit dans son homestead à Rich Valley. Tout en s'adonnant à son oeuvre littéraire et journalistique, il créa une plantation à partir de boutures obtenues de fermes expérimentales de divers pays et mit au point des variétés robustes qui résistaient aux hivers albertains.

Du vivant de Bugnet, l'importance de son oeuvre a été reconnue du public.

Alberta

This sign, installed in July, 1992 north of the intersection of Highways 43 and 33, suggests the growing recognition of Bugnet's formative role in Alberta culture. Photo from the files of Gamila Morcos.

achievement. Bugnet was born and educated in France, where he took his baccalaureate and studied for several years in a seminary. He decided against the priesthood, married, and came to Alberta to homestead in 1905. His early years in Alberta were taken up with farming and providing for his family. It was not until he was forty years old that he took up writing on his farm in Rich Valley, northwest of Edmonton.

Bugnet's first novel, *Le lys de sang* (Blood Lily), was published in installments in the newspaper *L'Union* in 1922/23, then in book form under the pseudonym Henri Doutremont. His second novel, *Nipsya,* was published in 1924 under the same name.[14] This novel fictionalized the life of an Alberta Métis, Octave Majeau (1841-1922), and dealt sympathetically with the Métis and the Riel rebellions.

In 1934, Bugnet published a peculiar philosophical book, *Siraf: étranges révélations* (Siraf: Strange Revelations), a dialogue between a spirit called Siraf and a contemporary man. Tougas describes it as the "thoughts of a recluse" who is well educated and very conservative.[15] It expresses both Bugnet's philosophical orientation and his seminary training. The following year,

Bugnet's fiction masterpiece *La Forêt* (The Forest) appeared. Tougas is kinder to this book, describing it as "a strong, true work, and one of the three or four greatest novels in French-Canadian literature."[16]

In *La Forêt,* nature is the dominant element, the controlling reality to which the human soul must respond and pay homage:

> The invisible hands of nature brought its emanations to her. She breathed them in, and she knew that her infant son breathed them as well. The scent of the new sprouts of wild mint crushed by her own heels. Then, from the banks of the lake, the stale odour of last season's moulding brown bulrushes. And the slightly bitter balsam fragrance of the black poplar leaves....Before her, behind her, all around her rose the high silent living barrier, turning green again—the million guardians of the soil upon whose resistance or welcome their future depended.[17]

Although *La Forêt* ended Bugnet's cycle of novels, it did not end his writing. In 1938, he published a small volume of poetry, *Voix de la solitude*, the finest book of poetry published by an Albertan prior to Earle Birney's 1941 classic, *David and Other Poems*.

Voix de la solitude consists of a long poem, "Hymne à la Nuit," a long prose-poem, "Le Pin du Maskeg," and several short poems, such as "Le Coyote." The poems are philosophical in tone, and one can easily picture Bugnet's experience of clear, star-filled nights and the thoughts and feelings that arose in him from this immense solitude. His motto was to seek "la grandeur dans la simplicité."[18] The poems express this "grandeur of the infinite universe," whom he calls "Mère de l'homme" (the mother of mankind).[19]

Bugnet did not publish after World War Two, although he lived until 1981. His literary achievement was recognized by a new generation of western French-Canadians who reissued his works. In 1978, Jean-Marcel Duciaume brought out a collection of Bugnet's poetry under the title *Poèmes*. In his introduction to that volume, Duciaume quotes Camille Roy, calling Bugnet "le poète de la nuit" (the night poet).[20] (Roy was a contemporary of Bugnet, a literary friend and the editor of the prestigious journal *Le Canada Français*.)

In 1988 Les Éditions des Plaines of St. Boniface issued a new edition of *Nipsya*, followed in 1990 by a critical edition; here, Guy Lecomte notes that Bugnet's life in the Alberta bush freed his style.[21] Lecomte describes Bugnet as

▤ *Georges Bugnet receives his honourary doctorate at age one hundred. Courtesy of Fonds Durocher, Institut de recherche de la Faculté Saint-Jean, Edmonton.*

more Albertan than most Albertans, a true convert to Canada, and a writer who drew his power from the vast natural world that surrounded him in north-central Alberta.[22] That same year, Gamila Morcos prepared a collection of previously unpublished essays, plays, and other works by Bugnet.

Jean Papen published *Georges Bugnet: homme de lettres canadien*, a literary biography, in 1985. Originally a doctoral dissertation written in the 1960s, the book took two decades to be published—an indicator of Bugnet's meagre literary status at the time. In the biography, Papen focuses on Bugnet's spirituality. He describes Bugnet as "l'un de nos poètes les plus lucides et les plus pénétrants dans l'exploration du mystère de la création et de sa présence à la fois immanente et transcendante" (one of our most lucid and penetrating writers in his exploration of the mystery of creation and the immanent presence of a transcendent faith).[23] Papen sees the origin of Bugnet's work partially in the solitude imposed by "un milieu anglophone."[24] That milieu, far from any powerful centres of French culture, meant that Bugnet fell into a crevasse separating literary worlds. His work was not easily incorporated into the Québec canon because it was from Alberta, and his distant, overly religious, provincial French sensibility was not of interest to Parisian thought; Alberta's English-speaking community did not welcome him either. Bugnet was an outsider in all the literary worlds he inhabited.

One of the most important aspects of Bugnet's literary life is that he stayed in Alberta and died here, unlike most other French writers of the period who visited only briefly. When Bugnet was one hundred years old, he was awarded an honourary doctorate by the University of Alberta. It was a belated recognition of his genius. For decades, Bugnet seemed to be lost to the literary consciousness of Alberta and Canada, although he did receive the French government's Chevalier de l'Ordre des Palmes Academiques in 1951. Tougas remarked in 1963 that, sadly, "Bugnet's renown has scarcely penetrated beyond a limited circle of French-Canadian and foreign readers."[25] When the English-language translation of La Forêt was finally published in 1976, it sold fewer than 4,000 copies in the five years before the author's death.[26] The translator, David Carpenter, himself a prairie writer, felt the novel was valuable because it combined a faithfulness to the "essential character of the region" with a "universal significance."[27]

Bugnet's sensibility as a writer can best be described as mystical: a cross-fertilization of a classical French education with the Alberta wilderness. In his introduction to Poèmes, Duciaume quotes from a letter Bugnet wrote in 1963, in which he refers to the parallels between his sensibility and the vision of the French Catholic mystic philosopher Teilhard de Chardin, who had an intense sense of the infinite mystery of the universe.[28] De Chardin was a scientist by training, and Bugnet also thought scientifically about the natural world. A striking symbol of Bugnet's talents is the beautiful Thérèse Bugnet Rose (named after his sister), which Bugnet developed by crossing the wild Alberta rose with a European variety, a hybrid for which he is known around the world. Bugnet's literary achievement is no less significant a creation, a hybrid that captured the essence of Alberta's impact on the immigrant mind.

The Ukrainian Tradition

After the French writers, the Ukrainian immigrant community of Alberta produced the largest and most varied body of non-English writing. The first

Ukrainian settlers came to Alberta in the early 1890s. These settlers were from western Ukraine, then a part of Austro-Hungary. They were called "Ruthenians" or "Galicians" at the time (the term "Ukrainian" did not come into wide use until the early twentieth century). These settlers were mostly peasants and were generally illiterate in their own language; at the turn of the century, literacy among Ukrainians was generally the preserve of either clergy, academics, or schoolteachers, few of whom emigrated.[29]

Ukrainians lived as minorities within the multinational empires of Austro-Hungary and Russia, and their national literature was routinely repressed or subject to assimilation. Because of this, Ukrainians brought to western Canada a strong, defensive sense of their identity. These values included a pro-active stance toward their culture and a desire for self-determination in literature as well as in politics. In the nineteenth century, Ukrainian literature was influenced by Romanticism, with its focus on popular folk culture and the vernacular. This spirit of national revival, combined with a strong agrarian idealism, generated the kind of religiously and nationalistically oriented writing that appeared in Alberta. Transplanted Ukrainian culture sought to validate itself, its former national identity, and its Eastern Christianity in an environment that was hostile, discriminatory, and anxious to assimilate these strangers to English-Canadian norms.

Considering the restrictions on its expression at home and the ignorance and poverty of the peasant immigrants, it should not be surprising that the Ukrainian community's literary productivity in Alberta prior to World War Two was small. The first Ukrainian-language description of the province appeared in a pro-emigration booklet published in Lviv, Ukraine, in 1895 by agronomist Osyp Olekskiv (1860-1903), who visited Alberta to investigate its agricultural potential. The first book-length work (fifty-six pages) to discuss Alberta in Ukrainian was published in Mt. Carmel, Pennsylvania, in 1897 by Nestor Dmytriw (1863-1925), a Ukrainian-Catholic priest who travelled from Winnipeg to Edmonton and back to visit the fledgling Ukrainian settlements of western Canada. The result was *Kanadiyska Rus: podorozhni vspomyn* (Canadian Ruthenia: Travel Memoirs).[30] Reverend Dmytriw provided this account of his experience:

The people gathered around me with genuine, sincere gratitude, and with tears in their eyes thanked me. They said to me, "Reverend Father, for two years we've sat like wild beasts in our sod-huts on Easter and sprinkled tears on our unblessed *paska* (Easter bread)." I had to flee into the school to do the Vesper service, because I myself could not keep from crying....In the course of three days 159 people made confession and I baptized and anointed 25 children....[31]

Dmytriw also wrote a short story set in Calgary in 1897, which was published in *Svoboda* (Liberty), a Pennsylvania-based Ukrainian newspaper.

As was the case with French-Canadian culture on the prairies, Winnipeg became the leading centre of Ukrainian-Canadian intellectual and literary life, while Edmonton lagged substantially behind.[32] In 1918, Joseph Yasenchuk (1893-1970) published *Kanadyiskyi Kobzar* (Canadian Minstrel), the first work of Ukrainian-Canadian literature with an Edmonton imprint. This sixty-four-page book contains Yasenchuk's poetry written with sincerity but with awkward rhymes. The poems imitate the national and religious themes of Taras Shevchenko, the nineteenth-century Ukrainian poet-laureate, with such titles as "To All My Brothers and Sisters" and "Oh My Land." Also included is a poem of historical interest called "A Few of My Words," which deals with Yasenchuk's internment as an "enemy alien" during the First World War. Yasenchuk late moved to Vancouver but for several decades figured prominently in Ukrainian cultural activities in rural Alberta.

Although many writers contributed poems and stories to immigrant periodicals, it was twenty years before another Ukrainian Albertan published a work of literature in Ukrainian. *Syny Zemli* (Sons of the Soil) was originally a 1100-page trilogy, published in Edmonton between 1939 and 1945; its author was Illia (Elias) Kiriak (1888-1955). The trilogy was abridged and translated into English by Ukrainian-Canadian parliamentarian Michael Luchkowich and published by Ryerson Press in 1959.

After a few years of working at various jobs in the West, Kiriak settled permanently in Alberta in 1911. He was involved with a series of short-lived, local Ukrainian-language newspapers, then earned his teaching certificate and taught for a number of years in Ukrainian districts in central Alberta. During his teaching career, he produced the first draft of *Sons of the Soil*. Kiriak had published short stories in Ukrainian-language publications, but it was not until 1937, when he retired from teaching, that he decided to publish his novel, a project he financed by soliciting subscriptions and funding subsequent volumes with income from the sale of previous ones. Ukrainian scholar Jars Balan describes *Sons of the Soil* as "the most ambitious literary undertaking in the history of Ukrainian writing in Canada."[33] The trilogy chronicles the forty-year history of several Ukrainian families told by an old settler, Hrehory Workun. The novel is rich with details of peasant folklore, cuisine, and customs. The following account of a wedding is typical of Kiriak's approach, which stresses authenticity and accurate sociological descriptions:

> One song followed another to the weeping of the violin and the tinkling of the cymbals, signifying the transition from innocent girlhood to responsible womanhood. And while the music developed the familiar theme, Teklia plaited the wedding wreaths, adding a bit of colour here, another there, and finally held it aloft for all to see. Then the singers responded. "The cranberry bud will come out white, Our little wreath will shine so bright...."[34]

It is fair to say Kiriak's novel is as important to the Ukrainian community of Alberta as Bugnet's is to the French.[35] Like Bugnet, Kiriak lived the pioneer immigrant experience, rooted himself in his ethnicity, and gave voice to a non-English tradition as it sought to make a home for itself in a new land. And like Bugnet's work, Kiriak's fiction has received primarily regional recognition.

The first Alberta contribution to non-fiction was William Czumer's collection of pioneer remembrances, *Spomyny pro perezlyvannya pershykh Ukrayinskykh pereselentsiv v Kanadi* (Memoirs of Immigrant Life by the First Ukrainians in Canada) (1942).[36] Written for the golden anniversary of Ukrainian immigration to Canada, this book commemorates the hardships of pioneer life. This story by Maria Eurchuk [Iuriichuk] of Hamlin, Alberta, about her 1899 immigration is representative of the many accounts Czumer related:

> Our husbands decided to look for homesteads...I was left alone with my little children in the Immigration Hall in Strathcona....The children cried. I thought I'd go insane from despair. Nobody would take us to Victoria

[the Victoria Settlement, northeast of Edmonton]. They wanted twenty dollars which we didn't have, nor was there any use staying in Strathcona because winter was coming and we had no money to live on. Finally my husband decided to put a raft together and float down the river, 120 miles east to Pasichny's, who lived at Victoria on the bank of the North Saskatchewan....[37]

In 1943, another book in a similar vein was compiled by Illia Kiriak in a format we would term "local history." The book celebrated the twenty-fifth anniversary of the M. Hrushevsky Institute in Edmonton.

Another aspect of Ukrainian cultural life in Alberta was live theatre. Drama found a large audience among Ukrainians in western Canada because it expressed their culture and heritage directly to audiences whose only other sources of Ukrainian culture were weekly papers and Sunday church services. Yasenchuk, for example, included two of his short plays in his book. Zygmund Bychynsky (1880-1947) was a teacher in 1909 when his play *V starim i novim kraiu* (In the Old and New Country*)* was staged in Vegreville; it was later published.[38] It was the first indigenously written Ukrainian-language play in Canada. Prior to World War One, Ukrainian-language plays, either from Ukraine or created by immigrant playwrights, were regularly staged in Edmonton, and plays continued to be produced after the War and into the 1930s. Pylyp Ostapchuk (1898-1967) worked in Edmonton in 1936 as a professional director for an amateur theatrical ensemble. The Edmonton Ukrainian bookstore published his (undated) one-act Depression comedy, *Soryshchemnona Kriza* (We'll Whistle at the Crisis). He authored more than two dozen political dramas and domestic comedies, under the *nom-de-plume* P. Pylypenko.[39] Jars Balan calculates that twenty-six Ukrainian-Canadian playwrights wrote one hundred new plays between 1910 and 1942, of which one-third were set in Canada.[40] The Alberta component was only a tiny fraction.

The publication of plays, fiction, non-fiction, and poetry expressed a wide range of literary endeavour by Albertans of Ukrainian descent. Although their production was small, it represented an important element of Alberta letters, and, with the work of Illia Kiriak, it attained significant stature.

Stephan G. Stephansson, c. 1925. Courtesy of the Glenbow Archives, NA 2613-1.

The Icelandic Tradition

Every national literary tradition has its strengths and weaknesses. Although most modern national traditions demonstrate a range of literary forms, from poetry to theatre to genre writing, some nations excel in one or two particular forms. This is true of the Icelandic tradition, in which poetry has come to be a fundamental expression of national culture.

Iceland was settled in the ninth century by Vikings from Norway, who brought two forms of poetry to the new land: mythological eddic poetry, which is anonymous, and heroic skaldic poetry, which is signed. These forms are complemented by Icelandic prose sagas. In the nineteenth century, the most popular form of Icelandic poetry was the *rimur*, a narrative poem that combines "a popular story line with the highly intricate style of the skaldic poems."[41] Using material from the ancient sagas but presenting it in a style accessible to everyone, *rimur* kept the Icelandic identity alive.

The first Icelanders migrated to western Canada in the 1870s, primarily to Manitoba. Icelandic immigration centred around Gimli, a town on Lake Winnipeg, which the immigrants called "New Iceland." Group settlement meant immigrants could preserve their language and culture. Manitoba became their cultural centre, just as it had for the French and Ukrainians, and Icelandic newspapers and writers were prevalent in Winnipeg. Despite this concentration in Manitoba, Alberta is honoured to be the home of the "most outstanding of Canada's Icelandic poets," Stephan Stephansson.[42]

Stephan Gudmundson Stephansson (1853-1927) was the Icelandic equivalent of Georges Bugnet in French and Illia Kiriak in Ukrainian. Stephansson wrote, "Without a poet you and yours / will disappear and leave no trace."[43] He saw himself as the bard for the Icelandic immigrant community. Stephannson came to Alberta in 1889, when he was thirty-six years old. He had originally immigrated to Wisconsin in 1873, when he was nineteen, then moved to North Dakota before settling near Red Deer in the Markerville area, where he farmed, set up a diary co-operative, and furthered education in the community, as well as composing copious amounts of poetry. He was considered a political and religious radical, who brought to his new land the populist views prevalent in nineteenth-century American agrarian society.

Stephansson's poetry was published in Reykjavik, the capital of Iceland, and in Winnipeg between 1909 and 1940. Poetry from Stephansson's six-volume set, titled *Andvøkur* (Sleepless Nights), was selected by Rognvaldur Petursson for a volume titled *Bref og ritgerdir* (Letters and Essays) (1939). The immigrant experience Stephansson described was often an unhappy one. Not only was there the terrible separation from one's homeland, there were feelings of guilt for leaving home, plus the discrimination faced by non-English speaking immigrants in Alberta, who were treated as second-class citizens because they weren't British. Stephansson wrote, "Somehow it has come upon me, / I've no fatherland."[44] The feeling of belonging to neither one's home country nor one's adopted nation creates a profound sense of alienation for the minority immigrant—one of the great problems of the immigrant voice.

Although Icelanders considered him one of their best poets, perhaps even the best Icelandic poet of the twentieth century, Stephansson's work was largely unavailable to Alberta's Anglophone reading public until Icelandic immigrant writer and scholar Kristjana Gunnars published her English translation of his work, *Stephan G. Stephansson: Selected Prose and Poetry* (1988).[45] Stephansson's poetry is apparently extremely difficult to translate into English.[46] Gunnars is a published poet in English and Icelandic, which facilitated her translation of his poetry into an idiom accessible to contemporary sensibility. Still, the book represents only a tiny portion of Stephansson's productivity. Stephansson wrote 1800 pages of poetry, as well as 1400 pages of letters and essays, so what it available today in English is a minuscule fraction of his work. The first English translation of Stephansson appeared in 1935 in *Canadian Overtones,* along with Ukrainian, Hungarian, Swedish, and other poetry. Watson Kirkconnell, a Canadian academic who worked tirelessly to further non-English Canadian writing, translated six of Stephansson's poems. "On the Train" is a typical rendering:

Out on the platform that coupled the cars,
    I drank in the night air alone;
For drugged in the thick, heavy vapors within,
    Each person sat like a stone.[47]

Kirkconnell praised Stephansson's poetry lavishly but concluded, "the impulse towards creative expression in a variety of European tongues will inevitably languish and die" unless new immigration revitalizes it.[48] "My Region" (*Sveitin min*), translated by Gunnars, captures a more contemporary idiom than Kirkconnell's lines:

Plains of gleam, palace of hills
blue slopes and rocky mountains,
chiselled with valleys and tributaries.
Aspen mound, the river blue
pastureland, peat marsh,
groves in the crusted range.[49]

Stephansson himself is a literary icon, but his work is not an influence on those who write poetry in English: it remains outside the mainstream. Icelandic critics of the Icelandic literature of North America call it "Western Icelandic," treating it as both similar to and distinct from the Icelandic literature produced in Iceland, an island nation with a current population of less

Stephansson House Historical Site. Provincial Archives of Alberta, A 5007.

than half a million.[50] Gunnars says that little critical work has been done on Stephansson in either English or Icelandic, and discusses the dichotomy of what it means to be a national poet in Iceland and an ethnic poet in Canada, where minority literature is still considered minor.

In Iceland, Stephansson is called "the poet of the Rocky Mountains," while in Alberta he is called "the Icelandic poet." Geography is traded: Icelanders make him Canadian, while Canadians make him Icelandic. Stephansson suggests this dual alienation in a letter he wrote describing his literary environment. "I have only the Icelandic books that were brought from home when we emigrated...," he relates sadly, apologetically, explaining that he has a large library of English books and is an avid reader of English-language periodicals.[51] Stephansson lived in a no-man's land between two cultures, typical of the immigrant experience.

Stephansson was not part of the Canadian canon when he was writing. For example, the 1926 *Canadian Poets* anthology, edited by John Garvin, included neither French nor non-English language poets. A half-century later, *The Poets of Canada* (1978), edited by John Robert Colombo, contained works translated from French and other languages used in Canada. The multicultural universe had officially arrived; in Stephansson's day, it was a utopian dream. But what is troubling is that these literary solitudes remain. The story of Stephansson's place in the Alberta canon is an example of the deep problem of non-English writing in Alberta and Canada overall. Stephansson was as influenced by Alberta as any writer, but in writing outside of English, he put himself outside its power to recognize and define.

Writing in Other Languages

A variety of national groups settled in Alberta with the agrarian settlement of the province. Besides the writers in French, Ukrainian, and Icelandic discussed above, there was a handful of writers in Danish, Polish, and German. Their works were generally written to tell people at home how settlement was progressing for people of their nationality. One exception was Anders Jensen Vester, a Danish homesteader who first came to Alberta in 1912, went to the United States, then returned for five years (1916-1921) before going back to Denmark. His pioneering account *Blandt Danske paa Kanadas Praerie* (A Danish Traveller in Prairie Canada) was published a year after returning to his native land. More typical is C. Mikkelsen's *Canada som fremtidsland: Danske udvandreres vilkaar* (Canada as a Future Homeland: The Conditions of Danish Immigrants) (1927), a Danish traveller's account of Canada; the Alberta section is illustrated with photographs of teepees and majestic mountains.

In 1989, *Ross Dane*, a translation of a 1928 Danish novel by Aksel Sandemose (1899-1965), was published. Sandemose came to Alberta in 1927 and spent less than two months in the Drumheller area, where he began making notes for a novel about Alberta. *A Sailor Goes Home* (1931) and *September* (1939) complete the trilogy, the latter two novels in Norwegian. The following excerpt suggests the flavour of *Ross Dane*:

It was high summer now. The prairie vegetation in places was a jungle— tall, bristly grass woven together with twining plants and prairie roses into an impenetrable tangle. Around the countless sloughs and marshes stood groups of young trees, deformed and singed stalks like collections of large scouring brushes.[52]

That a scant two months in Alberta would inspire a foreign novelist to produce a western Canadian trilogy suggests the power of Alberta's landscape upon the immigrant experience.

Roman Mazurkiewicz's *Polskie wychodztwo i osadnictwo w Kanadzie* (Polish Immigration and Settlement in Canada) (1929) describes Polish immigration and colonization in Canada. The Alberta section details the extent of Polish land-holding and agricultural activities in the province. A large body of similar writing was produced in German from 1922 to 1939—a half dozen volumes describe German pioneer settlements in Alberta. Heinz Lehmann's *Das Deutschtum in Westkanada* (Germans in Western Canada) (1939) is the most substantial of these, numbering 414 pages. Hermann Wagner's *Von Kueste zu Kueste* (From Coast to Coast) is a travel account, while Johannes Pietsch's *Dein den Deutschen in Westkanada* (Your German People in Western Canada) (1928) describes life for German settlers. Karl Karger's *14 Jahre unter Englaendern* (Fourteen Years Among the English) is a personal pioneering account; Karger, a German schoolteacher in Alberta, was deported from Canada in 1919. German-Swiss writer Jakob Stricker described Swiss settlement in Canada in *Erlebnisse eines Schweizers in Kanada* (Adventures among the Swiss in Canada) (1935).

These non-fiction accounts were written primarily by foreign travellers for a European audience. Except for Sandemose's trilogy, which has yet to be completely translated, works in German, Danish, and Polish have not had the literary impact of French, German, and Icelandic writers, who were more firmly rooted in the province.

The Place of Other Languages in the Alberta Tradition

Just as the question "What is Canadian writing?" has concerned Canadian nationalists, so the question "What is Alberta writing?" is central to this literary history. Nothing is more challenging to a definition of Alberta writing than non-English writing about and by people in Alberta, including those who spent only brief periods of their lives here (from a few days to a few years). The issue is the place of these writers in Alberta's literary tradition. In what sense can we include them in the canon, when historically they have been outside the dominant tradition because they did not write in English?

These writers were not exiles or expatriates from their own countries, but were either travellers or immigrants who came to Alberta voluntarily and who chose to live and write here. Because they wrote in languages other than English, they have been generally relegated to that distancing category of "ethnic" or "minority" writing, which places them outside the traditional English canon. The historic failure to integrate non-English writing into the wider tradition of Canadian literature greatly affects Alberta writing. When writing by writers of non-English heritage is considered in the Canadian tradition, only their writing in English seems to count. Certainly, many Canadian writers from ethnic minorities have written, and continue to write, in English. But for those who write in their native tongues, a problem of identification emerges. George Bisztray, a scholar of Hungarian-Canadian literature, notes that

> Literary history is not simply a sum total of written and/or published texts but a complex phenomenon whose development is analogous to the evolution of a cultural group [and its need for]...security, continuity, definable tendencies and the interaction between author and readership....[53]

The non-English writers in Alberta challenge the dominant cultural group's sense of "security, continuity, definable tendencies," as well as the relationship between author and reader. They have been defined as outsiders, belonging to some other cultural group, somehow not truly "Canadian." Their writing backgrounds are not English and they write out of and for a different consciousness, but literary figures such as Lacombe, Bugnet, Kiriak, and Stephansson are true Alberta voices, as much as Nellie McClung or Ralph Connor. Although Stephansson wrote in Icelandic, his literary world was mostly English. English-language culture influenced his work as much as the Alberta landscape and its society did. One cannot treat longtime residents of Alberta simply as transplanted nationals but, rather, as products of the general society in which they lived.

Alberta's nineteenth-century writing developed largely out of an English ideological and cultural framework, and it is easy to see the canon as organically English because it is Alberta's dominant language today. But we must realize such assumptions are seriously problematic. Ethnic literature scholar Tamara Palmer highlights the vital issue of the "vertical mosaic" in the acceptance of ethnic identities in Canada. In the literary works of immigrant writers, Palmer sees the socio-economic restraints that held back their integration into the mainstream: poverty, discrimination, and the generational struggle up the social ladder. The writer begins with buoyant hope for success in the promised land, which invariably turns to a profound sense of failure and victimization, which he is better able to express in his native tongue and to an ethnic audience who shares his experience and assumptions.[54]

This situation gives rise to a strong self-consciousness in non-English writing. One can sense this in Bugnet, Kiriak, and Stephansson. In response to the rejection and struggle associated with agrarian settlement, the literary personality seeks solace either in the ethnic community, as Kiriak did, or in nature, as Bugnet did. Palmer calls this "the divided soul of the immigrant," which is split among past, present, and an uncertain, problematic future.[55] Such fractures are characteristic of writing in a hostile foreign environment, and are seen not only in Alberta's non-English writing but in our earliest exploration journals and territorial writings, which tend to be multilingual to varying degrees. The settler's (and before him, the explorer's) anxiety of the unfamiliar and threatening takes from him the cultural security of a single culture, forcing him to embrace otherness.

Historian Howard Palmer described Alberta nativism, which was dominant up to the Depression, as "Anglo-Saxon, anti-Catholic and anti-radical."[56] Bugnet was French and Catholic; Kiriak was Ukrainian and Orthodox; Stephansson was a political radical. Neither they nor their writings fit the dominant discourse of Alberta as an outpost of English society and culture. Their work reminds the reader of other traditions, other voices. Just as aboriginal cultures need to be seen as one of the roots of the Alberta identity, so writing in languages other than English needs to be put on an equal footing with English works.

This history argues that the literary identity of Alberta is multicultural, multilingual, and multiracial. Albert Lacombe is no less an Albertan writer than Nellie McClung, although he was informed by a very different tradition and wrote for a very different purpose. Alberta's "canon" has previously been defined from outside itself—from a central Canadian perspective, as a part of a general "prairie" culture and as a minor stream in the greater English literary tradition. All of these perspectives privilege their exterior position, shaping Alberta's tradition into something "other" and marginal. The claiming of our "other literatures" resists the received monoculture of the dominant English tradition. Assimilation into English has often been considered the final and inevitable solution, but rethinking Alberta literature in a broader way could bring our lesser-known writers out of the shadows of the "ethnic" label, while preserving their cultural differences. Making their works fully a part of the canon is a first step toward the transformation of both the past and the future of Alberta's literary tradition.

If storytelling legitimizes our place in the world, the narratives of non-English Albertans can expand the definition of "Albertan." Narratives that have been placed "outside" the dominant discourse form a kind of dissident literature, whose oppositional project makes them integral to the creation of an Alberta literature. When Canadian cultural nationalism first tried to define itself against the dominant colonial British tradition, its narratives were belittled as worthless and primitive beside the grand imperial culture. This history strives to resist the same happening to Alberta writing. If we deny the plurality of our literary roots, Alberta literature will remain a colonized outpost of British and American consciousness, truly a provincial literature, even when it is absorbed into the national, Canadian identity. Alberta's strength lies in its diversity of originating voices.

The problem of integrating these diverse voices into the canon centres on two basic issues: origins and translation. Alberta has not traditionally sought its literary origins among the multiplicities of non-English literatures. But all origins are just that—origins. A history is long and evolutionary, full of transformation and change. Focusing simply on linguistic or cultural origins and using that focus to put aside certain narratives is to deny the evolutionary, transformational nature of our tradition.

When we include this writing in the canon, we create Alberta's literary identity as *fundamentally* multicultural and multilingual. Alberta writing is a literature with many origins. Because Alberta culture is predominantly English in expression, translation into English is a practical way to incorporate writing in languages other than English into the canon. Yet translation itself maintains the sense of difference, suggesting as it does a separation, an otherness. It is unsatisfying. Writers do not want to build their tradition upon translations, which seem indirect and secondary, but that is the challenge of originating Alberta literature in cultural plurality and linguistic variety. Only then will our history be founded in a cooperative sharing of traditions—read in translation or in their native tongues. The act of acknowledging and accepting these many works as collectively Albertan, while still respecting the unique qualities of each one, is a gesture of inclusion, of openness. It sets a much firmer foundation upon which to build Alberta's literary culture.

By incorporating the immigrant narrative and its values into a fundamental sense of what is "Albertan," the Alberta literary identity enriches itself and provides itself with a critical centrality. Without these literatures in translation Alberta writing is impoverished—trapped in an English-only paradigm. Non-English literatures in Alberta point to a richer, broader tradition. The authentic, indigenous voice of Alberta literature is found in the pluralism of its multiple origins.

7
Early
Literary
Institutions

EVERY CULTURE REACHES MATURITY through the presence of its own vigorous cultural institutions. This is especially relevant to literature, which requires a variety of institutional and corporate entities, from publishers to booksellers, to produce and market books. In the nineteenth century, territorial Alberta did not produce any books other than aboriginal-language religious texts. Its written word was either published elsewhere (London, New York, Montréal, or Toronto) or appeared in small, locally printed newspapers. As a hinterland, Alberta focused its literary identity on the metropolitan centres and the interests of those audiences. The development of an internal audience for its writings did occur until after provincehood, when the fledgling political entity gave voice to its new identity as a province of Canada and an immigrant-welcoming outpost of the British Empire. The early history books and immigrant fiction of the 1910s and 1920s were aimed at local as well as national audiences. These writings were usually processed through out-of-province publishers (although a few newspaper firms produced limited runs of books as spin-offs from their printing and advertising); but they represent the efforts of Alberta's settler society seeking to validate its image of itself through the written word.

Because they were not established at the start or transplanted directly from another culture, Alberta's cultural institutions developed naturally, in their own way. The very lack of traditional institutions at a time of burgeoning literary creativity actually aided the development of local forms of literary institutions. One might call this "the hinterland factor," in which a desire for self-expression drives the establishment of innovative cultural institutions, simply because of the distance from metropolitan cultural influences and the need for local support. Alberta's early literary institutions provided both instruction and audiences for local talent. The first was a public radio station.

CKUA

Radio came to Alberta in the early 1920s. Privately owned radio stations in both Calgary (CFCN) and Edmonton (CJCA) were founded to compete with the American stations that were already beaming their signals across the border. CFCN and CJCA provided mainstream entertainment and were driven by profit. The University of Alberta's Department of Extension decided to launch its own educational radio station in 1927 with the call-letters CKUA (the UA standing for University of Alberta).

The Government of Alberta provided a $5,000 grant to the Department of Extension to launch CKUA as a tool for province-wide public education. E.A. Corbett, Director of Extension, recalled later that, for him, radio-listening was the preserve of "bug-eyed enthusiasts [who] would sit up half the night glued to their crystal sets, listening to the crash, bang, whistle, wheeze, of remote signals and report breathlessly to their bored acquaintances next morning 'last night I got Texas.'"[1] Nonetheless, he supported the radio station idea.

As part of its educational mandate, CKUA pioneered radio theatre. According to Corbett, the "CKUA Players were among the first in Canada to produce one-act plays regularly on radio."[2] Canadian drama critic Howard Fink confirms that CKUA produced more radio drama on the prairies in the 1930s than any other station or network. He says the station had "no equal in Canada or the U.S. for much of the 1930s."[3] Young Edmonton playwrights Gwen Pharis Ringwood and Elsie Park Gowan were commissioned by CKUA program director Sheila Marryat to write a series of historical plays on great personalities of world history, for which they were paid $5 per script.[4] Both wrote numerous plays for radio throughout the 1930s and 1940s.

Another key player in developing indigenous playwriting was Elizabeth Sterling Haynes (1897-1957), who came to Edmonton in 1922. Haynes directed the University of Alberta's Dramatic Society and Edmonton's Little Theatre, and she was one of the founders of the Alberta Drama League in 1929. When the Carnegie Foundation granted $30,000 to the U of A's Department of Extension to develop a fine arts program in 1932, Haynes became its first drama specialist; she co-founded the Banff School of Drama (later the Banff School of Fine Arts) the following year. In 1935, the School hired Elsie Park Gowan to teach playwriting.

The combination of public education enthusiasts at the University of Alberta, indigenous populist governments such as the United Farmers of Alberta and Social Credit, and American funding from the Carnegie Foundation helped Alberta-based playwriting to develop quickly. In the midst of a terrible Depression, the University's radio station and the Banff School gave dramatic writing a new impetus.

The Banff School of Fine Arts

The second indigenous institution of literary culture was the Banff School of Fine Arts, which, in its sixty-plus years of existence, has developed an international reputation. From 1933 to 1936 it was known as the Banff School of Drama, but in 1936 it was renamed the Banff School of Fine Arts to reflect a multidisciplinary mandate. The literary stream of the Banff school began in 1935 with scriptwriting, taught by Elsie Park Gowan; that program continued until 1944, when the Alberta Folklore Project was introduced. Moira Day explains that the populist orientation of the pre-World War Two era is a significant feature of the Banff School's early years. "The original school of the 1930s had a unique and distinctive 'popular' character of its own born of the peculiar times and conditions of...Depression Canada," she says.[5] In a 1933 speech, Elizabeth Haynes declared "the people's theatre is an ageless idea springing everfresh from the hearts of humanity."[6] This populist orientation was very much a product of the radical 1930s.

In 1936, Gwen Pharis Ringwood's play *The Dragons of Kent*, a play for children, premiered while Ringwood was working as the School's secretary. The production of the folk play *Relief* (1935) is another example of the School's populist orientation. In 1937, the school launched a folk-playwriting program under the direction of Frederick Koch; its first summer saw the creation of four new plays with working-class and farm characters.

After Donald Cameron took over the school in 1936, the program's populist, social activist flavour waned, but the consciously Canadian bent persisted into the 1950s. Moira Day calculates that forty-one Canadian one-act plays were presented in the School's first two decades; but from 1953 to 1969 (Cameron's last year as director), only seven Canadian works were offered.[7] Donald Cameron (1903-1989) had a populist background (his father was a UFA-MLA from 1921-1935) and was, during the 1930s, interested in the "folk high schools" of Denmark. When Cameron recalled the early years of the Banff School in the mid-1950s, he wrote from the perspective of a successful cultural entrepreneur. He assessed the work done prior to his leadership with a fiscal metaphor, saying "good value had been obtained for the money spent."[8] He continues, "in the 1936 summer session, it was agreed that creative writing should be given a place of importance in the School curriculum. It was felt that this western country, just emerging from the first stages of pioneering, possessed the raw material for the playwright."[9] To mine this raw material the school decided to "invite as instructors to the School the leading men and women...regardless of where they lived."[10] Of course, this meant primarily non-Albertans, most often Americans. American playwriting instructors like Koch and Gard were also populists and supported the development of indigenous material by local writers. In *Grassroots Theatre,* Robert Gard comments on the local Alberta playwrights who "dramatized their own experience...wrote colourful plays about rodeos, pioneer stories and mangled crops, drought and dust...."[11]

Cameron described Dr. Frederick Koch of the University of North Carolina as "a showman and master advertiser," but believed the School did well by this marriage of raw material and foreign expertise because it gave Canada at least three successful playwrights: Gwen Pharis Ringwood, Elsie Park Gowan, and John Maclaren.[12] Cameron describes Ringwood as "a first cultural dividend of the Banff School and all its stands for."[13] Cameron apparently believed Alberta's cultural landscape could not become fecund of itself, but needed the active tillage of outsiders.

This approach reached its peak in the Alberta Folklore and History Project, funded by the Rockefeller Foundation. Cameron approached the Foundation in 1942 for funding to collect local history and folklore of Alberta. The

Foundation recommended Robert E. Gard, who was, at the time, in charge of the Rockefeller Folklore Project at Cornell University in Ithaca, New York. When Gard arrived in Banff in the summer of 1942, he suggested a similar folklore project for Alberta. Gard took on the Alberta Folklore and Local History project in 1943 and also replaced Frederick Koch, who had died, as instructor in playwriting. As project director, Gard travelled across Alberta, and, in Cameron's words, "met and interviewed some of the colourful characters and oldtimers whose exploits were already a legend in many parts of the country..."; he also helped to organize the Alberta Writers' Conference of 1944, as well as preparing his *Johnny Chinook* collection and overseeing the short-lived *Alberta Folklore Quarterly*, which incorporated the stories he collected.[14] Gwen Pharis Ringwood was Gard's assistant, who later wrote several Alberta-themed plays based on the material Gard gathered.

In August 1944, the School hosted a two-week Alberta Writers' Conference. The following year, the Conference evolved into a course on playwriting, short-story writing, and radio scriptwriting, under the direction of Gard.[15] It was continued by others after the war. The expansion of the playwriting program into other popular forms, such as radio drama and the short story, for which a large magazine market existed, suggests the Banff School's interest was, at least during this period, largely popular material.[16]

One aspect of early populist orientation is the culture of competitions. Contests enticed amateurs and first-time writers to submit creative work for evaluation and possible development. The Provincial Chapter of the International Order of the Daughters of the Empire (I.O.D.E.) joined the Department of Extension and the Banff School in sponsoring "The Creative Writing Competition for Alberta Schools" beginning in 1944. Hundreds of entries were received and hundreds of dollars in prizes and scholarships were awarded annually into the 1950s. That public institutions—CKUA and the Banff School—were the first major cultural bodies in Alberta involved in writing suggests the crucial role of the state in developing hinterland culture. Another important role was played by professional associations.

The Canadian Authors Association

The Canadian Authors Association (CAA) was organized by Canadian writers in 1921 "to develop a sense of cultural and literary solidarity among writers throughout Canada."[17] The original impetus for the organization came from concerns about copyright legislation that was being proposed at that time, which would have put Canadian writers at a disadvantage. Two years later, the CAA had 750 members in branches across Canada. The sense of national literary identity was sufficiently developed at this point to create a healthy, active organization.

The organization published its own magazine, *Canadian Author*, which later merged with another trade publication to become *Canadian Author and Bookman*. In the March 1945 issue, both the Calgary and Edmonton branches reported on local activities. Calgary listed meetings of the poetry and short story group, while Edmonton announced the publication of its 1945 *Alberta Poetry Year Book*. Both branches had been actively publishing poetry for some time.

The Edmonton branch began publishing in 1930 with the first *Alberta Poetry Year Book*, which declared that, in publishing the volume, the CAA was acting as "foster father to the versifiers."[18] Publication in the annual was the reward (along with a monetary prize) for successful competitors. At first, the competition was limited to Alberta residents, but it quickly grew to encompass the nation. By 1945, the contest was receiving more than 500 entries, and prizes were divided into half a dozen categories. The quality of submissions was uneven, to say the least!

The Calgary Branch jumped on the poetry bandwagon somewhat later with a chapbook titled *Collected Poems* (1935), representing its membership. The poetry group in Calgary had started in 1929, and the majority of its members were women. This first chapbook contained several poems each by Sara Carsley and novelist Flos Jewell Williams. In 1937, the Branch published a second chapbook, *Canadian Poems*, based on its own nation-wide poetry competition. The competition received 1,126 entries from 409 contestants, "divided as follows, 130 sonnets, 278 lyrics, 139 poems in Free Verse, 466 short poems any form and 113 poems on a Canadian theme."[19] One of the judges was renowned Canadian poet E.J. Pratt. The Prime Minister of Canada, R.B. Bennett, a former Calgary lawyer, provided a twenty-five-dollar first prize, while another Calgarian, the son of meat-packing magnate Patrick Burns, provided fifteen dollars for the Senator Patrick Burns Memorial Prize. The entry fee was fifty cents, and a copy of the chapbook cost thirty-five cents. Besides Flos Jewell Williams and Sara Carsley, a young P.K. Page numbered among the contributors; Page went on to a career as a celebrated Canadian poet.

The proliferation of poetry chapbooks and contests by local branches of the CAA led to the inauguration of *Canadian Poetry Magazine* in 1936, to provide a central focus for these branch-based activities. While the Edmonton Branch soldiered on for decades with its *Year Book*, the Calgary Branch ended its independent poetry competitions.

This culture of contests was born of the hinterland's lack of literary institutions. It was meant to fill a vacuum through the documentation, celebration, and validation of the Canadian experience. Competitions also stimulated local literary productivity, bringing the eyes of "expert judges" to the selection process and naming promising writers. Competitions appealed to educators, literary dilettantes, and those who saw themselves as patrons of the arts. The modest financial and publication rewards were an enticement for amateurs to venture into the literary arena without a large body of work—a single poem was enough. The contest model suited the hinterland well and became an enduring characteristic of Alberta's literary culture. A sense of both hinterland pride and inferiority, mingled with metropolitan aspirations, fuelled these early activities.

Writing and Public Institutions

The tension between the individual artist and cultural institutions is evident in this anecdote told by Walter Johns. He recounts that, at a 1971 dinner honouring Elsie Park Gowan, Senator Donald Cameron related how, in his capacity as president of the student's union in 1929, he had to fine Gowan fifteen dollars for a breach of student discipline. "At the time...she expressed the view that this 'Aggie from Innisfail' would never understand nor appreciate fine arts and she predicted a gloomy future for him."[20] Johns then commends Cameron as an outstanding cultural entrepreneur and educator; in that capacity, Cameron's commitment to the goals of the institution was paramount. For example, "The Alberta Writers' Conference as such was dropped...," Cameron wrote firmly, "because it had served its purpose. Arrangements were made to incorporate the work in more productive form as part of the classes in playwriting, short-story and radio writing."[21]

Self-directed writers fell outside the educational paradigm; they did not fit the pedagogical model of the uneducated (student) needing expert guidance (teacher). At the same time, writers themselves created institutions like the CAA and its local branches, which lacked the critical power of the academy. Occasionally, individuals like academic and novelist W.G. Hardy bridged the divide. As long as Alberta writers were viewed as needing primarily instruction in the literary arts, the institution encouraged their work; but any independent, non-directive effort on behalf of writers was outside its field of interest. Public education was important to the history of Alberta literary institutions, but its role was limited by its educational function.

An important exception to this limitation was F.M. (John) Salter. Salter (1895-1962) was a professor of English at the University of Alberta from the 1920s to the 1960s and was a vital supporter of the upcoming generation of Alberta writers. In 1939, Salter taught a course in creative writing, the first such course in Canada. After his death, Salter's students and colleagues collected his ideas on writing under the title *The Way of the Makers*, published

in 1967 by the Friends of the University as "a memorial to its author and as a means of continuing his work."[22] W.O. Mitchell, whose 1947 novel *Who Has Seen the Wind* has become a classic of Canadian literature, was one of Salter's students and considered him a key mentor.[23] Salter encouraged Mitchell to send his short stories to *Maclean's* and *Atlantic Monthly* during the war; Mitchell's literary career was launched when his stories were published in both of these prestigious periodicals. After the War, other writers nurtured by Salter included Christine Van Der Mark and Rudy Wiebe. Salter's teaching and his encouragement of student writers gave impetus to a new generation of Alberta writers, creating a lasting legacy at the University of Alberta.

Libraries are another integral part of literary culture. Alexander Calhoun (1879-1979), Calgary's first public librarian, exemplified the work of bringing literature to the public. "I have no creative gifts," he remarked in 1969, "only an interest in the arts because they have an important role to play in any community."[24] The Calgary Public Library's book holdings grew from 5,000 volumes in 1912 to 65,000 volumes in 1945, the year Calhoun retired.[25] In 1940, he resisted pressure to remove John Steinbeck's *The Grapes of Wrath* from the library's shelves, and in earlier years he addressed Calgary groups, such as the Women's Literary Club.[26] As one of the founders of the Co-operative Commonwealth Federation at its 1932 Calgary convention, Calhoun personified the populist impulse at the root of Alberta's literary institutions. Without a successful library system in both cities and rural areas, the book-reading public of Alberta would have been greatly diminished. Because libraries were public institutions, they must be considered alongside CKUA and the Banff School as important contributors to Alberta's literary culture.[27]

Alberta's early literary institutions reflected the province's small population (less than one million), its populist agrarian culture, and its desire to use foreign expertise to develop local talent. If an inferiority complex existed, it was compensated for by a fervent desire to overcome the cultural limitations of hinterland life by focusing on the value of local stories.

The inauguration of both CKUA and the Banff School was an initiative of the University of Alberta's Department of Extension, whose mandate was public education. But the educational goals of a university and its inherent values did not appeal to all writers. Writer-generated institutions like the Canadian Authors Association had their own grassroots nature, often practical and commercial in orientation. Alberta's early cultural institutions, however, while distinctive, were insufficient to represent a mature phase in literary affairs. The province had no book publishers. The CAA's poetry annual was a modest production. Booksellers were few and far between, and an emphasis on learning "how to" write only highlighted the seeming scarcity of professional literary talent. There were no literary magazines, and trade publications— such as Calgary's *Farm and Ranch Review* or the short-lived, Rockefeller-funded *Alberta Folklore Quarterly*—contributed little to developing literary culture. Literary life in Alberta was generally viewed as amateurish, despite the fact that nationally recognized writers lived here, because Alberta was seen as a source of raw resources needing development rather than a centre of accomplished literary leadership. Regrettably, it would be some time before this reputation was to change.

Conclusion

A HISTORICAL STUDY of a literary tradition that has never previously been named a tradition is both a destruction of a certain representation and the foundation of a new consciousness. But what can be said to have been destroyed if the thing had no identity or name until this text; what can be said to have been founded? Was something created *ex nihilo*? No; the tradition that was apparently absent was brought into being by the act of naming, by being represented as such.

The previous lack of an identified tradition was a kind of forgetfulness on our part, because the labelling of the past should truly matter to us.[1] This history's announcement of a tradition implies the existence of a body of Alberta literature expressive of the province's evolving identity.

Prior to World War Two, individual writers were acknowledged for their work, but not as part of an Alberta literary tradition. Rather, these Alberta writers were identified with the literary genres or styles in which they wrote, with ideologies they were thought to espouse, or with the cultures from which they came. They may have been identified as "prairie writers," or, in some cases, may not have been identified at all. Although the content of their work or the site of their residence placed them in Alberta, there was no discussion of how that placing might have created a tradition constituting an Alberta literature.

This volume of the literary history of Alberta is an attempt to construct a "history," a "tradition," and, ultimately, a literary canon, identifying writers and

171

texts that may be considered "Albertan." The simplicity of the criteria used (a book published and/or time spent in Alberta) to define "Alberta writing" has arisen out of a need to establish some ground for comparison and communication, some basis from which understanding might flow. Only after this can the process of refining and developing that definition begin.

This literary history of Alberta draws together facts, suppositions, evaluations, statements, biases, and interpretations. This volume ends in 1945 because that date divides writers of the present from writers and traditions that belong to the past, while volume two deals with writers who are, for the most part, still alive. And we know that what can be said in print about the living is different from what can be said about the dead. Nobel Laureate in Literature Nadine Gordimer calls writing "intellectual cannibalism," in which the imagination loots other lives and other texts.[2] This text has ingested other writers' work, creating a literary history by feeding upon their textual bodies. In volume two, this cannibalism will be modified, since the writers and their works are not bony skeletons to be exhumed but, rather, flesh and blood and mind. Their history will be constructed with this awareness.

The writers and the texts mentioned in this literary history were first identified by others, such as bibliographer Bruce Peel and literary critic Dick Harrison. By creating a history focused on Alberta, rather than on prairie writing, as previous scholars have done, this text has accomplished three things. First, it has created a *logos*, a rational order filled with names, titles, and individual stories. This is its linear chronology and genealogy—the logic of this history. Second, it has created a *mythos*, a form or shape for the whole that unifies the project. This is its interpretive centre, conceived as a dialectical evolution from aboriginal to European to an emerging global consciousness. And finally, it has created a *telos*, the author's goal or purpose, which was to name these writings as an Alberta canon *before he even knew the specifics of their existence*.

What this history has discovered is the richness and depth of Alberta literature, expressed in its centuries-long development from an aboriginal oral tradition through a patriarchal colonial consciousness to the emergence of polyphonic settlers' voices. By 1945, Alberta had contributed a number of major literary figures to Canadian culture, such as poet Earle Birney and novelists Ralph Connor and Nellie McClung. Alberta writing had evolved from the enigmatic images of Writing-on-Stone through imperial literature to novels that claimed this land. This history has revealed our literary biases, such as the difficulties poetry has faced in Alberta since its beginnings at the turn of the century and the marginalization of certain writers and their works for political and social reasons. It has dealt with the frontier stereotypes of "Mounties" and "Indians" that played a vital role in defining Alberta in the international literary imagination, beginning in the 1880s. It has also detailed the important place of women writers in Alberta's identity.

But the birth of a provincial literature and the existence of an Alberta canon must address the fact that a province is part of a nation and a national identity. As a hinterland province, Alberta has had a hinterland literary identity, because it lacked many of the cultural institutions normally found in metropolitan centres. Up to 1945, Alberta writers published their accounts in Toronto, Montréal, London, and New York. Alberta was a western province of a colonial country whose elite identified with the British Empire. So the "Alberta" part of any writer's identity is a distillation of other overlapping identities, such as "Canadian" or "British" or "French-Canadian." It is simply one of the multiple literary identities worn by each writer who has written about this place. "Alberta" does not exhaust or circumscribe other literary identities in which literary work may be situated. A writer's connections to other literary traditions provide both strengths and tensions that serve only to enrich his or her Alberta traces.

"A name should only be given to what deserves it and calls for it," writes Jacques Derrida. He continues, "the discourse is qualified or disqualified by what it relates to."[3] Alberta writing deserves a canon of its own, a literary tradition its writers can relate to as a shared heritage. The key belief of this history is that Alberta's literary history has resulted from both a *logical* and *mythological* discourse. Heidegger tells us, "the spoken word no longer speaks in the printed one" and "the written and printed text lacks the advantages of oral presentation."[4] The plural oralities of aboriginal culture, taken as the source of Alberta's literary identity in this narrative, offer a wholly other point of departure than English-identified, colonial print culture. The result is a contradiction, a fundamental difference between the spoken and written word at the core of the Alberta literary identity. By placing the origins of Alberta literature beyond both the English language and the printed word, this text claims an authentically indigenous Alberta expression beyond colonialism and imperialism.

Because this history is a printed text, it has been conceived and presented in "the old style of rational, linear discourse" that is historical writing as we know it.[5] The *logos* of such discourse is at odds with the *mythos* of the text, which seeks to stand closer to aboriginal orality. This text, then, expresses the contradictions between literate rationalism and oral narratives: seeking to fuse these outlooks into a new, global consciousness, turning the inclination of a line into the perpetuity of a circle.

Cultural critic Gary Taylor writes, "the history of literature is the history of innumerable struggles for cultural space and time...."[6] This history of Alberta writing is no different. Its overall goal has been to create a cultural space in which an Alberta literary history can be conceived and understood. It has sought to document and articulate various struggles within that contested space and, in so doing, create a record and a memory of literary activity in this province.

History is commonly considered a function of time rather than space. This text's overt sense of the past merely hides its deep sense of the varied geographic spaces of Alberta, which, by 1945, had yielded a variety of literatures, determined to a degree by the different economies of the province's physical regions. By 1945, there was already a mountain literature, a ranching literature, an agrarian literature, a northern forest literature, and an urban literature. The problems of relating time to space and the past to the present become evident in the text's organization. The chapters in volume one have been organized chronologically, while those in volume two will be organized by genre. The half-century covered in volume two (1946-1996) will be presented as a single period. This change in methodology will result in a different kind of story than the one told in this volume. Creating two volumes with different approaches signals an artificial break in historical reality but one that is, regrettably, unavoidable if we are to make sense of the myriad facts of a literary universe where past and present meet at mid-century.

Volume one of this literary history has explored the "promise" of Alberta writing up to 1945—the promise of a "new" literature in a "new" land. By 1945, that promise had materialized in some of Alberta's better writers, but its evolution after 1945 would also involve a threat: a threat to the dominant culture, as our literature moved from its British roots through a stage of Americanized, bicultural Canadian identity to a globalized multiculturalism at century's end. Volume one has told the story of the triumph of European literacy and colonialism over aboriginal orality; volume two will explain how that triumph has evolved into a wholly new sensibility.

Notes

Introduction: Toward a Literary History of Alberta

1 Robert Kroetsch, *Alberta* (Edmonton: NeWest Press, 1993), 281.

2 Kroetsch, *Alberta*, 52.

3 Gary Taylor, *Cultural Selection* (New York: Basic Books, 1996), 14.

4 This issue is particularly problematic because such texts may have acquired a twentieth-century patina through later editorial and critical processes.

5 The major literary/critical/historical work discussing Alberta writing was published under the designation "prairie" in the seminal texts of McCourt, Ricou, and Harrison. *The Literary History of Canada: Canadian Literature in English* includes many of the writers discussed in this history but from a different perspective.

6 Jacques Derrida, *On The Name* (Stanford: Stanford University Press, 1995), 89.

7 Derrida, *On The Name*, 91.

8 Quoted in Frances W. Kaye and Robert Thacker, "Gone Back to Alberta: Robert Kroetsch Rewriting the Great Plains," in *Great Plains Quarterly* (Issue 14, Summer 1994), 168.

9 Reiner Schurmann, *Heidegger on Being and Acting: From Principles to Anarchy* (Bloomington: Indiana University Press, 1987), 120.

1 Writing-on-Stone: The Aboriginal Tradition

1   The Milk River was called *Kin-nax-is-sa-ta* ("little river") by two
    Blackfoot chiefs who drew it on a map for Peter Fidler in 1801 while he
    was at Chesterfield House on the South Saskatchewan near the Red
    Deer River. Its Piegan name is *Inuksishuk*. A few years later (1805),
    American Captain Meriwether Lewis, while on his way to the Pacific,
    named the same river the Milk River, after seeing it where it joins the
    Missouri. The English name has remained.

2   P.S. Barry, *Mystical Themes in Milk River Rock Art* (Edmonton: University
    of Alberta Press, 1991), 18–19.

3   Mark Abley, *Beyond Forget: Rediscovering the Prairies* (Vancouver: Douglas
    & McIntyre, 1986), 205.

4   Barry, *Mystical Themes,* 16.

5   Derrick de Kerchove, *The Skin of Culture: Investigating the New Electronic
    Reality* (Toronto: Somerville House, 1995), 104.

6   de Kerchove, *Skin of Culture,* 107.

7   Abley, *Beyond Forget,* 202–203.

8   Abley, *Beyond Forget,* 204.

9   Grace Rajnovich, *Reading Rock Art: Interpreting the Indian Rock Paintings of
    the Canadian Shield* (Toronto: Natural Heritage/Natural History Inc.,
    1994), 10.

10 Rajnovich, *Reading Rock Art,* 19.

11 Rajnovich, *Reading Rock Art,* 124. From George Copway
    (*Kahegagagahbowh*), *The Traditional History and Characteristic Sketches of the
    Ojibway Nations* (London: Charles Gilpin, 1850).

12 "Interview with Leroy Little Bear," *Glenbow* 15, 1 (Spring 1995), 8.

13 Barry, *Mystical Themes,* 2, 3.

14 Rajnovich, *Reading Rock Art,* 21.

15 Gerald T. Conaty, "Pictograph Robes of the Plains First Nations,"
    Glenbow 14, 2 (Summer 1994), 5.

16 Michael Klassen and Martin Pagne, "The Management and
    Conservation of Alberta Rock Art: Background and Preliminary
    Recommendations," in M. Magne, *Archaeology in Alberta 1987:
    Archaeological Survey of Alberta Occasional Paper No. 32* (Edmonton: Alberta
    Culture and Multiculturalism, 1988), 65.

17 Conaty, "Pictograph Robes," 5.

18 Valerie Robertson, *Reclaiming History: Ledger Drawings by the Assiniboine Artist Hongeeyesa* (Calgary: Glenbow-Alberta Institute, 1993), 47. Bull Head of the T'su T'ina also had a robe of his exploits, which is now preserved in the National Museum in Ottawa.

19 Arni Brownstone, *War Paint: Blackfoot and Sarcee Painted Buffalo Robes in the Royal Ontario Museum* (Toronto: Royal Ontario Museum, 1993), 35. Letter of Father Leon Doucet to Edmund Morris, December 9, 1908 (Morris Papers: Manitoba Archives).

20 Brownstone, *War Paint*, 12.

21 Brownstone, *War Paint*, 38.

22 Brownstone, *War Paint*, 69.

23 Brownstone, *War Paint*, 69.

24 Hugh A. Dempsey, *A Blackfoot Winter Count*. Glenbow Occasional Paper No. 1 (Calgary: Glenbow-Alberta Institute, 1965), 3.

25 Ted Yellow-Fly, "Indian Tepee Designs and Their Derivations," in *The Calgary Daily Herald*, July 8, 1929.

26 Brownstone, *War Paint*, 10, 21, 38.

27 Brownstone, *War Paint*, 68. For example, the name glyph for one artist, Running Wolf (*Apisomakau*), was an image of a wolf with tracks behind it.

28 de Kerchove, *Skin of Culture*, 24.

29 de Kerchove, *Skin of Culture*, 80.

30 Quoted in Brownstone, *War Paint*, 16.

31 Brian Swann, ed., *Coming to Light: Contemporary Translations of the Native Literatures of North America* (New York: Random House, 1994), xiii.

32 Mary Louise Pratt, *Imperial Eyes: Travel Writing and Transculturation* (London: Routledge, 1992), 4.

33 Arnold Krupat, *The Voice in the Margin: Native American Literature and the Canon* (Berkeley: University of California Press, 1989), 39.

34 Paula Gunn Allen, *Voice of the Turtle: American Indian Literature 1900-1970* (New York: Random House, 1994), xiii.

35 Later, even these hybrid forms were rejected in favour of outright assimilation into the imperial culture, through such institutions as residential schools.

36 Eric Cheyfitz, *The Poetics of Imperialism: Translations and Colonization from The Tempest to Tarzan* (New York: Oxford University Press, 1991), 104.

See also Tejaswini Niranjana, *Siting Translation: History, Post-Structuralism and the Colonial Context* (Berkeley: University of California Press, 1992), 9.

37   Swann, *Coming to Light*, xxxi.

38   Krupat, *Voice in the Margin*, 141.

39   Albert Lacombe, *Dictionnaire de la langue des cris* (Montreal: Beauchemin & Valois, 1874), 509.

40   Robert Brightman, Angelique Linklater, and Henry Linklater, "Mistacayawasis, Big Belly Child" in Swann, *Coming to Light*, 192-3.

41   Brightman et al., "Big Belly Child," 200.

42   Robin Ridington, "Dunne-za Stories" in Swann, *Coming to Light*, 180.

43   Ron Scollon and Suzanne Scollon, *Narrative, Literacy and Face in Interethnic Communication* (Norwood, New Jersey: Ablex, 1981), 105.

44   Scollon and Scollon, *Interethnic Communication*, 108.

45   Scollon and Scollon, *Interethnic Communication*, 118.

46   Richard Glover, ed., *David Thompson's Narrative 1784-1812* (Toronto: Champlain Society, 1962), excerpted in Germaine Warkentin, ed., *Canadian Exploration Literature* (Toronto: Oxford University Press, 1993), 234.

47   Glover in Warkentin, *Canadian Exploration Literature*, 234.

48   Quoted in Warkentin, *Canadian Exploration Literature*, 234-235.

49   Quoted in Penny Petrone, *First People, First Voices* (Toronto: Oxford University Press, 1990), 64.

50   Scholars have challenged the authenticity of this attribution to Crowfoot. Robert Carlisle has argued that the quotation paraphrases a passage from Sir Henry Rider Haggard's 1880 novel *King Solomon's Mines.* But Muriel Whitaker attributes it to Bede's *Ecclesiastical History of the English People*, written in the eighth century, which is likely what Haggard drew upon for his own text.

51   C.C. Uhlenbeck, *Original Blackfoot Texts* (Amsterdam: Johannes Miller, 1911), iv.

52   Uhlenbeck, *Original Blackfoot Texts*, iv.

53   Conversation with Hugh Dempsey, Calgary, May 19, 1995.

54   The work was later reissued and expanded in 1960, including interviews done in 1926, and published by the National Museum of Canada as *Indian Days on the Western Prairies*. See Marius Barbeau, *Indian Days in the Canadian Rockies* (Toronto: Macmillan, 1923), 11.

55   Marius Barbeau, *Indian Days on the Western Prairies* (Ottawa: National Museum of Canada, 1974), 210.

56   Adolf Hungry Wolf, *The Blood People* (New York: Harper and Row, 1977), 290. Hugry Wolf was likely assisted by his second wife, Beverley, who was Blackfoot and who co-authored titles with him as well as writing her own English-language books on Blackfoot heritage.

57   H.C. Wolfart and J.F. Carroll, *Meet Cree: A Guide to the Language* (Edmonton: University of Alberta Press, 1981), xvi.

58   de Kerchove, *Skin of Culture*, 108.

59   For one example, see Laurence Nowry, *Man of Mana: Marius Barbeau* (Toronto: NCPress, 1996).

2   Exploration Literature: 1754–1869

1   Schurmann, *From Principles to Anarchy*, 25.

2   Schurmann, *From Principles to Anarchy*, 36.

3   Krupat, *Voice in the Margin*, 45.

4   R. Douglas Francis, *Images of the West: Responses to the Canadian Prairies* (Saskatoon: Western Producer Prairie Books, 1989), 231.

5   Victor G. Hopwood, "Explorers by Land to 1867" in Klinck, *Literary History of Canada*, Vol. 2, 19.

6   Glyndwr Williams, "The Puzzle of Anthony Henday's Journal, 1754-55," *The Beaver* (Winter 1978), 41.

7   Williams, "Anthony Henday's Journal," 48.

8   Williams, "Anthony Henday's Journal," 49.

9   I.S. MacLaren, "Exploration/Travel Literature and the Evolution of the Author," *International Journal of Canadian Studies/Revue internationale d'etudes canadiennes* 5 (Spring 1992), 41, 42.

10   Williams, "Anthony Henday's Journal," 45.

11   Quoted in E.E. Rich ed., *Cumberland House and Hudson House Journals* (London: Hudson's Bay Record Society, 1951), xxviii. Hearne's account of his overland trip from Hudson Bay to the Arctic was published posthumously in 1795. It was and continues to be a major work on the exploration of Canada. Although Hearne's narrative does not belong to Alberta literature as such, it did influence subsequent writers who were in Alberta and who sought to emulate Hearne's literary success.

12 Lawrence J. Burpee, ed., *An Adventurer From Hudson Bay: Journal of Matthew Cocking, from York Factor to the Blackfeet Country, 1772-73*. Transactions of the Royal Society of Canada, quoted in Germaine Warkentin, ed., *Canadian Exploration Literature* (Toronto: Oxford University Press, 1993), 148.

13 MacLaren, "Evolution of the Author," 56-57.

14 Hopwood, "Explorers by Land," 26-27.

15 Daniel Francis, ed., *Imagining Ourselves: Classics of Canadian Nonfiction* (Vancouver: Arsenal Pulp Press, 1994), 3.

16 Peter Fidler, *A Look at Peter Fidler's Journal: Journal of a Journey Over Land from Buckingham House to the Rocky Mountains in 1792 and 1793* (Lethbridge: Historical Resource Centre, 1991), 78.

17 Alice M. Johnson, *Saskatchewan Journals and Correspondence: Edmonton House 1795-1800, Chesterfield House 1800-1802* (London: Hudson's Bay Record Society, 1967), 85.

18 Robert Seaborn Miles, *Journals, 1818-1819*. Transcript by Bridget Fialkowski, 1983. Hudson's Bay Company Archives, Winnipeg. 151, 165.

19 Pond himself produced an account of his fur-trade life, but it stopped in 1775, before he set foot in Alberta. See Charles M. Gates, ed., *Five Fur Traders of the Northwest* (St. Paul: Minnesota Historical Society, 1965) for an explanation of why Pond's narrative did not go beyond 1775.

20 Harry W. Duckworth, ed., *The English River Book: A North West Company Journal and Account Books of 1786* (Montreal: McGill-Queen's University Press, 1990), xii.

21 Duckworth, *The English River Book,* 10.

22 T.D. MacLulich, "Alexander Mackenzie" in J. M. Heath, ed., *Profiles in Canadian Literature 5* (Toronto: Dundurn Press, 1986), 18.

23 MacLulich, "Alexander Mackenzie," 20. The ghost-writing claim was made by Franz Montgomery in "Alexander Mackenzie's Literary Assistant," *Canadian Historical Review* 18 (1937), 301-303.

24 Barbara Belyea, "Mackenzie Meets Moodie in the Great Divide," *Journal of Canadian Studies* 23, 3 (Autumn 1988), 124.

25 Hopwood, "Explorers by Land to 1867," 30.

26 Alexander Mackenzie, *Voyages from Montreal in the River St. Lawrence through the Continent of North America to the Frozen and Pacific Oceans...* (London: Cadell and Davis, 1801), 187.

27   Interview with I.S. MacLaren, Edmonton, Alberta, June 30, 1995.

28   Interview with Barbara Belyea, Canmore, Alberta, April 19, 1995.

29   Correspondence from Belyea to Melnyk.

30   Warkentin, *Canadian Exploration Literature*, 261.

31   J. B. Tyrrell, ed., *David Thompson: Narrative of his Explorations in Western America 1784-1812* (Toronto: Champlain Society, 1916); re-issued in 1962 with an introduction by Richard Glover and an additional chapter. Victor Hopwood's edition, *Travels in Western North America 1784-1812,* came out in 1972, while Barbara Belyea's version, *Columbia Journals,* was published in 1994.

32   John Warkentin, ed., *The Western Interior of Canada: A Record of Geographical Discovery 1612-1812* (Toronto: McClelland and Stewart, 1964), 63.

33   Quoted in I.S. MacLaren, "David Thompson's Imaginative Mapping of the Canadian Northwest 1784-1812," *Ariel* 15:2 (April 1984), 99.

34   David Thompson, *Columbia Journals,* Barbara Belyea, ed. (Montreal: McGill-Queen's University Press, 1994), 202.

35   The manuscript was originally titled *Some Account of the Trade Carried on by the North West Company* but was changed for publication.

36   A.S. Morton, *A History of the Canadian West to 1870-71* (Toronto: Thomas Nelson & Sons, 1939), 466.

37   Hopwood, "Explorers by Land to 1867," 32-33.

38   Hopwood, "Explorers by Land to 1867," 31.

39   W. Kaye Lamb, ed., *Sixteen Years in the Indian Country: The Journal of Daniel Williams Harmon 1800-1816* (Toronto: Macmillan, 1957), 120.

40   Daniel Williams Harmon, *A Journal of Voyages and Travels in the Interior of North America...* (Toronto: Courier Press, 1911), xiii.

41   Belyea, "Mackenzie Meets Moodie," 121.

42   Brian Patton, *Tales from the Canadian Rockies* (Edmonton: Hurtig, 1994), 21.

43   Malcolm McLeod, ed. *Peace River: A Canoe Voyage from Hudson's Bay to Pacific by Sir George Simpson, Journal of the late Chief Factor, Archibald McDonald* (Rutland, Vermont: Tuttle, 1971), xxiii. Originally published 1872.

44   The key identifying words were "narrative" to denote a story; "journey" to denote land and "voyage" when dealing with water and "expedition" when one was in some official capacity and in a group.

45 I.S. MacLaren, "Touring at High Speed: Fur-Trade Landscape in the Writings of Frances and George Simpson" *Musk-Ox* 34, 1986, 78.

46 James MacGregor, *A History of Alberta* (Edmonton: Hurtig, 1977), 66.

47 Warkentin, *Exploration Literature,* 201.

48 MacLaren, "Touring at High Speed," 83.

49 MacLaren, "Touring at High Speed," 85.

50 Hugh A. Dempsey, ed., *The Rundle Journals 1840-48* (Calgary: Historical Society of Alberta, 1977), xiii.

51 Pierre-Jean de Smet, *Oregon Missions and Travels Over the Rocky Mountains in 1845-46* (New York: Edward Dunigan, 1847).

52 de Smet, *Oregon Missions,* 163.

53 de Smet, *Oregon Missions,* 185.

54 Captain H. Warre, *Sketches in North America and the Oregon Territory* (London: Dickinson & Co., 1848), 2.

55 Paul Kane, *Wanderings of an Artist Among the Indians of North America: From Canada to Vancouver Island and Oregon through the Hudson's Bay Company Territory and Back Again* (London: Longman, Brown, Green, 1859), 385.

56 Paul Kane, *Wanderings of an Artist* (Toronto: Radisson Society, 1925), xxv.

57 Kane, *Wanderings* (1925), xxxi.

58 I.S. MacLaren, "Notes Toward a Reconstruction of Paul Kane's Art and Prose," *Canadian Literature* 113-114 (1987), 192; I.S. MacLaren, "Wanderings in Search of Paul Kane's *Wanderings of an Artist,*" *Prairie Fire* 10:3 (September 1989), 32.

59 MacLaren, "Notes Toward Reconstruction," 201, 202.

60 Samuel Hearne had been paid 200 pounds for his manuscript in 1792, the equivalent of 20 years' wages for a HBC clerk.

61 I.S. MacLaren, "Creating Travel Literature: The Case of Paul Kane," *Papers of the Bibliographic Society of Canada* 27 (1988), 81.

62 Warkentin, *Exploration Literature,* 437.

63 Captain John Palliser, *The Journals, Detailed Reports and Observations Relative to the Exploration of Captain Palliser of a Portion of British North America...* (London: Queen's Printer, 1863), 15.

64 The journal on which the book was based was published in 1931.

65 Mary Quayle Innis, *Travellers West* (Toronto: Clarke Irwin, 1956), 106.

66   This route was considered a tough slog, having been used the previous year by colonists (later called the Overlanders), who had made a perilous trip to reach the Cariboo over land from the east.

67   Innis, *Travellers West*, 215.

68   Earl Southesk, *Saskatchewan and the Rocky Mountains* (Edmonton: Hurtig, 1969), 154. Originally published 1875.

69   Innis, *Travellers West*, 17.

70   Peter Erasmus, *Buffalo Days and Nights* (Calgary: Glenbow-Alberta Institute, 1976), xi.

71   Erasmus, *Buffalo Days and Nights*, 210.

72   Pratt, *Imperial Eyes*, 4.

73   Pratt, *Imperial Eyes*, 7.

74   Northrope Frye, *The Great Code: The Bible and Literature* (Toronto: The Academic Press, 1982), 108.

75   Frye, *The Great Code*, 206.

76   Interview with Ian MacLaren, Edmonton, Alberta, June 30, 1995.

77   Ian MacLaren, "Evolution of the Author," 56.

3 Territorial Literature: 1870–1904

1   Jurgen Habermas, *The Philosophical Discourse of Modernity: Twelve Lectures* (Cambridge, Mass: MIT Press, 1992), 80.

2   Macmillan of Canada published the seventeenth edition of *The Great Lone Land* in 1910, the year Butler died, and Hurtig published a reprint in 1968. I myself own a 1924 edition.

3   W.F. Butler, *The Great Lone Land: A Narrative of Travel and Adventure in the North-West of America* (London: Sampson, Low, 1872), 199–200.

4   Butler, *Great Lone Land*, 256.

5   Butler, *Great Lone Land*, 241.

6   W.F. Butler, *Introductory Report to Adam Archibald, Lieut.-Governor of Manitoba of a trip from Ft. Garry to Edmonton in 1870-71*, 14.

7   W.F. Butler, *Sir William Butler: An Autobiography* (London: Constable & Co., 1911), 144.

8   Butler, *Autobiography*, 258.

9   George M. Grant, *Ocean to Ocean: Sandford Fleming's Expedition Through Canada in 1872* (Toronto: James Campbell, 1873), 228.

10 Elizabeth Waterston, "Travel Books 1860–1920", in Klinck, *Literary History of Canada,* Vol. 1, 363.

11 Sandford Fleming, *England and Canada: A Summer Tour Between Old and New Westminster* (London: Sampson, Low, 1884), 219.

12 Morley Roberts, *The Western Avernus, or Toil and Tavels in Further North America* (London: Brown, Langham & Co., 1904), 52.

13 Morley Roberts, *On the Old Trail* (London: Nash & Grayson, 1927), 42.

14 Stuart Chamberlain, *Queen's Highway: From Ocean to Ocean* (London: Sampson, Low, 1884), 170.

15 Chamberlain, *Queen's Highway*, 173.

16 A.J. Church, *Making A Start in Canada: Letters From Two Young Immigrants* (London: Seedy, 1889), 142.

17 A. C. Garrioch, *A Hatchet Mark in Duplicate* (Toronto: Ryerson, 1929), 232.

18 Garrioch, *Hatchet Mark*, 254.

19 John MacLean, *Lone Land Lights* (Toronto: William Briggs, 1882).

20 MacLean, *Lone Land Lights*.

21 This work was reprinted in 1983 by the University of Alberta Press, Edmonton.

22 E.B. Glass, *Primer and English Language Lessons in Cree* (Toronto: William Briggs, 1888), 32, 104.

23 Sarah Carter, "The Missionaries' Indian: The Publications of John McDougall, John Maclean and Egerton Ryerson Young," *Prairie Forum* 9:1 (1984), 27.

24 John McDougall, *In the Days of the Red River Rebellion: Life and Adventure in the Far West of Canada 1868-72* (Toronto: William Briggs, 1903), 32.

25 McDougall, *Red River Rebellion*, 233, 235.

26 Bruce Fairley, ed., *The Canadian Mountaineering Anthology* (Edmonton: Lone Pine Publishing, 1994), 10.

27 Patton, *Tales From the Canadian Rockies,* 126.

28 William Spotswood Green, *Among the Selkirk Glaciers* (London: Macmillan, 1890), 126.

29 Fairley, *Canadian Mountaineering Anthology*, 42.

30 Walter Dwight Wilcox, *Camping in the Rockies* (New York: Putnam, 1896), 51.

31 H. Stutfield and J.N. Collie, *Climbs and Explorations in the Canadian Rockies* (London: Longmans, Green, 1903), 334–335.

32 James Outram, *In the Heart of the Canadian Rockies* (London: Macmillan, 1905), 438.

33 John Mackie, *The Heart of the Prairie* (London: Nisbet, 1899).

34 Dick Harrison, *Unnamed Country: The Struggle for a Canadian Prairie Fiction* (Edmonton: University of Alberta Press, 1977), 71.

35 W.A. Fraser, *Mooswa and Others of the Boundaries* (New York: Scribners, 1900), ix.

36 For example, Canadian writer Ernest Seton Thompson's 1898 classic *Wild Animals I Have Known* was translated into fifteen languages!

37 Ralph Connor, *Black Rock: A Tale of the Selkirks* (Toronto: Westminster, 1898).

38 Ralph Connor, *The Sky Pilot: A Tale of the Foothills* (Toronto: Westminster, 1899).

39 Connor, *The Sky Pilot*, 50.

40 Frank Davey, *Canadian Literary Power* (Edmonton: NeWest Press, 1994), 139.

41 A. Spragge, *From Ontario to the Pacific by the C.P.R.* (Toronto: Blackett Robinson, 1888), 46.

42 Charles F.P. Conybeare, *Vahnfried* (London: Kegan Paul, 1902), 169.

43 Charles F.P. Conybeare, *Lyrics from the West* (Toronto: W. Briggs, 1907), 63.

44 Harrison, *Unnamed Country*, 45.

45 Harrison, *Unnamed Country*, 86.

4 Provincial Literature: 1905–1929

1 Rudyard Kipling, *Letters to the Family* (Toronto: Macmillan, 1908), 60.

2 Quoted in Greg Gatenby, ed., *The Very Richness of that Past: Canada Through the Eyes of Foreign Writers, Volume 2* (Toronto: Alfred A. Knopf Canada, 1995), 339.

3 Gatenby, *Very Richness of that Past,* 310.

4 In 1980, Ted Hart of the Whyte Museum of the Rockies published *A Hunter of Peace* (Banff: The Whyte Foundation, 1980), a study of Mary Schäffer that included material from the 1911 book as well as some previously unpublished material.

5 Mary T.S. Schäffer, *Old Indian Trails: Incidents of Camp and Tail Life, Covering Two Years' Exploration through the Rocky Mountains of Canada* (New York: Putnam, 1911), 310-311.

6 Francis, *Images of the West,* 109, 114.

7 Frank Yeigh, *Through the Heart of Canada* (Toronto: Frowde, 1910), 215, 217, 219.

8 J. Burgon Bickerseth, *The Land of Open Doors: Being Letters From Western Canada 1911-1913* (Toronto: University of Toronto Press, 1976), 165.

9 Stanley Washburn, *Trails, Trappers, and Tenderfeet in the New Empire of Western Canada* (London: Andrew Melrose, 1912), xv.

10 Frank Carrel, *Canada West & Further West* (Quebec: Telegraph Printing Co. 1911), 73.

11 Agnes Deans Cameron, *The New North: Being Some Account of a Woman's Journey Through Canada to the Arctic* (New York: Appleton, 1909), 33.

12 Cameron, *The New North,* 375.

13 Elizabeth B. Mitchell, *In Western Canada Before the War: A Study of Communities* (London: John Murray, 1915), 46.

14 Mitchell, *In Western Canada Before the War,* 46.

15 Rupert Brooke, *Letters from America* (London: Sidgwick & Jackson, 1916), 128.

16 Geoffrey Keynes, ed., *The Letters of Rupert Brooke* (New York: Harcourt, Brace, 1968), 500.

17 Mary Fitz-Gibbon, ed., *The Diaries of Edmund Montague Morris: Western Journeys 1907-1910* (Toronto: Royal Ontario Museum, 1985), 112.

18 Walter McClintock, *The Old North Trail or Life, Legends and Religion of the Blackfeet Indians* (London: Macmillan, 1910), 384.

19 McClintock, *Old North Trail,* 482.

20 L.V. Kelly, *The Range Men: The Story of the Ranchers and Indians of Alberta* (Toronto: Briggs, 1913), 430. This volume was reprinted in a limited-edition, coffee-table format by Willow Creek Publishing of High River in 1988. In 1972, the Glenbow-Alberta Institute published Kelly's newspaper accounts of a 1910 trip to the Peace River country in book form, under the title *North With Peace River Jim.*

21 Gertude Balmer Watt, *Town and Trail* (Edmonton: News Publishing Co., 1908), 17.

22 Lacombe died in 1916 in Midnapore, south of Calgary.

23 Padraig O'Siadhail, "Katherine Hughes: Irish Political Activist" in Bob Hesketh and Francis Swyripa, eds., *Edmonton: The Life of a City* (Edmonton: NeWest Press, 1995), 82.

24 O'Siadhail, "Katherine Hughes," 86.

25 Nellie L. McClung, *The Next of Kin or Those Who Wait and Wonder* (Toronto: T. Allen, 1917), 243.

26 Emily Ferguson (Murphy), *Janey Canuck in the West* (Toronto: Cassell & Co., 1910), 282.

27 Emily Ferguson Murphy, *The Black Candle* (Toronto: T. Allen, 1922), 7.

28 A. Carter Goodloe, *At the Foot of the Rockies* (New York: Scribner & Sons, 1905), viii.

29 These two novels were collected in a single volume titled *Northern Trails Omnibus* (1920), along with a similar novel, *Law of the North* by S.A. White.

30 Harrison, *Unnamed Country,* 161.

31 James Oliver Curwood, *The Grizzly King, A Romance of the Wild* (New York: Grosset & Dunlap, 1915), 18-19. Interestingly, Curwood no longer agreed with hunting. In the preface to the book, he writes, "It is with something like a confession that I offer this second of my nature books to the public—a confession, and a hope: the confession of one who for years hunted and killed before he learned that the wild offered a more thrilling sport than slaughter—and the hope that what I have written may make others feel and understand that the greatest thrill of the hunt is not in killing, but in letting live.... I now regard myself as having been almost a criminal—for killing for the excitement of killing can be little less than murder." (vii-viii)

32 James Oliver Curwood, *The Flaming Forest: A Novel of the Canadian Northwest* (Toronto: Copp Clark, 1923), 2.

33 Gatenby, *Very Richness of that Past,* 371.

34 Harrison, *Unnamed Country,* 83.

35 G. Roper et al., "Writers of Fiction: 1880-1920" in Klinck, *Literary History of Canada,* Vol. 1, 339.

36 Victor Lauriston, *Arthur Stringer: Son of the North* (Toronto: Ryerson Press, 1941), 149.

37   Arthur Stringer, *The Mud Lark* (Toronto: McClelland & Stewart, 1932), 67.

38   Robert Stead, *The Cow Puncher* (Toronto: Musson, 1918), 3.

39   Howard Palmer with Tamara Palmer, *Alberta: A New History* (Edmonton: Hurtig, 1990), 237.

40   Harrison, *Unnamed Country*, 75.

41   Candace Savage, *Our Nell: A Scrapbook Biography of Nellie L. McClung* (Saskatoon: Western Producer Prairie Books, 1979), i.

42   Randi R. Warne, *Literature as Pulpit: The Christian Social Activism of Nellie L. McClung* (Waterloo: Wilfred Laurier University Press, 1993), 12.

43   Nellie McClung, *The Stream Runs Fast: My Own Story* (Toronto: Thomas Allen, 1946), 144.

44   Savage, *Our Nell*, 1.

45   Mary Hallet and Marilyn Davis, *Firing the Heather: The Life and Times of Nellie McClung* (Saskatoon: Fifth House, 1993), 228.

46   Hallet and Davis, *Firing the Heather*, 253, 269.

47   Arun P. Mukherjee, "In a Class of Her Own" in *The Literary Review of Canada* (July/August 1995), 20.

48   Robert J.C. Stead, *Kitchener and Other Poems* (Toronto: Musson, 1917), 142.

49   Bruce Peel reports Sivell bought two stallions with the proceeds from the sale of *Voices From the Range*. See Bruce Peel, *A Bibliography of the Prairie Provinces to 1953* (Toronto: University of Toronto Press, 1973), 754.

50   Rhoda Sivell, *Voices From the Range* (Toronto: T. Eaton Co., 1911), 18.

51   Robert T. Anderson, *Canadian Born and Other Poems* (Edmonton: Esdale Press, 1913), 16.

52   Anthony Mardiros, *William Irvine: The Life of a Prairie Radical* (Toronto: Lorimer, 1979), 98.

53   Hugh Dempsey, ed., *The Best of Bob Edwards* (Edmonton: Hurtig, 1975), 15.

54   Hugh Dempsey, ed., *The Wit and Wisdom of Bob Edwards* (Edmonton: Hurtig, 1976), 7.

55   Bob Edwards, *Bob Edwards Summer Annual* (Toronto: Musson, 1921), 5.

56   Grant MacEwan, *Eye Opener Bob: The Story of Bob Edwards* (Edmonton: Institute of Applied Art, 1957), I.

57   Louise Rourke, *The Land of the Frozen Tide: An Account of the Life of the Author for Two Years at Fort Chipewyan* (London: Hutchinson, 1928), 11.

58   Rourke, *Land of the Frozen Tide*, 11.

59 Rourke, *Land of the Frozen Tide,* 13. She continues this commentary by telling of a "well-known writer" who was planning a trip to Fort Chipewyan but who never made it beyond Edmonton. She notes, "...yet, later on, we heard that a thrilling story 'picturing the mighty wastes of the North' might shortly be expected from his pen!" (13, 14)

60 H. E. Church, *An Emigrant in the Canadian Northwest* (London: Metheun, 1929), 132.

61 Donald Smith, "From Sylvester Long to Chief Buffalo Child Long Lance" in James A. Clifton, ed., *Being and Becoming Indian* (Chicago: Dorsey Press, 1989), 202.

62 Donald Smith, *Long Lance: The True Story of an Imposter* (Toronto: Macmillan, 1982), 148.

63 Harwood E.R. Steele, *Spirit-of-Iron (Manitou-pewabic): An Authentic Novel of the North-west Mounted Police* (New York: A.L. Burt, 1923), vii–viii.

64 Will James, *Cowboys North and South* (New York: Arno Press, 1975 [1924]), vii. For further discussion on James' persona, see Greg Stott, "Wanted: Will James" in *Equinox* (March/April 1995), 60.

65 Paul A. W. Wallace, *Baptiste Larocque: Legends of French Canada* (Toronto: Musson, 1923), 59.

66 Charlotte Gordon, *Red Gold, A True Story of an Englishwoman's Development in the West* (Vancouver: McBeath-Campbell, 1928), 35. The authorship of this novel is disputed. Cultural historian Francis Kaye claims that May Florence Weller (1881-1964), who lived in Calgary between 1909 and 1944, was the actual writer. Interview with Francis Kaye, Lincoln, Nebraska, April 5, 1997.

67 Flos Jewell Williams, *New Furrows: A Story of the Alberta Foothills* (Ottawa: Graphic Press, 1926), 1.

68 Augustus Bridle, *Hansen: A Novel of Canadianization* (Toronto: Macmillan, 1924), vi.

69 Harold Loeb, *The Professors Like Vodka* (Carbondale: Southern Illinois University Press, 1974), 264-265.

70 Edward McCourt, *The Canadian West in Fiction* (Toronto: Ryerson, 1970), 75. McCourt made this assessment in the 1940s, when the West was still dominated by its agrarian and ethnic identity.

71 Laura Goodman Salverson, *Confessions of an Immigrant's Daughter* (Toronto: Ryerson, 1929), 511.

72 Salverson, *Confessions*, 512.

73 The McClungs also moved to Calgary, and Nellie McClung later hired Laura Salverson's secretarial assistant to work for her.

74 Salverson received a second Governor General's award for *Confessions of an Immigrant's Daughter* (1939), her autobiography.

75 Laura Goodman Salverson, *Wayside Gleams* (Toronto: McClelland & Stewart, 1925), 72.

76 Onoto Watanna, *Cattle* (Toronto: Musson, 1923), 56.

77 Linda Popp Di Biase, "The Alberta Years of Winnifred Eaton Babcock Reeve," *Alberta History* 39:2 (Spring 1991), 3, 5.

78 George Bugnet, *Nipsya* (New York: Louise Carrier, 1929), 257.

79 Interestingly, none of the major western Canadian literary critics, such as McCourt or Harrison, mention Bugnet. There is obviously some important work still to be done.

5   Depression and War: 1930–1945

1 A.J.P. Taylor, "Two Rebels: Lafayette and Riel," *Manchester Guardian*, June 26, 1936, 7. Taylor's assessment was accurate because the book was reprinted in the 1960s and again in 1992, making it one of the few historical texts from the first half of this century still considered relevant.

2 G.F.G. Stanley, "A Historical Footnote" in *Riel Project Bulletin No. 5* (April 1981), 4.

3 In the 1980s, Stanley was the General Editor of the Louis Riel Project at the University of Alberta, which published Riel's complete work.

4 Robert E. Gard, *Johnny Chinook: Tall Tales and True from the Canadian West* (Toronto: Longmans, Green, 1945), xix.

5 Gard, *Johnny Chinook,* 139.

6 Robert E. Gard, *Grassroots Theatre: A Search for Regional Arts in America* (Madison: University of Wisconsin Press, 1955), 71.

7 Frederick Niven, *Canada West* (London: J.M. Dent & Sons, 1930), 97.

8 Edmund Kemper Broadus, *Saturday and Sunday* (Toronto: Macmillan, 1935).

9 Broadus, *Saturday and Sunday*.

10 Broadus, *Saturday and Sunday,* 21. From today's vantage point, a student-professor ratio of eleven to one seems utterly delightful!

11 Lovat Dickson, *The Ante-Room* (Toronto: Macmillan, 1959), 221.

12 Lovat Dickson, "A Grown Man and the Alberta Boy He Used to Be," *The Globe Magazine,* March 5, 1971, 4-5.

13 Matthew Halton, *Ten Years to Alamein* (Toronto: Reginald Saunders, 1944), 177.

14 He is also the Griesbach for whom one of Edmonton's military bases was named.

15 The book was republished in 1995 under the title *Suitable for the Wilds: Letters from Northern Alberta 1929-1931* (Toronto: University of Toronto Press); the new edition includes a biographical introduction by Janice Dickin-McGinnis.

16 Jackson, *Suitable for the Wilds,* 13-14.

17 Jackson, *Suitable for the Wilds,* 156.

18 Kathleen Strange, *With the West in Her Eyes: The Story of a Modern Pioneer* (Toronto: MacLeod, 1937), 213-14.

19 Dan McCowan, *A Naturalist in Canada* (Toronto: Macmillan, 1941), 81.

20 Bob Dyker, *Get Your Man: An Autobiography of the North-west Mounted* (London: Low, Marsden, 1934), 134.

21 Wilfred Eggleston, *Literary Friends* (Ottawa: Borealis, 1980), 12.

22 Ronald Ross Annett, *Especially Babe* (Edmonton: Treefrog, 1978), 11. This is a reprint of the 1942 edition, with an introduction by Rudy Wiebe.

23 Interview with Ken Conibear, Vancouver, B.C., September 21, 1995.

24 Interview with Ken Conibear, Vancouver, B.C., September. 21, 1995.

25 This volume was published by Peter Davies, who took over the Dickson imprint, then sold out to Macmillan.

26 The author himself has only one copy of each of his three books. Interview with Ken Coniber, Vancouver, B.C., September 21, 1995.

27 No doubt Dickson was acquainted with Hardy from his student days at U of A.

28 W.G. Hardy, *Father Abraham* (London: Lovat Dickson, 1935), 292.

29 Howard O'Hagan, *Tay John* (Toronto: McClelland & Stewart, 1989), 265.

30 O'Hagan, *Tay John,* 156.

31 In 1977 and 1978, a few years before O'Hagan's death, Talonbooks reprinted both books; they were later combined in one collection, *Trees Are Lonely Company* (1993). Talonbooks also published O'Hagen's 1977 novel, *The School-Marm Tree,* set in Jasper in the 1920s. It was originally a short story, but in the 1950s, O'Hagan turned it into a novel.

32   Howard O'Hagan, *The Woman Who Got on at Jasper Station and Other Stories* (Vancouver: Talonbooks, 1977), 131.

33   Sara E. Carsley, *Alchemy and Other Poems* (Toronto: Macmillan, 1935), 9.

34   *Alberta Poetry Year Book 1930* (Edmonton: Canadian Author's Association, 1930).

35   *Alberta Poetry Year Book 1930*, 3.

36   In 1950, for example, there were 454 entries. Sara Carsley won first prize that year in the "Sonnet" category for her poem "The Refugee's Story," as well as awards in other categories. See *Alberta Poetry Yearbook 1950* (Edmonton: Canadian Author's Association, 1950).

37   Earle Birney, *The Collected Poems of Earle Birney* (Toronto: McClelland & Stewart, 1975), 113.

38   Bruce Nesbitt, ed., *Earle Birney* (Toronto: McGraw-Hill Ryerson, 1974), 8.

39   Nesbitt, ed., *Earle Birney*, 169.

40   Nesbitt, ed., *Earle Birney*, 14.

41   Nesbitt, ed., *Earle Birney*, 70.

42   Brian Brennan, "Rockies shaped Earle Birney's life and work," in *Calgary Herald,* September 27, 1995, B2.

43   Elsie Park Gowan was also the writer of a series of patriotic wartime broadcasts for schoolchildren. "Proud Procession," a series of "stories of pioneering in various fields of Canadian achievement today, stressing the variety of opportunity and stimulating the desire for accomplishment," aired in 1943/44 as a part of the Alberta School Broadcast program. From "The 1943-44 Alberta School Broadcast Schedule", reproduced in Mary J. Lyseng, "History of Educational Radio in Alberta" (Master's Thesis, Department of Education, University of Alberta, 1978), 99.

44   Moira Day, ed., *The Hungry Spirit: Selected Plays and Prose by Elsie Park Gowan* (Edmonton: NeWest Press, 1992), 10.

45   Typescript page 6 of an undated panel discussion at U of A Studio Theatre with Elsie Park Gowan, Henry Kreisel, and Robert Gard, probably between 1955 and 1958. Courtesy of Prof. Diane Bessai, University of Alberta.

46   Ibid., 5.

47   Day, *Hungry Spirit*, 32.

48   Geraldine Anthony, *Gwen Pharis Ringwood* (Boston: Twayne, 1981), ii.

Ringwood's first professionally performed play was *The Dragon of Kent* (1935).

49 E. Delgatty Rutland, *The Collected Plays of Gwen Pharis Ringwood* (Ottawa: Borealis, 1982), xviii.

50 A number of Ringwood's plays, such as *Lament for Harmonica* and *Pasque Flower*, were published in the 1970s, suggesting the continuing significance and appeal of her work.

51 Anthony, *Ringwood* , iv.

52 Gowan's works for both stage and radio number almost 200, while Ringwood's number about 60.

53 Day, *Hungry Spirit*, 8–9.

6 Francophone and Other Literatures: 1820–1945

1 In 1969, the Champlain Society published a critical bilingual edition, using Franchère's original manuscript in a new translation.

2 Bibliographer Bruce Peel mentions a private collector who claimed to possess a book by a Frenchman named LeHaiye, whose account of a trip with the Norwest brigade to Lake Athabasca in 1811 was supposedly published in Paris in 1813. Peel never saw the book and its existence has not been verified, nor is it known whether LeHaiye got as far as Fort Chipewyan in Alberta. If the book could be verified, it would predate Franchère's work, which is the only French-language book from the exploration period that can presently be confirmed.

3 A. Trottier et al., *Aspects du passé franco-albertain* (Edmonton: Salon d'historie de la francophonie albertaine, 1980), 78.

4 Gerard Tougas, *History of French-Canadian Literature*, Alta Lind Cook, translator (Westport, CT: Greenwood Press, 1976), 2.

5 Robert Choquette, *The Oblate Assault on Canada's Northwest* (Ottawa: University of Ottawa Press, 1995), 194.

6 James G. MacGregor, *Father Lacombe* (Edmonton: Hurtig, 1975), 241.

7 E. Grouard, *Souvenir des mes soixante ans d'aspostolat dans L'Athbaska-Mackenzie* (Winnipeg: La Liberté, 1922), 50.

8 M. Charles Benoist, *Les Français et le nord-ouest canadien* (Bar-Le-Duc: Imprimerie de l'Ouevre de Saint-Paul, 1895), 1.

9 Benoist, *Les Français*, 100, 109.

10 In the same vein, the Archbishop of St. Boniface's foreword to the book refers to the Manitoba Schools Question, which was dividing English and French-speaking Canada at the time.

11 Louis-Frederic Rouquette, *L'épopée blanche* (Paris: Ferenczi, 1926), 18.

12 W. Toye, ed., *The Oxford Companion to Canadian Literature* (Toronto: Oxford University Press, 1983), 718.

13 Morinville, a town northwest of Edmonton, is named after Morin.

14 This novel was published in English translation in 1929 in both Canada and the United States.

15 Tougas, *French-Canadian Literature,* 117.

16 Tougas, *French-Canadian Literature,* 117.

17 Georges Bugnet, *The Forest,* David Carpenter, translator (Montreal: Harvest House, 1976), 107.

18 Georges Bugnet, *Voix de la solitude* (Montreal: Éditions du Totem, 1938), 6.

19 Bugnet, *Voix de la solitude,* 26.

20 Georges Bugnet, *Poèmes,* Jean-Marcel Duciaume, ed. (Edmonton: Éditions de l'egantier, 1978), 21.

21 Georges Bugnet, *Nipsya* (St. Boniface: Éditions des Plaines, 1990), 37. Originally published 1924.

22 Georges Bugnet, *Albertaines*, Gamila Morcos, ed., (St. Boniface: Éditions des Plaines, 1990), vii.

23 Jean Papen, *Georges Bugnet: L'homme des lettres canadien* (St. Boniface: Les Éditions des Plaines, 1985), 196.

24 Papen, *Georges Bugnet,* 205.

25 Tougas, *French-Canadian Literature*, 118.

26 Bugnet, *The Forest*, 87.

27 Bugnet, *The Forest*, 66.

28 Bugnet, *Poèmes*, 21.

29 Jars Balan cites a 1916 study of Ukrainian-Canadian settlements that found forty-eight percent of men and seventy percent of women were illiterate in their own language. See "The Writing of a History of the Ukrainian Literary Institution" in Joseph Pivato, ed., *Literatures of Lesser Diffusion* (Edmonton: Research Institute for Comparative Literature, 1990).

30 The book was published in a new edition in 1972.

31 Translation courtesy of Jars Balan.

32 Edmonton received its first press with Cyrillic type in 1911.

33 Jars Balan, "Elias Kiriak: Chronicler of Alberta's Ukrainian Pioneers" in
    The Review (March 16, 1993), 14.

34 I. Kiriak, "Ukrainian Wedding" in J.P. Gillese, ed., *Chinook Arch*
    (Edmonton: Government of Alberta, 1967), 187.

35 The importance of Kiriak's work to Alberta letters was recognized when
    an excerpt from the novel was published in the 1967 anthology of
    Alberta writing, *Chinook Arch*. The Ukrainian-language edition was
    republished in 1973-74 by Trident Press of Winnipeg, and in 1979 by the
    Alberta Department of Education, while the English translation was also
    reprinted by Trident, most recently in 1983.

36 This small, illustrated book was later translated into English by Louis
    Laychuk and published by the Canadian Institute of Ukrainian Studies at
    the University of Alberta in 1981 as *Recollections About the Life of the First
    Ukrainian Settlers in Canada.*

37 William A. Czumer, *Recollections About the Life of the First Ukrainian
    Settlers in Alberta*, 1967), 187.

38 Information courtesy of Jars Balan.

39 Information courtesy of Jars Balan.

40 See Jars Balan, "Ukrainian Theatre: Showtime on the North
    Saskatchewan" in B. Hesketh and F. Swyripa, eds., *Edmonton: The Life of a
    City* (Edmonton: NeWest Press, 1995), 88-95; Pivato, ed., *Literatures of a
    Lesser Diffusion*, 196.

41 D.L. Neijmann, *The Icelandic Voice in Canadian Letters* (Amsterdam: Vrije
    University, 1994), 37.

42 Peel, *Bibliography of the Prairie Provinces,* 757.

43 Peel, *Bibliography of the Prairie Provinces,* 127.

44 Neijmann, *The Icelandic Voice,* 107.

45 A *Selected Translations* had appeared in 1982, when Stephannson's house in
    Markerville was declared a historic site. These poems had appeared in
    various anthologies, such as *Canadian Overtones* (1935) and *Chinook Arch*
    (1967), but the volume lacked the coherent vision brought to translation
    by Gunnars.

46 Neijmann, *The Icelandic Voice*, 127.

47 Watson Kirkconnell, *Canadian Overtones* (Winnipeg: Columbia Press, 1935), 21.

48 Kirkconnell, *Canadian Overtones,* 3.

49 Stephan G. Stephansson, *Selected Prose and Poetry,* K. Gunnars, translator (Red Deer: Red Deer College Press, 1988), 43.

50 Neijmann, *The Icelandic Voice,* 97.

51 Neijmann, *The Icelandic Voice,* 20.

52 Aksel Sandemose, *Ross Dane* (Winnipeg: Gunnars & Campbell,1989), 18. Professor Tamara Seiler of the University of Calgary brought this book to my attention.

53 George Bisztray, *Hungarian-Canadian Literature* (Toronto: University of Toronto Press, 1987), 11.

54 Tamara J. Palmer, "The Fictionalization of the Vertical Mosaic: The Immigrant, Success and National Mythology" in J. Pivato, ed., *Literatures of Lesser Diffusion*, 85.

55 Palmer, "Vertical Mosaic," 101.

56 Howard Palmer, *Patterns of Prejudice: A History of Nativism in Alberta* (Toronto: McClelland & Stewart, 1982), 168.

7 Early Literary Institutions

1 E.A. Corbett, *We Have With Us Tonight* (Toronto: Ryerson, 1957), 51.

2 Corbett, *We Have With Us Tonight,* 101.

3 Howard Fink, "Radio Drama in English," in Eugene Benson and I.W. Conolly, eds., *The Oxford Companion to Canadian Theatre* (Toronto: Oxford University Press, 1989), 456.

4 Anne Nothof, "Making Community History: The Radio Plays of Ringwood and Gowan," in Bob Hesketh and Frances Swyripa, eds., *Edmonton: The Life of a City* (Edmonton: NeWest, 1995), 172.

5 Moria Day, "The Banff School of Fine Arts 1933-69: A Theatre of the People," *Alberta* 2:1 (1989), 47.

6 Quoted in Day, "Banff School," 49.

7 Day, "Banff School," 56.

8 Donald Cameron, *Campus in the Clouds* (Toronto: McClelland & Stewart, 1956), 15.

9 Cameron, *Campus in the Clouds,* 19.

10 Cameron, *Campus in the Clouds,* 19.

11 Gard, *Grassroots Theatre,* 47.

12 Cameron, *Campus in the Clouds,* 21.

13 Cameron, *Campus in the Clouds,* 30.

14 Cameron, *Campus in the Clouds,* 39.

15 David and Peggy Leighton, *Artists, Builders and Dreamers: 50 Years at the Banff School* (Toronto: McClelland & Stewart, 1982), 53.

16 The replacement of American funding with private Alberta money for Banff occurred immediately after the War. Cameron went in search of capital funding to the boardrooms of corporate Montreal, where he was rejected on the grounds that the Banff school was a public state-funded institution. But a new era was inaugurated in 1946 when Mrs. J.H. Woods, widow of the publisher of the *Calgary Herald,* donated $100,000 to the school. Donald Cameron was eventually named a Senator. Such bourgeois associations and the new climate of the Cold War spelled the end of populism at the Banff School. After the War, the school became increasingly interested in music, the performing arts and the visual arts as cultural artifacts for middle-class audiences. The focus on playwriting began to recede.

17 John Lennox, "Canadian Authors Association" in William Toye, ed., *The Oxford Companion to Canadian Literature* (Toronto: Oxford University Press, 1983), 100.

18 *Alberta Poetry Year Book 1930* (Edmonton: Canadian Authors Association, 1930).

19 *Canadian Poems* (Edmonton: Canadian Authors Association, 1937), 3.

20 Walter Johns, *A History of the University of Alberta: 1908-1969* (Edmonton: University of Alberta Press, 1981), 116.

21 Cameron, *Campus in the Clouds,* 40.

22 *The Way of the Makers* (Edmonton: The Friends of the Univeristy of Alberta, 1967), dust jacket. The book was followed in 1971 by *The Art of Writing,* a similar volume published by Ryerson Press and edited by H.V. Weekes.

23 Interview with W.O. Mitchell, Calgary, June 12, 1996.

24 Ken Bolton, *The Albertans* (Edmonton: Lone Pine Publishing, 1981), 94.

25 Brian Brennan, "Calgary's first librarian left rich legacy," *Calgary Herald* August 13, 1994, B2.

26 Donna Lohnes and Barbara Nicholson, *Alexander Calhoun* (Calgary: Calgary Public Library, 1987), 13.

27 For example, the first public library in Calgary, built by the Carnegie Foundation, served many decades later as the home of the Calgary Public Library's writer-in-residence program, as well as a place for book launches by local authors and workshops on writing. And when the Alberta Foundation for the Literary Arts was formed by the Government of Alberta in 1984, libraries joined with writers and publishers to establish a significant funding program for the literary arts.

Conclusion: Establishing a Canon

1 Dominique Janicaud, "Overcoming Metaphysics?" in D. Janicaud and Jean-Francois Mattei, ed., *Heidegger From Metaphysics to Thought*, M. Gendre, translator (Albany: SUNY Press, 1995), 3.

2 Nadine Gordimer, *Writing and Being* (Cambridge: Harvard University Press, 1995), 1.

3 Jacques Derrida, *On The Name* (Stanford: Stanford University Press, 1995), 91.

4 Martin Heidegger, *Nietzsche: The Will to Power as Art* (New York: Harper and Row, 1979), xvi.

5 Glenn Willmott, *McLuhan or Modernism in Reverse* (Toronto: University of Toronto Press, 1996), xiii.

6 Taylor, *Cultural Selection*, 19.

Bibliography

Abley, Mark. *Beyond Forget: Rediscovering the Prairies.* Vancouver: Douglas & McIntyre, 1986.

Alberta Poetry Yearbook 1930. Edmonton: Canadian Authors Association, 1930

Alberta Poetry Yearbook 1950. Edmonton: Canadian Authors Associaton, 1950

Allan, Luke. *The Blue Wolf: A Tale of the Cypress Hills.* London: H. Jenkins, 1913.

_____. *Blue Pete, Half Breed: A Story of the Cowboy West.* London: H. Jenkins, 1921.

_____. *The Lone Trail.* London: H. Jenkins, 1922.

_____. *The Return of Blue Pete.* New York: George H. Doran Company, 1922.

_____. *The Westerner.* London: Herbert Jenkins Limited, 1924.

_____. *Blue Pete: Horse Thief.* London: Herbert Jenkins Limited, 1938.

Anderson, Robert T. *Old Timers and Other Poems.* Edmonton: Edmonton Printing and Publishing Co., 1909.

_____. *Canadian Born and Other Poems.* Edmonton: Esdale Press, 1913.

_____. *Troopers in France.* Edmonton: Coles, 1932.

Annett, Ronald Ross. *Especially Babe.* Edmonton: Treefrog, 1978 (1942).

Anthony, Geraldine. *Gwen Pharis Ringwood.* Boston: Twayne, 1981.

Argyll, John Douglas. *Canadian Pictures.* London: The Religious Tract Society, 1884.

Back, Sir George. *Narrative of the Arctic Land Expedition to the Moth of the Great Fish River and along the Shores of the Arctic Ocean in the Years 1833, 1834 and 1835.* London: J. Murray, 1836.

Balan, Jars. "The Writing of a History of the Ukrainian Literary Institution." *Literatures of Lesser Diffusion.* Joseph Pivato, ed. Edmonton: Research Institute for Comparative Literature, 1990: 191–208.

_____. "Elias Kiriak: Chronicler of Alberta's Ukrainian Pioneers." *The Review* (Redwater, AB) March 16, 1993: 14.

_____. "Ukrainian Theatre: Showtime on the North Saskatchewan." *Edmonton: The Life of a City.* B. Hesketh and F. Swyripa, eds. Edmonton: NeWest Press, 1995: 88–95.

Barbeau, Marius. *Indian Days in the Canadian Rockies.* Toronto: Macmillan, 1923.

Barry, P.S. *Mystical Themes in Mild River Rock Art.* Edmonton: University of Alberta Press, 1991.

_____. *Indian Days on the Western Prairies.* Ottawa: National Museum of Canada, 1974.

Belyea, Barbara. "Mackenzie Meets Moodie in the Great Divide." *Journal of Canadian Studies* 23:3 (Autumn, 1988): 118–29.

Benoist, Charles. *Les Français et le nord-ouest canadien.* Bar-Le-Duc: l'Ouevre de Saint-Paul, 1895.

Bickerseth, J. Burgon. *The Land of Open Doors: Being Letters From Western Canada 1911-13.* Toronto: University of Toronto Press, 1976 (1914).

Bindloss, Harold. *The Mistress of Bonaventure.* New York: F.A. Stokes, 1907.

_____. *Winston of the Prairie.* New York: F.A. Stokes, 1907.

_____. *The Impostor.* New York: F.A. Stokes, 1908.

_____. *Lorimer of the North-West.* New York: F.A. Stokes, 1909.

_____. *Ranching for Sylvia.* New York: A.L. Burt, 1913.

_____. *Pine Creek Ranch.* New York: F.A. Stokes, 1926.

Birney, Earle. *David and Other Poems.* Toronto: The Ryerson Press, 1942.

_____. *Now Is Time.* Toronto: The Ryerson Press, 1945.

_____. *Trial of a City and Other Verse.* Toronto: Ryerson Press, 1952.

_____. *The Collected Poems of Earle Birney.* Toronto: McClelland & Stewart, 1975.

_____. *Spreading Time: Remarks on Canadian Writing and Writers Book 1: 1904-1949.* Montreal: Vehicule Press, 1980.

Bisztray, George. *Hungarian-Canadian Literature.* Toronto: University of
    Toronto Press, 1987.

Bloomfield, Leonard. *Sacred Stories of the Sweet Grass Cree.* Ottawa: F.A.
    Acland, 1930.

_____. *Plains Cree Texts.* New York: G.E. Stechert & Co., 1934.

Blue, John. *Alberta Past and Present; Historical and Biographical.* Chicago:
    Pioneer Historical Publishing Co., 1924.

Bolton, Ken. *The Albertans.* Edmonton: Lone Pine Publishing, 1981.

Borel, André. *Croquis du Far-West canadiens: gens, bêtes, choses, travaux.* Paris:V.
    Attinger, 1928.

_____. *Le Robinson de la Red Deer.* Neuchatel, France:V. Attinger, 1930.

Brennan, Brian. "Calgary's first librarian left rich legacy." *Calgary Herald*
    August 13, 1994: B2.

_____. "Rockies shaped Earle Birney's life and work." *Calgary Herald*
    September 27, 1995: B2.

Bridle, Augustus. *Hansen: A Novel of Canadianization.* Toronto: Macmillan,
    1924.

Brightman, Robert, Angelique Linklater, and Henry Linklater.
    "Mistacayawasis: Big Belly Child." In Swann, *Coming to Light:* 190-207.

Broadus, Edmund Kemper. *Saturday and Sunday.* Toronto: Macmillan, 1935.

Brooke, Rupert. *Letters from America.* London: Sidgwick & Jackson, 1916.

Brownstone, Arni. *War Paint: Blackfoot and Sarcee Painted Buffalo Robes in the
    Royal Ontario Museum.* Toronto: Royal Ontario Museum, 1993.

Bruce, Eva. *Call Her Rosie.* New York. I. Washburn, 1942.

Bugnet, Georges. *Le lys de sang.* Montreal: Éditions Eduouard Garaud, 1923.

_____. *Nipsya.* English trans. New York: Louise Carrier, 1929.

_____. *Siraf: étranges révélations.* Montreal: Éditions du Totem, 1934.

_____. *La forêt.* Montreal: Éditions du Totem, 1935.

_____. *Voix de la solitude.* Montreal: Totem, 1938.

_____. *The Forest.* David Carpenter, trans. Montreal: Harvest House, 1976.

_____. *Poèmes.* Jean-Marcel Duciaume, ed. Edmonton: Éditions de l'églantier,
    1978.

_____. *Albertaines.* Gamila Morcos, ed. St. Boniface: Éditions des Plaines, 1990.

_____. *Nipsya.* St. Boniface: Éditions des Plaines, 1990 (1924).

Burpee, Lawrence J., ed. *An Adventurer From Hudson Bay: Journal of Matthew
    Cocking, from York Factor to the Blackfeet Country, 1772-73.* In *Exploration*

Literature, Germaine Warkentin ed. Toronto: Oxford University Press, 1993.

Butler, W.F. *Introductory Report to Adam Archibald, Lieut.-Governor of Manitoba of a Trip from Ft. Garry to Edmonton in 1870-71.* Winnipeg: Manitoba Public Archives.

_____. *The Great Lone Land: A Narrative of Travel and Adventure in the North-West of America.* London: Sampson, Low, 1872.

_____. *The Wild North Land: The Story of a Winter Journey with Dogs across Northern North America.* London: Sampson, Low, 1873.

_____. *Red Cloud: The Solitary Sioux.* London: S. Low, Marston, Searle, & Rivington, 1882.

_____. *Sir William Butler: An Autobiography.* London: Constable & Co., 1911.

Cameron, Agnes Deans. *The New North: Being Some Account of a Woman's Journey Through Canada to the Arctic.* New York: Appleton, 1909.

Cameron, Donald. *Campus in the Clouds.* Toronto: McClelland & Stewart, 1956.

Canadian Poems. Edmonton: Canadian Authors Association, 1937.

Carlisle, Robert S. "Crowfoot's Dying Speech" *Alberta History* 38:3 (Summer 1990): 16-17.

Carrel, Frank. *Canada's West & Further West.* Quebec: Telegraph Printing Co., 1911.

Carsley, Sara E. *Alchemy and Other Poems.* Toronto: Macmillan, 1935.

_____. *The Artisan.* Toronto: The Ryerson Press, 1941.

Carter, Sarah. "The Missionaries' Indian: The Publciations of John McDougall, John Maclean and Egerton Ryerson Young." *Prairie Forum* 9:1 (1984): 27-44.

Chamberlain, Stuart. *Queen's Highway: From Ocean to Ocean.* London: Sampson, Low, 1884.

Cheyfitz, Eric. *The Poetics of Imperialism: Translations and Colonization from* The Tempest *to* Tarzan. New York: Oxford University Press, 1991.

Choquette, Robert. *The Oblate Assault on Canada's Northwest.* Ottawa: University of Ottawa Press, 1995.

Church, A.J. *Making a Start in Canada: Letters From Two Young Immigrants.* London: Seedy, 1889.

Church, H.E. *An Emigrant in the Canadian Northwest.* London: Metheun, 1929.

Collected Poems. Calgary: Canadian Authors Association, 1935.

Colombo, John Robert. *The Poets of Canada.* Edmonton: Hurtig, 1978.

Conaty, Gerald T. "Pictograph Robes of the Plains First Nations." *Glenbow* 14:2 (Summer 1994): 5-7.

Conibear, Kenneth. *North Land Footprints; or Lives on Little Bent Tree Lake.* London: Lovat Dickson, 1936.

_____. *Northward to Eden.* London: P. Davies, 1939.

Connor, Ralph. *Black Rock: A Tale of the Selkirks.* Toronto: Westminster, 1898.

_____. *The Sky Pilot: A Tale of the Foothills.* Toronto: Westminster, 1899.

_____. *The Prospector: A Tale of the Crow's Nest Pass.* New York: Revell, 1904.

_____. *Corporal Cameron of the North West Mounted Police.* New York: Hodder & Stoughton, 1912.

_____. *The Patrol of the Sun Dance Trail.* New York: Hodder & Stoughton, 1914.

Conybeare, Charles F.P. *Vahnfried.* London: Kegan Paul, 1902.

_____. *Lyrics from the West.* Toronto: W. Briggs, 1907.

Copway, George. *The Traditional History and Characteristic Sketches of the Ojibway Nations.* London: Charles Gilpin, 1850.

Corbett, E.A. *Blackfoot Trails.* Toronto: Macmillan, 1934.

_____. *McQueen of Edmonton.* Toronto: Ryerson, 1934.

_____. *Father, God Bless Him.* Toronto: Ryerson Press, 1953.

_____. *Henry Marshall Tory, Beloved Canadian.* Toronto: Ryerson Press, 1954.

_____. *We Have With Us Tonight.* Toronto: Ryerson Press, 1957.

Craig, John Roderick. *Ranching with Lords and Commoners; or Twenty Years on the Range.* Toronto: Briggs, 1903.

Cumberland, Stuart. *The Queen's Highway: From Ocean to Ocean.* London: Sampson, Low, 1887.

Curwood, James Oliver. *Philip Steele of the Royal Northwest Mounted Police.* Toronto: McLeod & Allen, 1911.

_____. *The Grizzly King: A Romance of the Wild.* New York: Grosset & Dunlap, 1915.

_____. *The Flaming Forest: A Novel of the Canadian Northwest.* Toronto: Copp Clark, 1923.

Czumer, William A. *Recollections About the Life of the First Ukrainian Settlers in Alberta.* L. T. Laychuk, trans. Edmonton: Canadian Institute of Ukrainian Studies, 1981.

Davey, Frank. *Canadian Literary Power.* Edmonton: NeWest Press, 1994.

Day, Moira. "The Banff School of Fine Arts 1933-69: A Theatre of the People." *Alberta* 2:1 (1989).

_____, ed. *The Hungry Spirit: Selected Plays and Prose by Elsie Park Gowan.* Edmonton: NeWest Press, 1992.

Dempsey, Hugh, ed. *The Best of Bob Edwards.* Edmonton: Hurtig, 1975.

de Kerchove, Derrick. *The Skin of Culture: Investigating the New Electronic Reality.* Toronto: Somerville House, 1995.

de Smet, Pierre-Jean. *Oregon Missions and Travels Over the Rocky Mountains in 1845-46.* New York: Edward Dunigan, 1847.

Dempsey, Hugh A. *A Blackfoot Winter Count.* Calgary: Glenbow Occasional Paper No. 1, 1965.

_____, ed. *The Rundle Journals 1840-48.* Calgary: Historical Society of Alberta, 1977.

_____. *The Wit and Wisdom of Bob Edwards.* Edmonton: Hurtig, 1976.

Derrida, Jacques. *On the Name.* English trans. Stanford: Stanford University Press, 1995.

Dickson, Lovat. *Out of the West Land.* Toronto: Collins, 1944.

_____. *The Ante-Room.* Toronto: Macmillan, 1959.

_____. "A Grown Man and the Alberta Boy He Used to Be." *The Globe Magazine* March 5, 1971: 4-5.

Dmytriw, Nestor. *Kanadiyaska Rus: podorozhi vspomyn.* Mount Carmel, Pennsylvania: Svoboda, 1897.

Doyle, Sir Arthur Conan. *Memories and Adventures.* London: Hodder & Stoughton, 1924.

Duckworth, Harry W., ed. *The English River Book: A North West Company Journal and Account Books of 1786.* Montreal: McGill-Queen's University Press, 1990.

Dyker, Bob. *Get Your Man: An Autobiography of the North-west Mounted.* London: Low, Marsden, 1934.

Edwards, Bob. *Bob Edwards Summer Annual.* Toronto: Musson, 1920.

_____. *Bob Edwards Summer Annual.* Toronto: Musson, 1921. Eggleston, Wilfred. *Prairie Moonlight and Other Lyrics.* Published privately, 1927.

_____. *The High Plains.* Toronto: Macmillan, 1938.

_____. *Prairie Symphony.* Ottawa: Borealis Press, 1978.

_____. *Literary Friends.* Ottawa: Borealis, 1980.

Erasmus, Peter. *Buffalo Days and Nights.* Calgary: Glenbow–Alberta Institute, 1976.

Erskine, Laurie York. *Renfrew of the Royal Mounted.* New York: D. Appleton & Co., 1922.

_____. *Renfrew Rides the Range.* New York: D. Appleton-Century Co., 1935.

_____. *Renfrew's Long Trail.* New York: D. Appleton-Century, 1933.

_____. *Renfrew in the Valley of Vanished Men.* New York: D. Appleton-Century, 1936.

_____. *Renfrew Flies Again.* New York: Grosset & Dunlop, 1942.

Evans, James. *Cree Syllabic Hymn Book.* Toronto: Bibliographical Society of Canada, 1954. Originally published Norway House, 1841.

Fairley, Bruce, ed. *The Canadian Mountaineering Anthology.* Edmonton: Lone Pine Publishing, 1994.

Fidler, Peter. *A Look at Peter Fidler's Journal: Hournal of a Journey Over Land from Buckingham House to the Rocky Mountains in 1792 and 1793.* Lethbridge: Historical Resource Centre, 1991.

Fink, Howard. "Radio Drama in English." *The Oxford Companion to Canadian Theatre.* Eugene Benson and I.W. Connolly, eds. Toronto: Oxford University Press, 1989: 452–456.

Fitz-Gibbon, Mary, ed. *The Diaries of Edmund Montague Morris: Western Journeys 1907-10.* Toronto: Royal Ontario Museum, 1985.

Fleming, Sandford. *England and Canada: A Summer Tour Between Old and New Westminster.* London: Sampson, Low, 1884.

Footner, Hulbert. *Two on the Trail: A Story of the Far Northwest.* London: Methuen, 1911.

_____. *Jack Chanty: A Story of Athabasca.* Garden City, New York: Doubleday, Page & Co., 1913.

Franchère, Gabriel. *Relation d'un voyage à la côte du nord-ouest de l'Amerique septentrionale dans les années 1810, 1811, 1812, 1813 et 1814.* Montreal: C.B. Pasteur, 1820.

Francis, Daniel, ed. *Imagining Ourselves: Classics of Canadian Nonfiction.* Vancouver: Arsenal Pulp Press, 1994.

Francis, Douglas R. *Images of the West: Responses to the Canadian Prairies.* Saskatoon: Western Producer Prairie Books, 1989.

Franklin, Sir John. *Narrative of a Journey to the Shores of the Polar Sea in the Years 1819-20-21.* London: J. Murray, 1824.

_____. *Narrative of a Second Expedition to the Shores of the Polar Sea, in the Years 1825, 1826 and 1827.* London: J. Murray, 1828.

Fraser, William Alexander. *The Eye of a God and Other Tales of East and West.* New York: Doubleday & McClure, 1899.

Francisco, Ramón (Francis Cecil Whitehouse). *Rebels and Other Love Poems.* Ottawa: The Graphic Publishers, 1929.

Fraser, W.A. *Mooswa and Others of the Boundaries.* New York: Scribners, 1900.

Frye, Northrop. *The Great Code: The Bible and Literature.* Toronto: The Academic Press, 1982.

Gard, Robert E. *Johnny Chinook: Tall Tales and True from the Canadian West.* Toronto: Longmans, Green, 1945.

_____. *Grassroots Theatre: A Search for Regional Arts in America.* Madison: University of Wisconsin Press, 1955.

Garrioch, A.C. *The Gospel of St. Mark.* London: Society for Promoting Christian Knowledge, 1886.

_____. *Manual of Devotion in the Beaver Indian Language.* London: Society for Promoting Christian Knowledge, 1886.

_____. *The Far and Furry North: A Story of Life and Love and Travel in the Days of the Hudson's Bay Company.* Winnipeg: Douglass-McIntyre, 1925.

_____. *A Hatchet Mark in Duplicate.* Toronto: Ryerson Press, 1929.

Garvin, John William, ed. *Canadian Poets.* Toronto: McClelland & Stewart, 1926.

Gatenby, Greg, ed. *The Very Richness of the Past: Canada Through the Eyes of Foreign Writers.* Vol. 2. Toronto: Knopf, 1995

Gates, Charles M., ed. *Five Fur Traders of the Northwest.* St. Paul: Minnesota Historical Society, 1965.

Glass, E.B. *Primer and English Language Lessons in Cree.* Toronto: William Briggs, 1888.

Gard, Robert E. *Grassroots Theatre.* Madison: University of Wisconsin Press, 1955.

Glover, George, ed. *David Thompson's Narrative 1784-1812.* Toronto: The Champlain Society, 1962.

Gordimer, Nadine: *Writing and Being.* Cambridge: Harvard University Press, 1995.

Goodloe, Abbe Carter. *At the Foot of the Rockies.* New York: Scribner & Sons, 1905.

Gordon, Charlotte. *Red Gold, A True Story of an Englishwoman's Development in the West.* Vancouver: McBeath-Campbell, 1928.

Gowan, Elsie Park. *The Royal Touch.* In *Canadian School Plays.* Emrys Maldwyn Jones, ed. Toronto: Ryerson Press, 1948.

_____. *Breeches from Bond Street.* New York: S. French, 1952.

Grant, George M. *Ocean to Ocean: Sandford Fleming's Expedition Through Canada in 1872.* Toronto: James Campbell, 1873.

Green, William Spotswood. *Among the Selkirk Glaciers.* London: Macmillan, 1890.

Griesbach, William. *I Remember.* Toronto: Ryerson, 1946.

Grouard, E. *Prières, cantiques et catechisme en langue montagnaise ou chipewyan.* La La Biche, 1887.

_____. *Souvenir des mes soixante ans d'aspostolat dans L'Athbaska-Mackenzie.* Winnipeg: La Liberté, 1922.

Gunn Allen, Paula. *Voice of the Turtle: American Indian Literature 1900-1970.* New York: Random House, 1994.

Habermas, Jurgen. *The Philosophical Discourse of Modernity: Twelve Lectures.* Cambridge: MIT Press, 1992.

Hallet, Mary and Marilyn Davis. *Firing the Heather: The Life and Times of Nellie McClung.* Saskatoon: Fifth House, 1993.

Halton, Mathew. *Ten Years to Alamein.* Toronto: Reginald Saunders, 1944.

Hardy, W.G. *Father Abraham.* London: Lovat Dickson, 1935.

_____. *Turn Back the River.* Toronto: Macmillan of Canada, 1938.

_____. *All the Trumpets Sounded; A Novel Based on the Life of Moses.* New York: Coward-McCann, 1942.

_____, ed. *Alberta Golden Jubilee Anthology.* Toronto: McClelland & Stewart, 1955.

_____, ed. *Alberta: A Natural History.* Edmonton: The Patrons, 1967.

_____. *The City of Libertines.* Toronto: McClelland & Stewart, 1957.

_____. *The Scarlet Mantle: A Novel of Julius Caesar.* Toronto: Macmillan of Canada, 1978.

Harmon, Daniel Williams. *A Journal of Voyages and Travels in the Interior of North America....* Toronto: Courier Press, 1911.

Harrison, Dick. *Unnamed Country: The Struggle for a Canadian Prairie Fiction.* Edmonton: University of Alberta Press, 1977.

Heidegger, Martin. *Nietzsche: The Will to Power as Art.* English trans. New York: Harper and Row, 1979.

Higinbotham, John D. *When the West Was Young*. Toronto: Ryerson Press, 1978 (1933).

_____. *Foothill and Prairie Memories: A Group of Poems*. Lethbridge: n.p., 1978.

Hill, Alexander Stavely. *From Home to Home: Autumn Wanderings in the North-West in the Years 1881, 1882, 1883, 1884*. London: Sampson, Low, Marston, Searle & Rivington, 1885.

Hopwood, Victor G. *David Thompson: Travels in Western North America, 1784-1812*. Toronto: Macmillan, 1972.

_____. "Explorers by Land to 1867." In Klinck, *Literary History of Canada*, Vol 1: 19-53.

Hughes, Katherine. *Archbishop O'Brien, Man and Churchman*. Ottawa: R.L. Crain, 1906.

_____. *Father Lacombe: The Black-Robe Voyageur*. Toronto: McClelland & Stewart, 1920.

Hungry Wolf, Adolf. *The Blood People*. New York: Harper and Row, 1977.

Innis, Mary Quayle. *Travellers West*. Toronto: Clarke, Irwin, 1956.

"Interview with Leroy Little Bear," *Glenbow* 15, 1 (Spring 1995).

Irvine, William. *The Farmers in Politics*. Toronto: McClelland & Stewart, 1920.

_____. *Co-operative Government*. Ottawa: Mutual Press, 1930.

_____. *The Brains We Trust*. Toronto: Thomas Nelson, 1935.

Jackson, Dr. Mary Percy. *On the Last Frontier: Pioneering in the Peace River Block*. London: The Sheldon Press, 1933.

_____. *Suitable for the Wilds: Letters from Northern Alberta 1929-31*. Janice Dickin-McGinnis, ed. Toronto: University of Toronto Press, 1995.

James, Will. *Cowboys North and South*. New York: Arno Press, 1975 (1924).

Janicaud, Dominique and Jean-Francois Mattei. *Heidegger: From Metaphysics to Thought*. M. Gendre, trans. Albany: SUNY Press, 1995.

Johns, Walter. *A History of the University of Alberta: 1908-1969*. Edmonton: University of Alberta Press, 1981.

Johnson, Alice M. *Saskatchewan Journals and Correspondence: Edmonton House 1795-1800, Chesterfield House 1800-1802*. London: Hudson's Bay Record Society, 1967.

Kain, Conrad. *Where the Clouds Can Go*. New York: American Alpine Club, 1935.

Kane, Paul. *Wanderings of an Artist Among the Indians of North America: From Canada to Vancouver Island and Oregon Through the Hudson's Bay Company Territory and Back Again*. London: Longman, Brown, Green, 1859.

_____. *Wanderings of an Artist.* Toronto: Radisson Society, 1925.

Kaye, Francis W. and Robert Thacker. "Gone Back to Alberta: Robert Kroetsch Rewriting the Great Plains." *Great Plains Quarterly* 14:3: (Summer 1994): 167-184.

Kelly, L.V. *The Range Men: The Story of the Ranchers and Indians of Alberta.* Toronto: Briggs, 1913.

Kendall, Ralph Selwood. *Benton of the Royal Mounted.* New York: John Lane Company, 1918.

_____. *The Luck of the Mounted.* New York: John Lane Company, 1920.

_____. *Northern Trails Omnibus.* New York: Grosset, 1920. (Includes Samuel Alexander White, *Law of the North.*)

Keynes, Geoffrey, ed. *The Letters of Rupert Brooke.* New York: Harcourt, Brace, 1968.

Kipling, Rudyard. *From Sea to Sea: Writings in Prose and Verse.* New York: Scribner, 1897.

_____. *Letters to the Family.* Toronto: Macmillan, 1908.

Kiriak, I. *Syny Zemli.* Edmonton: The Institute Press, 1939-1945.

_____. "Ukrainian Wedding." *Chinook Arch.* J.P. Gillese, ed. Edmonton: Government of Alberta, 1967.

Kirkconnell, Watson. *Canadian Overtones.* Winnipeg: Columbia Press, 1935.

Klassen, Michael and Martin Pagne. "The Management and Conservation of Alberta Rock: Background and Preliminary Recommendations." *Archaeology in Alberta 1987,* Magne, M., ed. Occasional Paper No. 32. Edmonton: Alberta Culture and Multiculturaism, 1988.

Klinck, Carl F., ed. *The Literary History of Canada: Canadian Literature in English.* Second edition. Toronto: University of Toronto Press, 1977.

Kroetsch, Robert. *Alberta.* Edmonton: NeWest Press, 1993 (1967).

Krupat, Arnold. *The Voice in the Margin: Native American Literature and the Canon.* Berkeley: University of California Press, 1989.

Lacombe, Albert. *Dictionnaire et grammaire de la langue Crise.* Montreal: Beauchemin & Valois, 1872.

_____. *Dictionnaire de la langue des Cris.* Montreal: Beauchemin & Valois, 1874.

_____. *Grammaire de la langue des Cris.* Montreal: Beauchemin & Valois, 1874.

Lambe, W. Kaye, ed. *Sixteen Years in the Indian Country: The Journal of Daniel Williams Harmon 1800-1816.* Toronto: Macmillan, 1957.

Lauriston, Victor. *Arthur Stringer: Son of the North.* Toronto: Ryerson Press, 1941.

Lavaille, E. *The Life of Father De Smet S.J.* New York: Kennedy & Sons, 1915.

Le Chevalier, Jule Jean Marie Joseph. *Esquisse sur l'origine et les premiers développements de Calgary 1883-1930.* Calgary: Paroisse Sainte-Famille, 1936.

Lehmann, Heinz. *Das Deutschtum in Westkanada.* Berlin: Junker und Dännhaupt, 1939.

Leighton, David and Peggy. *Artists, Builders and Dreamers: 50 Years at the Banff School.* Toronto: McClelland & Stewart, 1982.

Leighton, Robert. *Woolly of the Wilds: A Story of Pluck and Adventure in North-West Canada.* London: Ward, Lock, 190?.

_____. *Rattlesnake Ranch: A Story of Adventure in the Great Northwest.* London: C. Arthur Pearson, 1912.

Lennox, John. "Canadian Authors Association" in *The Oxford Companion to Canadian Literature.* William Toye, ed. Toronto: Oxford University Press, 1983: 100-101.

Lionnet, Jean. *Chez les Français du Canada.* Paris: Plan-Nourrit et cie, 1908.

Loeb, Harold. *Tumbling Mustard.* New York: H. Liveright, 1929.

_____. *The Professors Like Vodka.* Carbondale: Southern Illinois University Press, 1974.

Lohnes, Donna and Barbara Nicholson. *Alexander Calhoun.* Calgary: Calgary Public Library, 1987.

Long Lance, Buffalo Child (Sylvester C. Long). *Long Lance, The Autobiography of a Blackfoot Indian Chief.* New York: Cosmopolitan Book Corp., 1928.

Lyseng, Mary J. "History of Educational Radio in Alberta." Master's thesis, Department of Education, Univesity of Alberta, 1978.

MacEwan, Grant. *Eye-Opener Bob: The Story of Bob Edwards.* Edmonton: Institute of Applied Art, 1957.

MacGregor, James. *Father Lacombe.* Edmonton: Hurtig, 1975.

_____. *A History of Alberta.* Edmonton: Hurtig, 1977.

Mackenzie, Alexander. *Voyages from Montreal in the River St. Lawrence through the Continent of North America to the frozen and Pacific Oceans....* London: Cadell and Davis, 1801.

Mackie, John. *The Devil's Playground: A Story of the Wild North-West.* London: T.F. Unwin, 1894.

_____. *Sinners Twain: A Romance of the Great Lone Land.* London: T.F. Unwin, 1895.

_____. *The Heart of the Prairie.* London: Nisbet, 1899.

_____. *The Prodigal's Brother: A Story of Western Life.* London: Jarrold, 1899.

_____. *The Rising of the Red Man: A Romance of the Louise Riel Rebellion.* London: Jarrold, n.d.

MacLaren, I.S. "David Thompson's Imaginative Mapping of the Canadian Northwest 1784-1812." *Ariel: A Review of International English Literature* 15:2 (April 1984): 89-106.

_____. "Touring at High Speed: Fur-Trade Landscape in the Writings of Frances and George Simpson." *Musk-Ox* 34 (1986): 78-87.

_____. "Notes Toward a Reconstruction of Paul Kane's Art and Prose." *Canadian Literature* 113 & 114 (1987): 179-205.

_____. "Creating Travel Literature: The Case of Paul Kane." *Papers of the Bibliographic Society of Canada* 27 (1988): 80-95.

_____. "Wanderings in Search of Paul Kane's *Wanderings of an Artist.*" *Prairie Fire* 10:3 (September, 1989): 28-43.

_____. "Exploration/Travel Literature and the Evolution of the Author." *International Journal of Canadian Studies/Revue internationale d'etudes canadiennes,* No. 5 (Spring 1992): 39-68.

Maclean, John. *Lone Land Lights.* Toronto: William Briggs, 1882.

_____. *The Indians, Their Manners and Customs.* Toronto: William Briggs, 1889.

_____. *James Evans: Inventor of the Syllabic System of the Cree Language.* Toronto: Methodist Mission Rooms, 1890.

_____. *Canadian Savage Folk: The Native Tribes of Canada.* Toronto: Briggs, 1896.

_____. *The Warden of the Plains and Other Stories of Life in the Canadian Northwest.* Toronto: W. Briggs, 1896.

_____. *McDougall of Alberta: A Life of Rev. John McDougall, Pathfinder of Empire and Prophet of the Plains.* Toronto: Ryerson, 1927.

MacLulich, T.D. "Alexander Mackenzie" in *Profiles in Canadian Literature* 5. J. M. Heath, ed. Toronto: Dundurn Press, 1986: 17-24.

MacRae, Archibald Oswald. *History of the Province of Alberta.* Calgary: The Western Canada History Co., 1912.

Mallery, G. *Picture-Writing of the American Indians.* 2 vols. New York: Dover, 1972 (1893).

Marchant, Bessie. *Athabasca Bill: A Tale of the Far West.* London: Society for Promoting Christian Knowledge, 1906.

_____. *Daughter of the Ranges: A Story of Western Canada.* London: Blackie, 1906.

Mardiros, Anthony. *William Irvine: The Life of a Prairie Radical.* Toronto: Lorimer, 1979.

Markwell, Mary. *Aweena: An Indian Story of a Christmas Tryst in the Early Days.* Winnipeg: n.p., 1906.

Martineau, L. *The Rocks Begin to Speak.* Las Vegas: KC Publications, 1973.

Mazurkiewicz, Roman. Polskie wychodztwo i osadnictwo w Kanadzie. Warsaw: Naukowy Instytut Emigracyjny, 1929.

McClellan, Catherine. "The Girl Who Married the Bear." *Coming to Light,* Brian Swann, ed. New York: Random House, 1994: 124-137.

McClintock, Gray. *The Wolves at Cooking Lake and Other Stories.* Albany: J.B. Lyon Company, 1932.

McClintock, Walter. *The Old North Trail or Life, Legends and Religion of the Blackfeet Indians.* London: Macmillan, 1910.

McClung, Nellie L. *Sowing Seeds in Danny.* New York: Grosset & Dunlop, 1908.

_____. *The Second Chance.* New York: Doubleday, 1910.

_____. *Black Creek Stopping-House and Other Stories.* Toronto: W. Briggs, 1912.

_____. *The Next of Kin or Those Who Wait and Wonder.* Toronto: T. Allen, 1917.

_____. *Three Times and Out.* Toronto: T. Allen, 1918.

_____. *Purple Springs.* Toronto: T. Allen, 1921.

_____. *When Christmas Crossed the Peace.* Toronto: T. Allen, 1923.

_____. *Painted Fires.* Toronto: Ryerson Press, 1925.

_____. *All We Like Sheep, and Other Stories.* Toronto: T. Allen, 1926.

_____. *Be Good to Yourself: A Book of Short Stories.* Toronto: T. Allen, 1930.

_____. *Flowers for the Living: A Book of Short Stories.* Toronto: A. Allen, 1931.

_____. *Clearing in the West: My Own Story.* Toronto: Thomas Allen, 1936.

_____. *The Stream Runs Fast: My Own Story.* Toronto: Thomas Allen, 1946.

McCourt, Edward. *The Canadian West in Fiction.* Toronto: Ryerson, 1970.

McCowan, Daniel. *Animals of the Canadian Rockies.* Toronto: Macmillan, 1936.

_____. *A Naturalist in Canada.* Toronto: Macmillan, 1941.

_____. *Outdoors with a Camera in Canada.* Toronto: Macmillan, 1947.

_____. *Hill-top Tales.* Toronto: Macmillan, 1948.

_____. *Tidewater to Timberline.* Toronto: Macmillan, 1951.

_____. *Upland Trails.* Toronto: Macmillan, 1955.

McDougall, John. *Cree Hymn Book.* Toronto: Methodist Mission Rooms, 1888.

_____. *George Millward McDougall: The Pioneer, Patriot and Missionary.* Toronto: W. Briggs, 1888.

_____. *Primer and Language Lessons in English and Cree.* Toronto: W. Briggs, 1890.

_____. *Forest, Lake, and Prairie: Twenty Years of Frontier Life in Western Canada 1842-62.* Toronto: William Briggs, 1895.

_____. *Saddle, Sled and Snowshoe: Pioneering on the Saskatchewan in the Sixties.* Toronto: William Briggs, 1896.

_____. *Pathfinding on Plain and Prairie: Stirring Scenes of Life in the Canadian Northwest.* Toronto: Briggs, 1898.

_____. *In the Days of the Red River Rebellion: Life and Adventure in the Far West of Canada 1868-72.* Toronto: William Briggs, 1903.

McLeod, Malcolm, ed. *Peace River: A Canoe Voyages from Hudson's Bay to the Pacific by Sir George Simpson, Journal of the late Chief Factor, Archibald McDonald.* Rutland, Vermont: Tuttle, 1971 (1872).

Mercier, Anne and Violet Watt. *A Home in the Northwest: Being a Record of Experience.* London: Society for Promoting Christian Knowledge, 1894.

_____. *The Red House by the Rockies: A tale of Riel's Rebellion.* Toronto: Musson, 1896.

Mikkleson, Chr. *Canada som fremtidsland: Danske udvandreres vilkaar.* Copenhagen: H. Aschehoug, 1927.

Miles, Robert Seaborn. *Journals 1818-1819.* Bridget Fialkowski, ed. Typescript. Winnipeg: Hudson's Bay Archives, 1983.

Mitchell, Elizabeth B. *In Western Canada Before the War: A Study of Communities.* London: John Murray, 1915.

Mitchell, Peter. *The West and North-West: Notes of a Holiday Trip.* Montreal, 1880.

Mitchell, W.O. *Who Has Seen the Wind.* Boston: Little, Brown, 1947.

Montgomery, Franz. "Alexander Mackenzie's Literary Assistant." *Canadian Historical Review* 18 (1937): 301-303.

Moore, A. Bromley. *Canada and Her Colonies; or, Home Rule for Alberta.* London: W. Stewart & Co., 1911.

Morice, Adrien Gabriel. *Edmonton et l'Alberta français: impressions et statistiques.* Edmonton: Le Courier, 1914.

Morin, Jean-Baptiste. *Journal d'un missionaire-colonisateur, 1890-1897.* Edmonton: Salon d'histoire de la francophonie albertaine, 1984.

Morton, A.S. *A History of the Canadian West to 1870-71.* Toronto: Thomas Nelson & Sons, 1939.

Mukherjee, Arun P. "In a Class of Her Own." *The Literary Review of Canada* (July/August 1995): 20-22.

Murphy, Emily Ferguson. *Janey Canuck in the West.* London: Cassell, 1910.

_____. *Open Trails.* London: Cassell, 1912.

_____. *Seeds of Pine.* London: Hodder & Stoughton, 1914.

_____. *The Black Candle.* Toronto: T. Allen, 1922.

Neijmann, D.L. *The Icelandic Voice in Canadian Letters.* Amsterdam: Vrije University, 1994.

Nesbitt, Bruce, ed. *Earle Birney.* Toronto: McGraw-Hill Ryerson, 1974.

Niranjana, Tejaswini. *Siting Translation: History, Post-Structuralism and the Colonial Context.* Berkeley: University of California Press, 1992.

Niven, Frederick. *Canada West.* London: J.M. Dent & Sons, 1930.

_____ and Walter Joseph Philips. *Colour in the Canadian Rockies.* Toronto: T. Nelson, 1937.

Nothof, Anne. "Making Community History: The Radio Plays of Ringwood and Gowan." *Edmonton: The Life of a City.* Bob Hesketh and Frances Swyripa, eds. Edmonton: NeWest Press, 1995: 170-177.

Nowry, Laurence. *Man of Mana: Marius Barbea.* Toronto: NC Press, 1996.

O'Hagan, Howard. *The School-Marm Tree.* Vancouver: Talonbooks, 1977.

_____. *The Woman Who Got on at Jasper Station and Other Stories.* Vancouver: Talonbooks, 1977.

_____. *Wilderness Men.* Vancouver: Talonbooks, 1978.

_____. *Tay John.* Toronto: McClelland & Stewart, 1989 (1939).

_____. *Trees Are Lonely Company.* Vancouver: Talonbooks, 1993.

O'Siadhail, Padraig, "Katherine Hughes: Irish Political Activist." *Edmonton: The Life of a City.* Edmonton: NeWest Press, 1995: 78-87.

Outram, James. *In the Heart of the Canadian Rockies.* London: Macmillan, 1905.

Palliser, Captain John. *The Journals, Detailed Reports and Observations relative to the Exploration of Captain Palliser of a Portion of British North America during the Years 1857, 1858, 1859 and 1860.* London: Queen's Printer, 1863.

Palmer, Howard. *Patterns of Prejudice: A History of Nativism in Alberta.* Toronto: McClelland & Stewart, 1982.

_____ (with Tamara Palmer). *Alberta: A New History*. Edmonton: Hurtig, 1990.

Palmer, Tamara. "The Fictionalization of the Vertical Mosaic: The Immigrant, Success and National Mythology." *Literatures of Lesser Diffusion*. Joseph Pivato, ed. Edmonton: Research Institute for Comparative Literature, 1990: 65-101.

Papen, Jean. *Georges Bugnet, homme de lettres canadien*. Saint-Boniface, Manitoba: Éditions des Plaines, 1985.

Paterson, Isabel. *The Shadow Riders*. London: John Lane, 1916.

_____. *The Magpie's Nest*. Toronto: S.B. Gundy, 1917.

Patton, Brian. *Tales from the Canadian Rockies*. Edmonton: Hurtig, 1984.

Peel, Bruce. *A Bibliography of the Prairie Provinces to 1953*. Toronto: University of Toronto Press, 1973.

Le Père Lacombe: "l'homme au bon coeur," après ses mémoires et souvenirs. Montreal: Le Devoir, 1916.

Peterson, C.W. *Fruits of the Earth: A Story of the Canadian Prairies*. Ottawa: Ru-Mi-Lou Books, 1928.

Petrone, Penny. *First People, First Voices*. Toronto: Oxford Univeristy Press, 1990.

Plummer, Norman M. *The Goad: A Human Story of the last great west in the early part of the twentieth century based mainly on facts*. London: Stockwell, 1931.

_____. *The Long Arm*. London: Thomas Nelson, 1939.

Pocock, Henry Roger. *Tales of Western Life*. Ottawa: C.W. Mitchell, 1888.

_____. *The Arctic Night*. London: Chapman & Hall, 1896.

_____. *The Wolf Trail*. New York: D. Appleton and Co., 1923.

Pomeroy, Earl. *In Search of the Golden West: The Tourist in Western America*. New York: Knopf, 1957.

Popp Di Biase, Linda. "The Alberta Years of Winnifred Eaton Babcock Reeve." *Alberta History* 39:2 (Spring 1991): 1-8.

Pratt, Mary Louise. *Imperial Eyes: Travel Writing and Transculturation*. London: Routledge, 1992.

Rajnovich, Grace. *Reading Rock Art: Interpreting the Indian Rock Paintings of the Canadian Shield*. Toronto: Natural Heritage/Natural History Inc, 1994.

Rich, E.E., ed. *Cumberland House and Hudson House Journals*. London: Hudson's Bay Record Society, 1951.

Ricou, Laurence. *Vertical Man, Horizontal World: Man and Landscapes in Canadian Prairie Fiction.* Vancouver: University of British Columbia Press, 1973.

Ridington, Robin. "Dunne-za Stories" in *Coming to Light,* Brian Swann, ed. New York: Random House, 1994: 176-189.

Ringwood, Gwen Pharis. *Still Stands the House.* S. French, 1939.

_____. *Dark Harvest: A Tragedy of the Canadian Prairie.* Toronto: Nelson, 1945.

Roberts, Morley. *The Western Avernus, or Toil and Travels in Further North America.* London: Brown, Langham & Co., 1904.

_____. *On The Old Trail.* London: Nash & Grayson, 1927.

Robertson, Valerie. *Reclaiming History: Ledger Drawings by the Assiniboine Artist Hongeeyesa.* Calgary: Glenbow-Alberta Institute, 1993.

Roper, G. et al. "Writers of Fiction: 1880-1920." In Klinck, *Literary History of Canada* Vol. 1: 327-353.

Rouquette, Louis-Frédéric. *L'épopée blanche.* Paris: Ferenczi, 1926.

Rourke, Louise. *The Land of the Frozen Tide: An Account of the Life of the Author for Two Years at Fort Chipewyan.* London: Hutchinson, 1928.

Rouse, John James. *Pioneer Work in Canada, Practically Presented.* Kilmarnack, Scotland: John Ritchie, 1935.

Roy, Irene. *Junette or Are Women Just to One Another.* Edmonton: douglas Co., 1919.

Rutland, E. Delgatty, ed. *The Collected Plays of Gwen Pharis Ringwood.* Ottawa: Borealis, 1982.

Salter, F.M. *The Way of the Makers: A New Rationale of the Art of Writing.* Edmonton: The Friends of the University of Alerta, 1967.

_____. *The Art of Writing.* H.V. Weekes, ed. Toronto: Ryerson, 1971.

Salverson, Laura Goodman. *The Viking Heart.* Toronto: McClelland & Stewart, 1925.

_____. *Wayside Gleams.* Toronto: McClelland & Stewart, 1925.

_____. *When Sparrows Fall.* Toronto: Thomas Allen, 1925.

_____. *Lord of the Silver Dragon.* Toronto: McClelland & Stewart, 1927.

_____. *Confessions of an Immigrant's Daughter.* Toronto: Ryerson, 1929.

Sandemose, Aksel. *Ross Dane.* English trans. Winnipeg: Gunnars & Campbell, 1989.

Savage, Candace. *Our Nell: A Scrapbook Biography of Nellie L. McClung.* Saskatoon: Western Producer Prairie Books, 1979.

Schäffer, Mary T.S. *Old Indian Trails: Incidents of Camp and Trail Life, Covering Two Years' Exploration Through the Rocky Mountains of Canada*. New York: Putnam, 1911.

_____. *A Hunter of Peace: Mary T.S. Schäffer's Old Indian Trails of the Canadian Rockies*. Banff: Whyte Museum of the Canadian Rockies, 1980.

Schurmann, Reiner. *Heidegger on Being and Acting: From Principles to Anarchy*. Bloomington: Indiana University Press, 1987.

Scollon, Ron and Suzanne Scollon. *Narrative, Literacy and Face in Interethnic Communication*. Norwood, New Jersey: Ablex, 1981.

Sivell, Rhoda. *Voices From the Range*. Toronto: T. Eaton Co., 1911.

Smith, Donald. *Long Lance: The True Story of an Imposter*. Toronto: Macmillan, 1982.

_____. "From Sylvester Long to Chief Buffalo Child Long Lance." *Being and Becoming Indian*. James A. Clifton, ed. Chicago: Dorsey Press, 1989.

Southesk, Earl. *Saskatchewan and the Rocky Mountains*. Edmonton: Hurtig, 1969 (1875).

Spragge, A. *From Ontario to the Pacific by the C.P.R.* Toronto: Blackett Robinson, 1888.

Stanley, G.F.G. *The Birth of Western Canada: A History of the Riel Rebellions*. London: Longmans, Green, 1936.

_____. "A Historical Footnote." *Riel Project Bulletin No.5* (April 1981): 4-7.

Stead, Robert. *The Empire Builders and Other Poems*. Toronto: W. Briggs, 1908.

_____. *Prairie-Born and Other Poems*. Toronto: W. Briggs, 1911.

_____. *The Bail Jumper*. London: T. Fisher Unwin, 1914.

_____. *The Homesteaders: A Novel of the Canadian West*. Toronto: Musson, 1916.

_____. *Kitchener and Other Poems*. Toronto, Musson 1917

_____. *The Cow Puncher*. Toronto: Musson, 1918.

_____. *Dennison Grant: A Novel of Today*. Toronto: Musson, 1920. (Published in England as *Zen of the Y.D.: A Novel of the Foothills*. London: Hodder & Stoughton, 1925.)

_____. *The Smoking Flax*. Toronto: McClelland & Stewart, 1924.

_____. *Grain*. Toronto: McClelland & Stewart, 1926.

Steele, Harwood E.R. *Cleared for Action*. London: T. Fisher Unwin, 1914.

_____. *Spirit-of-Iron (Manitou-pewabic): An Authentic Novel of the North-west Mounted Police*. New York: A.L. Burt, 1923.

_____. *The Ninth Circle*. New York: A.L. Burt, 1927.

_____. *To Effect an Arrest, Adventures of the Royal Canadian Mounted Police.* Toronto: Ryerson Press, 1947.

_____. *Ghosts Returning.* Toronto: Ryerson Press, 1950.

Stephansson, Stephan G. *Andvøkur.* Reykjavøk: Kostnadormenn nokkrir øslendigar ø vesturheimi, 1909–1923.

_____. *Selected Prose and Poetry.* K. Gunnars, trans. Red Deer: Red Deer College Press, 1988.

Stott, Greg. "Wanted: Will James." *Equinox* (March/April 1995).

Strange, Harry and Kathleen. *Never a Dull Moment.* Toronto: Macmillan, 1941.

Strange, Kathleen. *With the West in Her Eyes: The Story of a Modern Pioneer.* Toronto: MacLeod, 1937.

Stringer, Arthur. *The Prairie Wife.* New York: A.L. Burt, 1915.

_____. *The Prairie Mother.* Toronto: McClelland & Stewart, 1920.

_____. *The Prairie Child.* New York: A.L. Burt, 1922.

_____. *Prairie Stories.* New York: A.L. Burt, 1922.

_____. *The Mud Lark.* Toronto: McClelland & Stewart, 1932.

Stutfield, H. and J.N. Collie. *Climbs and Explorations in the Canadian Rockies.* London: Longmans, Green, 1903.

Swann, Brian, ed. *Coming to Light: Contemporary Translations of the Native Literatures of North America.* New York: Random House, 1994.

Taylor, A.J.P. "Two Rebels: Lafayette and Riel." *Manchester Guardian* June 26, 1938: 7.

Taylor, Gary. *Cultural Selection.* New York: Basic Books, 1996.

Teetgen, Ada B. *A White Passion.* London: Wells Gardner, 1912.

Thompson, David. *Columbia Journals.* Barbara Belyea, ed. Montreal: McGill-Queen's University Press, 1994.

Thompson, Ernest Seton. *Wild Animal I Have Known.* New York: Grossett Dunlap 1966 (1898).

Tougas, Gerard. *History of French-Canadian Literature.* Westport: Greenwood Press, 1976.

Toye, W., ed. *The Oxford Companion to Canadian Literature.* Alta Lind Cook, trans. Toronto: Oxford University Press, 1983.

Trottier, A. et al. *Aspects du passé franco-albertain.* Edmonton: Salon d'histoire de la francophonie albertaine, 1980.

Tyrrell, J.B., ed. *David Thompson: Narrative of his Explorations in Western America 1784-1812.* Toronto: Champlain Society, 1916.

Uhlenbeck, C.C. *Original Blackfoot Texts.* Amsterdam: Johannes Miller, 1911.

Vaughan, Walter. *The Life and Work of Sir William Van Horne.* New York: Century, 1920.

Wagner, Hermann. *Von Kueste zu Kueste bei deutschen Auswanderern in Kanada.* Hamburg: Verlag der Ev. luth. Auswanderdermission, 1929.

Wallace, J.N. *The Wintering Partners on Peace River from the Earliest Records to the Union in 1821.* Ottawa: Thorburn and Abbott, 1929.

Wallace, Paul A.W. *Baptiste Larocque: Legends of French Canada.* Toronto: Musson, 1923.

Warkentin, Germaine ed. *Canadian Exploration Literature.* Toronto: Oxford University Press, 1993.

Warkentin, John, ed. *The Western Interior of Canada: A Record of Geographical Discovery 1612-1812.* Toronto: McClelland & Stewart, 1964.

Warne, Randi. *Literature as Pulpit: The Christian Social Activism of Nellie L. McClung.* Waterloo: Wilfred Laurier University Press, 1993.

Washburn, Stanley. *Trails, Trappers, and Tenderfeet in the New Empire of Western Canada.* London: Andrew Melrose, 1912.

Warre, Captain H. *Sketches in North America and the Oregon Territory.* London: Dickinson & Co., 1848.

Watanna, Onoto. *A Japanese Nightingale.* New York: Harper & Bros., 1901.

_____. *Sunny-San,* New York: George H. Doran Company, 1922.

_____. *Cattle.* Toronto: Musson, 1923.

_____. *His Royal Nibs.* New York: W.J. Watt & Co., 1925.

Waterston, Elizabeth. "Travel Books 1860-1920." In Klinck, *Literary History of Canada* Vol. 1: 361-379.

Watt, Gertrude Balmer. *A Woman in the West.* Edmonton: News Publishing Co., 1907.

_____. *Town and Trail.* Edmonton: News Publishing Co., 1908.

Whitehouse, Francis Cecil. *Plain Folks.* Ottawa: Graphic Press, 1926.

_____. *Canadian and Other Poems.* Toronto: The Ryerson Press, 1934.

Wilcox, Walter Dwight. *Camping in the Rockies.* New York: Putnam, 1896.

Williams, Flos Jewell. *The Judgment of Solomon.* Toronto: Musson, 1925.

_____. *New Furrows: A Story of the Alberta Foothills.* Ottawa: Graphic Press, 1926.

_____. *Broken Goods.* Ottawa: The Graphic Publishers, 1930.

_____. *Fold Home.* Toronto: Ryerson Press, 1950.

Williams, Glyndwr. "The Puzzle of Anthony Henday's Journal, 1754-55." *The Beaver* (Winter 1978): 40-56.

Williams, M.B. *Through the Heart of the Rockies and Selkirks.* Ottawa: Published under the direction of Hon. Charles Stewart, Minister of the Interior, 1924.

Willmott, Glenn. *McLuhan or Modernism in Reverse.* Toronto: University of Toronto Press, 1996.

Wolfart, H.C. and Carroll, J.F. *Meet Cree: A Guide to the Language.* Edmonton: University of Alberta Press, 1981.

Yasenchuk, Joseph. *Kanadyiskyi Kobzar.* Edmonton: Ukrainska Knyharnia, 1918.

Yeigh, Frank. *Through the Heart of Canada.* Toronto: Frowde, 1911.

Yellow-Fly, Ted. "Indian Teepee Designs and Their Derivations." *Calgary Daily Herald* July 8, 1929.

Index

Paterson, Isabel, 85
  The Magpie's Nest, 85
  The Shadow Riders, 85
Pathfinding on Plain and Prairie
      (McDougall), 58
The Patrol of the Sun Dance Trail
      (Connor), 66
Peace River district, 11, 116
Peel, Bruce, 172
Persons Case, 83, 93
Peterson, Charles, 102-03
  Fruits of the Earth, 102
Petursson, Rognvaldur, 151
Philip Steele (Curwood), 86
Phillips, Walter J., 113
  Colour in the Canadian Rockies, 113
Piegan Indians, 5, 12, 14
Pietsch, Johannes, 155
  Dein den Deutschen, 155
Pilgrim of the Wild (Grey Owl), 114
Pine Creek Ranch (Bindloss), 88
Pioneer Work in Canada (Rouse), 115
Plains Cree Texts (Bloomfield), 16
Plummer, Norman, 118-19
  The Goad, 118
  The Long Arm, 118
Pocock, Henry, 61-62
  Arctic Night, 61-62
  Tales of Western Life, 61
  The Wolf Trail, 62
Poèmes (Bugnet), 143, 145
The Poets of Canada (Colombo), 153
Polish literature, 154-155
Polskie wychodztwo i osadnictwo w
      Kanadzie (Mazurkiewicz),
      155
Pomeroy, Earl, 53-54
  In Search of the Golden West, 53-54
Pond, Peter, 26
Portraits from the Plains (MacEwan), 12
Prairie-Born (Stead), 93
The Prairie Child (Stringer), 89

Prairie Moonlight (Eggleston), 119
The Prairie Mother (Stringer), 89
Prairie Stories (Stringer), 89
Prairie Symphony (Eggleston), 119
The Prairie Wife (Stringer), 89
Pratt, E.J., 126
Pratt, Mary Louise, 8, 44
  Imperial Eyes, 44
Prières, cantiques et catechisme
      (Grouard), 139
Primer and Language Lessons in English
      and Cree (McDougall), 57
The Prodigal Son (Mackie), 63
The Prospector (Connor), 65-66
Purple Springs (McClung), 92
Pylypenko, P. (Zygmund
      Bychynsky), 149

The Queen's Highway (Cumberland),
      53

radio drama, 162
railway travel accounts, 52-54
Rajnovich, Grace, 2, 5
Ranching for Sylvia (Bindloss), 88
Ranching with Lords and Commons
      (Craig), 80
The Range Men (Kelly), 81
Rattlesnake Ranch (Leighton), 88
Recueil de Voyages au Nord (Bernard), 134
Red Cloud (Butler), 48
Red Gold (Gordon), 102
The Red House by the Rockies (Mercier
      and Watt), 66
Reeve, Winnifred Eaton Babcock *see*
      Watanna, Onoto
Relations d'un voyage à la côte du Nord-
      ouest (Franchère), 135
Renfrew in the Valley of Vanished Men
      (Erskine), 100